AN EVENT IN SPACE

JoAnne Akalaitis in Rehearsal

AN EVENT IN SPACE

JoAnne Akalaitis in Rehearsal

Deborah Saivetz

CAREER DEVELOPMENT SERIES

A Smith and Kraus Book

Published by
Smith and Kraus, Inc.
177 Lyme Road, Hanover, New Hampshire 03755
www.SmithKraus.com

Cover and Text Design by Julia Hill Gignoux, Freedom Hill Design
Front cover photo: Enrico Ferorelli, 1999
Back cover photos: Left, Jo Ellen Allen (Governess) tries
to convince Lauren Tom (Princess Lena) of the importance of
her future marriage. The Guthrie Theater's 1987 production of
Leon & Lena (and lenz). *Right, The Guthrie Theater's 1989 production*
of The Screens *cast.Both photos by Joe Gianetti.*

Chapter IV, "The Physical Exercises," appeared in a substantially
different version in *TDR: The Journal of Performance Studies,*
42.2 (T 158): 132–156.

"An Interview with JoAnne Akalaitis,"
was first published in *New Theatre Quarterly,* 13.52: 329–338.

First edition: November 2000
9 8 7 6 5 4 3 2 1

The Library of Congress Cataloging-In-Publication Data
Saivetz, Deborah.
An event in space : JoAnne Akalaitis in rehearsal / by Deborah Saivetz. —1st ed.
p. cm. — (Career development series)
Includes bibliographical references.
ISBN 1-57525-239-2
1. Akalaitis, JoAnne—Criticism and interpretation. 2. Mabou Mines (Theater group)
I. Title. II. Series.
PN2287.A445 S25 2001
792'.0233'092—dc21   00-045003

The stage will therefore be a site
not where reflections spend themselves
but where bursts of light meet and collide.

JEAN GENET

Contents

Preface

I don't think anybody has ever been able
to objectively explain process.

SAM SHEPARD

After a brief interview with JoAnne Akalaitis in the winter of 1990, I was hired to be her assistant on John Ford's Jacobean tragedy 'Tis Pity She's a Whore to be produced by Chicago's Goodman Theatre. While in rehearsal for that production, Akalaitis invited me to perform in The Mormon Project workshop that was to take place later that year at the Atlantic Center for the Arts in New Smyrna Beach, Florida. Needless to say, I was thrilled to be able to work as an actress and apprentice director with an artist as fascinating as Akalaitis. I was also eager to write about these two rehearsal processes, particularly because I had been given the opportunity to experience Akalaitis's work from a number of different vantage points. The first project involved assisting Akalaitis in her re-visioning of a classical text, and the second involved collaborating on the development of an original theater piece. During the months that we worked together, I had the privilege of talking at length with Akalaitis about such topics as her experiences as an actress and director with Mabou Mines theater company; her artistic encounters with Beckett, Brecht, and Genet; her views on the relationship between art and politics; and her thoughts about acting, dramaturgy and design.

What I found most intriguing, however, about Akalaitis's way of working in the theater was her fundamental belief in the connection between the physical and the emotional in performance. While Akalaitis occasionally spoke about this matter, she was less interested in theorizing than in getting up on her feet with her actors and, as she puts it, "moving around." At the start of each rehearsal day, she guided the actors through a series of physical exercises, each accompanied by detailed instructions, each with a desired effect. Far from serving as a simple cast warm-up, the exercises appeared to release a kind of psychophysical energy within and among the actors, strengthening their connection to each other and to the scenic space around them. This book is about these exercises, and the way in which they illuminate a central aspect of Akalaitis's directing process— specifically, her emphasis on the physicality of performance. It is also about the artistic vision of the woman who created them, a director who believes that theater is first and foremost an event in space.

Akalaitis is a theater artist who redefines herself with every project she undertakes. Writing about an artist whose work is constantly evolving and changing is problematic. Writing about Akalaitis poses a further challenge because, as she herself admits, much of her creative process occurs on an unconscious level that defies logic or explanation. She is mercurial, does not easily or willingly articulate her process or her goals, and can be resistant to questioning and interviews. Her productions are beautiful, sensuous, complex, and at times, difficult—to understand, to enjoy, simply to experience. Both the popular and critical response to her work have been mixed. While I sought a clearer understanding of the unease that surrounds Akalaitis's work, my aim has been neither to defend nor demonize but rather to analyze and reflect upon her directing process from a point of view at once sensitive and critical, personal and fair-minded.

Witnessing Akalaitis's work from the multiple perspectives of director's assistant, performer, audience member, and researcher, I felt myself to be both an "outsider" and an "insider" in relation to the rehearsal processes I was attempting to document. This duality also colored my relationship to the artistic communities that existed around the two productions. To function simultaneously as scholar and artist, observer and participant, "outsider" and "insider," is to occupy a liminal position that brings with it dangers as well as privileges. The "outsider" may become so seduced by her own critical agenda that she risks losing sight of the subject itself. And the "insider" may develop such an attachment to and investment in this very subject that he risks losing sight of his own critical perceptions.

Because I sought the trust of the professional artists I was observing and working with, I fought to keep my critical agenda from insinuating itself into the artistic process. I thought of myself as an undercover researcher despite the fact that Akalaitis, a few of the designers and several of the actors were aware that I was writing about the rehearsal process. I refrained from taking notes if it distracted the actors, from interviewing Akalaitis if it intruded upon her privacy, from questioning her collaborators if it disturbed their concentration. I trusted that either my mind or my body would somehow remember the important experiences that occurred each day in the rehearsal room. Above all, I attempted to keep rigid theoretical constructs and reductive hypotheses from clouding my view of the complex theatrical work that was taking shape in front of me. Throughout the writing of this book I grappled with the at times complimentary, at times contradictory activities of making and researching theater, and searched for the intersection between the two.

The first two chapters chronicle Akalaitis's work as a performer, director, writer, and designer with Mabou Mines, and discuss the influence of this work upon her directing process and style. Since its founding in 1970, Mabou Mines has been a laboratory for artistic exploration, a collective of individuals with vastly different backgrounds, temperaments, and skills who relate to each other as both collaborators and foils. For Akalaitis, Mabou Mines was above all a group of people empowered to think creatively about all aspects of theater, including production, aesthetics, and text. A number of Akalaitis's intellectual and aesthetic priorities, particularly her emphasis upon the physicality of performance, have their roots in her work with Mabou Mines.

The third chapter lays out in detail the various physical exercises Akalaitis has developed as an essential aspect of her rehearsal process, and it discusses their importance for director, actors, and audience. I explain the way in which the exercises create a kind of "dreaming consciousness" in the actors, allowing them to feel as if they are both agents and observers of the dramatic action. The actors see the space around them, but they also see *themselves* in that space; they see images in the scenic environment, but they also see *themselves* as images. As the actors enter more consciously into the image-making aspect of theater, the membrane between acting and design becomes more permeable. The actors begin to perform with, or within, the design instead of simply in front of it. Akalaitis's physical exercises may thus be viewed as a structured means of connecting the inner life of the actors with the scenic elements of theatrical production.

Chapters Four and Five document the rehearsal processes of two very different theater projects, demonstrating specific ways that Akalaitis uses the exercises to investigate text, scenography, and personal imagery. Chapter Four is devoted to the rehearsal process for the 1990 Goodman Theatre production of John Ford's Jacobean revenge tragedy, *'Tis Pity She's a Whore*. This production had an eight-week rehearsal period, a generous budget, and a team of nationally renowned designers serving as Akalaitis's collaborators. Chapter Five describes the rehearsal process for the 1990 workshop of *The Mormon Project*, an original theater piece about religion in America presented at The Atlantic Center for the Arts in New Smyrna Beach, Florida. The workshop had a three-week rehearsal period, a limited budget, and few technical resources; its focus was the composition of a performance text from found sources and original writings. In addition to situating the physical exercises within the context of these two specific rehearsal and performance processes, I discuss Akalaitis's concept and artistic goals for each of the projects, as well as various ideas, images, and questions sparked in Akalaitis's imagination by the dramatic text.

The final chapter discusses the firing of Akalaitis as artistic director of the New York Shakespeare Festival, the response to this event by the New York press and professional theater community, and its implications for nonprofit theater in the United States. After an overview of Akalaitis's current projects, the book concludes with a summary of the key elements of Akalaitis's directing process, and my suggestion that the integration of acting and design, while not always achieved in production, is fundamental to Akalaitis's theatrical vision.

This book is neither an exhaustive study of Akalaitis's directorial oeuvre, nor a comprehensive survey of the work of Mabou Mines, the theater company she co-founded. Rather, it is limited to a thorough documentation of two rehearsal processes and their resulting productions. These two contrasting processes serve to illuminate a central aspect of Akalaitis's directing process—specifically, her emphasis on the physicality of performance as manifested in the relationship between acting and design.

Akalaitis describes a rehearsal process as a journey that in and of itself is far more important than its destination. Likewise, this book chronicles a number of complementary and contradictory journeys. Negotiating a relationship between theater practice and theater scholarship can be tricky. Academic and professional theater communities have traditionally looked askance at each other despite the fact that they share interests, methods, and values. Professional actors, directors, and designers are not eager to welcome an academic "spy" into their midst during what, for many of them, is an intimate and volatile process. At the same time, members of the academic community can become impatient with the demands the theater itself places upon a scholar's time, energy, and emotional life. Yet, as Akalaitis's own work demonstrates, conflict and tension are unavoidable, and perhaps even essential, aspects of the creative endeavor.

I have attended numerous conferences, seminars, and lectures that aim to bring theater scholars and practitioners together. The two groups sit alongside each other on panels devoted to the relationship between theory and practice, speak their individual pieces, and engage in polite conversation or mild debate. More often than not, I am left wondering whether these two communities have anything to say to each other. Might questions on the minds of intelligent theater practitioners have anything to say to those who study and write about the form? Similarly, might questions on the minds of imaginative theater scholars have anything to say to those working in the profession? These are questions with which I continue to struggle and that have inspired this book about a theater artist who approaches her work, and her life, as an investigation.

Introduction

Studies show that communication is only seven percent words.
JoAnne is interested in the other ninety-three percent, which is why her work
is sometimes baffling and threatening to her audiences. Her work says,
"Wake up! Look a little deeper, and then look again."

LAUREN TOM

JoAnne Akalaitis is one of America's most innovative and controversial theater directors whose work ranges from original theater pieces to unconventional interpretations of classic plays. Noted for her imagistic and sculptural approach to staging, Akalaitis's multilayered, collage-like works combine text, acting, and design to create highly evocative theatrical environments. Her approach to creating theater is, above all, a profoundly physical one. In her work the dramatic event is palpably present in the bodies of the actors and in the scenic architecture of space, image, light, sound, and music. While Akalaitis considers these concrete, physical aspects of theater to be compositional elements, they do more than contribute structure and form to her work; they convey emotion as well. Theatrical space is psychological space; physical geography is emotional geography. What matters most of all, according to this iconoclastic director, is "the inside and the outside coming together."[1]

For twenty years, Akalaitis was a member of Mabou Mines, the collaborative theater group she co-founded in 1970 with Lee Breuer, Ruth Maleczech, David Warrilow, and Philip Glass. Mabou Mines is often mentioned in the same breath as the contemporaneous but more overtly political performance ensembles such as Julian Beck and Judith Malina's Living Theatre, Joseph Chaikin's Open Theatre, and Richard Schechner's Performance Group, which formed a part of New York's downtown experimental theater scene during the late 1960s and early 1970s. Mabou Mines has distinguished itself, however, by a complex visual sensibility, intellectual rigor, democratic operating principles, and a tradition of collaborating with artists from various disciplines. Throughout its history, Mabou Mines has remained dedicated to the creative process rather than the commercial product, developing its theater pieces over lengthy rehearsal periods and keeping them in the repertory for several years. The company has won numerous awards for performance, direction, and design, and it has been recognized in the New York press as "a microcosm of the American experimental theater" and "a model of avant-garde theatricality—in writing, in acting, in directing, in production, in technology, and in collaboration."[2]

During the early years of Mabou Mines, Akalaitis performed in Samuel Beckett's *Play* (1967) and *Come and Go* (1971), and Lee Breuer's *Animations* (1970–78). Her first directing venture was a fully staged adaptation of Beckett's radio play *Cascando* in 1975. *Cascando* won a *Village Voice* Obie award, as did nearly every project Akalaitis directed for Mabou Mines including *Dressed Like an Egg* (1977), a dramatic collage adapted from the life and writings of French novelist Colette; *Southern Exposure* (1979), inspired by the biography of Antartic explorerer Robert Scott; *Dead End Kids* (1980/81), a multimedia history of nuclear power; and German playwright Francis Xavier Kroetz's *Request Concert* (1981) and *Through the Leaves* (1984), a gritty work about the abusive relationship between a middle-aged female butcher and her construction worker boyfriend.

In the early 1980s, Akalaitis branched out from her work with Mabou Mines and began directing large-scale works at major regional theaters across the United States. Her idiosyncratic and often irreverent stagings of classic plays both exhilarated and infuriated audiences unaccustomed to work that flirted dangerously with thematic and aesthetic disorder. These radically reinterpreted, though textually faithful, productions included a production of Beckett's *Endgame* (1984) set in a post-apocalyptic subway car and denounced by the author's spokespeople and a Latin American version of Genet's *The Balcony* (1986) with a musical score by Rubén Blades, both at the American Repertory Theatre; *Green Card* (1988), an original work about immigration in Los Angeles, developed at the Mark Taper Forum; two acclaimed productions at the Guthrie Theater: Büchner's *Leon and Lena (and lenz)* (1987) and Genet's *The Screens* (1989); and Ford's *'Tis Pity She's a Whore* (1990), whose notorious "cunt" graffito shocked and enraged audiences at Chicago's Goodman Theatre. For the New York Shakespeare Festival, Akalaitis directed a critically savaged production of Shakespeare's *Cymbeline* (1989), Parts One and Two of Shakespeare's *Henry IV* (1990), a restaging of *'Tis Pity She's a Whore* (1992), and a production of Büchner's *Woyzek* (1992/93).

Akalaitis's other directing projects include the 1983 *Stop Making Sense* tour for the band Talking Heads; *Red and Blue* (1982), an actorless theater piece consisting of a conversation between red and blue light bulbs; and her staging of contemporary American playwright Len Jenkin's *American Notes* (1988). She last appeared as an actress in 1981, playing the role of Mrs. Lammle, a specialist in "coincidences," in Jenkin's *Dark Ride* at New York's Soho Repertory Theater. In May of 1991, Joseph Papp, the founder and producer of the New York Shakespeare Festival, named Akalaitis as his artistic associate. Three months later, she was appointed Papp's successor, and upon his death in the autumn of 1991, took over as artistic director of the Festival. In March of 1993, after a stormy twenty-month tenure, Akalaitis was fired by the theater's board of directors.

Since that time, Akalaitis's stagings have included Calderón de la Barca's *Life's a Dream* at Chicago's Court Theatre (1999); *The Iphigenia Cycle*, a pairing of Euripides' *Iphigenia at Aulis* and *Iphigenia in Tauris* at the Court Theatre (1997) and New York's Theatre for a New Audience (1999); *Ti Jean Blues*, a theater piece based on the life and work of Jack Kerouac, at the Actors Theatre of Louisville's Humana Festival of New American Plays (1998); Euripides' *The Trojan Women* at the Shakespeare Theatre in Washington, D.C. (1998); August Strindberg's *The Dance of Death* at the Arena Stage in Washington, D.C. (1996); *Suddenly Last Summer* by Tennessee Williams at Hartford Stage (1994); Aphra Behn's *The Rover* at the Guthrie (1994); and Jane Bowles's *In the Summer House* at Lincoln Center (1993). She is the recipient of a 1993 Obie Award for Sustained Achievement, the 1993 Edwin Booth Award, four Obie Awards for Distinguished Direction and Production, a Guggenheim Fellowship for experimental theater, and Rockefeller and National Endowment for the Arts grants for playwriting. Her recent projects include a remounting of *The Screens* at New York Theatre Workshop and an opera based on Franz Kafka's *In the Penal Colony* with music by Philip Glass. She has served as co-chair of the MFA Directing Program at the Juilliard School and is the chair of the Theater department at Bard College.

Akalaitis has for years been considered a provocative director of at times astounding, at times flawed, experimental work. Yet, particularly since her brief tenure as Artistic Director of the New York Shakespeare Fesival, she has suffered a staggering amount of negative press. She has been referred to as cold, insecure, distant, defensive, and difficult; she has been accused of being "an abrasive ideologue" and "a terrorist [who is] destructive of institutions."[3] While her work has been praised for its originality, intelligence, and boldness of vision, it has also been accused of impenetrability, humorlessness, overly elaborate physical productions, actors who lack the ability to speak the text, gimmicky anachronism, and a mystifying system of color- and gender-blind casting—all of which are cited as eclipsing or obliterating "the text."

Akalaitis's directorial work also provokes grumbling because she values the visual, spatial, and compositional aspects of theater, which causes certain critics and audience members to conclude that she must therefore devalue the inner processes of the actor. In fact, not only does Akalaitis respect the actor's emotional life, but she also considers her actors to be intelligent and active collaborators in the overall fabric of her productions. Yet it is perhaps her emphasis on the physicality of the actor—the sense, in her work, that the actor is image as well as agent (i.e., the transmitter of "the play")—that has caused certain members of the critical community to fiercely defend the primacy of the dramatic text that they accuse Akalaitis of disrespecting. Despite their professed admiration of *auteur* directors and their fascination with the jump-cut images of music videos, they become uneasy if they do not "get" the story and are disturbed by gestures that appear to have iconographic rather than narrative value.

Performance theorist Philip Ausslander suggests that certain works of art may contain no overt political content yet are "transgressive" or "resistant" in their very existence. The political statement expressed in these works, according to Ausslander, is not encoded in words or gestures but is present in a style of performance that questions or ignores accepted aesthetic values, such as those of beauty or formal seamlessness.[4] Perhaps it is the "transgressive" nature of Akalaitis's theater that both captivates and disturbs audiences. Her productions are cauldrons where psychology, sociology, and even politics boil together, where dramatic characters may at times appear more as spokespeople for ethnic, racial, religious, gender, or class groups than as unique individuals. (At a rehearsal for 'Tis Pity She's a Whore, Akalaitis wondered aloud why all the dramaturgs she knew dressed like "the proletariat," in work shirts and jeans.)

Akalaitis herself is a director who defies easy categorization and subverts aesthetic boundaries, shrugging off attempts by even the most appreciative critics and scholars to describe her work, her style, her taste. Her imagination is as intrigued by social structures and systems of power relationships, as it is by her own dreams. Her work encourages us to reflect upon the many ways of telling stories, to question the redundancy of the label "visually-oriented" director, to wonder what kind of director eschews "concepts." For Joseph Papp, Akalaitis's refusal to be aesthetically inscribed was an asset. Defending her as the perfect person to guide the New York Shakespeare Festival in difficult economic times, Papp asserted that "JoAnne has the most original mind in the theater today. As a leader, she is independent. She doesn't recognize boundaries and you can't pigeonhole her."[5] Akalaitis is a theater artist who grapples with complex social, philosophical, and aesthetic questions, without settling for easy answers. And she expects no less of her colleagues, critics, and audiences.

Akalaitis's emphasis on the physicality of performance is, in part, what makes her work exhilarating for actors and audiences; it is also what makes it difficult. During the early stages of working with actors on a scene, she may begin not by analyzing or interpreting the text but by suggesting strong physical choices as a way to explore character. She may ask the actors to experiment with a deformity, an article of clothing, or a dialect, or suggest they exaggerate their physical movements and gestures as a way to arrive ultimately at truthful behavior. Watching Jesse Borrego as the strung-out title character in *Woyzeck,* Ruth Maleczech and Frederick Neumann as a pair of economically and romantically oppressed workers in *Through the Leaves,* or Joan McIntosh as a woman silently preparing her suicide in *Request Concert* is to witness a torrent of emotional, sexual, social, and historical forces at once pressing in on these characters from the "outside" and surging up in them from somewhere deep within their bodies. Woyzeck, for instance, tormented equally by his own paranoid temperament, a morally bereft society, and the hard, gray sky above him, is periodically overtaken by fits of epilectic-like shaking. He falls to the floor, only to jump back up again a few seconds later as if nothing unusual had occurred. This is a fully physicalized and felt response arising from the actor's inner condition; at the same time, it is the actor's reponse to outer images present in the scenic environment. Odd though it may be, Borrego/Woyzeck's behavior is riveting.

For Akalaitis, the primal element of theater, the "bottom line" as she puts it, is bodies moving in space onstage. Even her critics have remarked upon her unique sense of composition, her ability to shape bodies, music, and design into worlds of ideas and feelings. Several of Akalaitis's colleagues have mentioned that the actors in her productions exhibit a strong connection to each other and to the space around them. On occasion, the actors' ability to be viscerally activated by the space around them is more pronounced than either their technical or emotional prowess. Yet however chaotic, murky, or flawed the production may be, there is always a strangely powerful emotional atmosphere emanating from the stage. Defending Akalaitis's directorial talents, Joseph Papp confessed that, while he "used to say that all you needed to do Shakespeare was two planks and a passion, I don't feel that way anymore. You need a psychological milieu which JoAnne knows how to create."[6]

Akalaitis's allies in imaging and sculpting her scenic landscapes are, of course, designers, and, less obviously, actors. At the Second Annual New York University Design Symposium, which focused on the relationship between design and the performer, Akalaitis spoke about her willingness to use design to challenge actors, as well as her interest in working with actors who "can see it all—who can both see the space and see themselves in that space." She believes that a physically demanding set poses no problem for actors and is in fact desireable because it contributes an "interesting tension" to the performance.[7] Akalaitis feels that actors work in a very private, hermetic, deeply subjective manner, which they then must translate into a way of working that is public, objective, and physicalized:

> The actor has to put himself or herself into space, and that's a very hard thing to do. Actors say, "Oh, the set is so hard to work on." They all say that. They should say that. They need to say that. And then they need to get on to the next step, which is to understand that the set supports them and embraces them. And they have to figure out how to dominate. I often say that the actors have to possess the space. And they usually do.

Interestingly, Akalaitis uses the very same words—*support* and *embrace*—to describe the function that Philip Glass and Foday Musa Suso's musical score, another aspect of scenic space, performs for Jean Genet's text in her production of *The Screens*.[8]

Akalaitis believes that all great plays require the actor to be "prenarrative," to be able to exist in a kind of primeval, subconscious state that is open to the world, or worlds, of the play. To this end, and inspired by her work with specific companies of actors, Akalaitis has developed a series of physical exercises that are central to her directing process. The exercises, performed by the entire cast of actors throughout the rehearsal period, are not about creating improvisational situations or scenes. Rather, their focus is to establish this prenarrative, open, alert state on the part of the actors in a manner that avoids defining the *actual* physicality of their characters too early on in the rehearsal process. Once established, this foundation of primitive physicality will underly the more detailed, articulated scenework that Akalaitis and her actors engage in as they continue their exploration of the play.

Although each exercise has its own particular set of instructions, Akalaitis continually side-coaches the actors to be aware of the physical sensation of the space around them as well as the space between themselves and their fellow actors. She coaches the actors to put any images contained in and conjured by the space "inside," and, as mentioned above, to see both the space itself and themselves in that space. Over time, the exercises strengthen the actors' connection to each other and to the space around them, a space that eventually will contain scenery, props, lighting, and music. In this way, the actors become accustomed to working as an ensemble, and to creating a vocabulary of images, movement, and gestures that can be invoked throughout the rehearsal process. More importantly, by following Akalaitis's instruction to "see both the space and yourselves in that space," the actors come to view themselves not merely as components but also as shapers of the entire stage picture.

It is customary, even expected, for actors to influence and be influenced by the emotional geography of a play.[9] Encouraging actors to activate and be activated by *scenic* geography goes a step futher, intensifying their involvement in the performance event and bestowing on them an extraordinary degree of compositional responsibility. The actors become active image-makers rather than passive images in the theatrical process. Moreoever, the interaction of actor-as-image with scenography-as-image forges an unusually strong link between acting and design. Some might argue that it is the rare, or perhaps ignorant, director who fails to recognize that actors are shapers of scenic space. I suggest, however, that it is rare indeed for actors to be overtly empowered by the director, throughout an entire rehearsal process, to see themselves as active image-makers.

Akalaitis has stated that "chaos, not conflict, is the essence of drama." The illogical, the disruptive, and the reckless are interesting to her. She habitually unearths the strange and perverse in history, politics, and culture. While Akalaitis frequently stages works written by and about people from cultures other than the United States, her imagination is caught by those aspects of the collective American psyche that are twisted, demented, ugly, and frightening, and that, with our peculiar tendency toward naive optimism, we sentimentalize or repress. Her productions have dealt with such disturbing subjects as the intertwining of political failure and sexual tragedy in Fascist Italy; the sexism and patriarchy surrounding the development of atomic energy; and the current of hypocrisy and fraud that runs through the Mormon religion.

Fight director and longtime collaborator David Leong remarks that, "JoAnne has a socio-political-feminist approach to the classics that, if you allow it, can strike you in a deep way. And she is able to touch upon the issues that lie at the base of the play and stir them up. She doesn't try to provide answers but she gets those issues rumbling within you. You go away with all that jumbled up inside and it's yours to do with as you will."[10] Akalaitis gives theatrical form to material that has provoked varying degrees of appreciation, bafflement, and irritation among audiences and co-workers. Watching her productions, one senses something hellish thrashing around "in there" trying to get out. Participating in her work, from either the stage or the audience, requires venturing into the darker emotional realms of humiliation, frustration, revenge, loneliness, depression, and violence—territory that may be psychologically chaotic and politically suspect.

One of the few influences Akalaitis acknowledges is that of German theater and film director Rainer Werner Fassbinder.[11] She speaks admiringly of Fassbinder's 1973 film, *Ali, Fear Eats the Soul*, which concerns the love between an elderly German cleaning woman named Emmi and a young Moroccan immigrant named Ali. When Emmi confesses to Ali that she is terrified by the rude stares and comments of her neighbors and co-workers, Ali replies, "Fear no good.

Fear eats the soul." Obsessed by what he saw as the criminality of oppression, Fassbinder became increasingly enraged at the horrors he witnessed in the news and in his own life, eventually coming to believe that "all stories are crime stories." His films deal in large part with the humiliation and oppression of those whom mainstream society regards as foreigners or outcasts, a theme that runs through much of Akalaitis's theater work. Critic Michael Töteberg argues that while it would be a mistake to assume Fassbinder's films provide direct access to his biography, "they are autobiographical in the true sense: they attempt to confer shape and meaning on a chaotic, sometimes scandalous life subject to the distortions of what Fassbinder perceived as a catastrophic social and political environment."[12] In a strange way, Töteberg's observation brings to mind a dynamic present in Akalaitis's theater work. Many of her dramatic characters are "Fassbinderesque" in that they lead chaotic, scandalous lives in catastrophic sociopolitical environments. And it is Akalaitis's very act of bringing them from the page to the stage that endows them with physical form (shape) and the capacity to evoke feeling (meaning).

Akalaitis has also been deeply inspired and influenced by Jean Genet, who, like Fassbinder, addresses aspects of chaos in the individual and in society. Both Genet and Fassbinder people their works with characters who exist at the margins of society: the depraved, the persecuted, the downtrodden, as well as those who possess violent, insatiable appetites for power. Akalaitis recalls that, for years, she would mention Genet's *The Screens* whenever artistic directors asked her what plays she would like to direct. The artistic directors would then unfailingly argue that *The Screens* was too expensive to produce and dramaturgically a disaster. But Akalaitis suspects that beneath these completely justifiable complaints lay something even more troubling to potential producers: namely, that Genet himself was a profoundly subversive, profoundly anti-bourgeois theater artist who wrote about the Arab Third World. Pointing out that Genet was also an apolitical homosexual who wrote about heterosexual politics, and an avowed criminal and prostitute who was an extraordinary poet, she suggests that Genet's unpopularity may have something to do with the fact that most theaters are run by white, middle-aged, heterosexual men. Despite the apparent "Genetphobia" among American theatrical producers, Akalaitis's imagination is very much captured by this playwright who transcended and transgressed boundaries both in his personal life and in his professional career.[13]

Fortunately, Garland Wright, Artistic Director of the Guthrie Theater, saw the value of producing an unruly work staged by a subversive director. The very idea of a flagship institutional theater producing a politically volatile, aesthetically demanding and economically risky work was in itself subversive. The Guthrie boldly poured its resources into a long developmental workshop followed by a period of reflection and twelve weeks of rehearsal. For many reviewers and critics, *The Screens* was a high point of nationwide theatrical activity. Jack Kroll of *Newsweek* referred to the production as "one of the major events of the decade in American regional theater." Richard Christiansen of *The Chicago Tribune* described *The Screens* as "a triumph." Lucille Johnson Stelling of *Theater Week* stated that "theater history was made in Minneapolis . . . when *The Screens* opened at the Guthrie Theatre." And Don Shewey wrote in the *Village Voice* that "in Akalaitis, Sartre's St. Genet finds an ideal disciple. . . . she is a master of world-sickness. You may try and try to push it away, but she makes you feel the flies on your face."[14]

Akalaitis recalls that, at one point, the publicity for *The Screens* read "Five Hours of Rage and Despair." She points out that, "Yes, there was 'rage and despair' but there was also healing poetry, soaring lyric beauty and, as it turned out, a lot of humor."[15] Shewey suggests that *The Screens,* with nearly one hundred speaking roles and a running time of more than five hours, is "one of the most daunting plays of the century," and is, like all of Genet's work, "an act of radical identification with disenfranchised populations":

> Unlike even the best contemporary theater aimed at inducing in middle-class theatergoers liberal sympathy for the underclass or the ethnic Other, (cf. *Nicholas Nickleby, The Mahabharata, Les Miserables,* Steppenwolf's *The Grapes of Wrath*), *The Screens* offers no palliatives, no figures of heroic sympathy. Instead, it demands of the audience something really scary—to identify with the anger, the

hopelessness, the destructiveness (both outward- and inward-directed) of "the wretched of the earth."[16]

In contrast to the success of *The Screens,* Akalaitis's earlier production of Genet's *The Balcony* alienated many of the American Repertory Theatre's intellectually sophisticated subscribers. Akalaitis recalls that audiences, particularly the men, were "even disturbed by the props."[17] In the scene where the The Archbishop receives communion, for example, Akalaitis substituted a diaphragm for the host. The diaphragm was upsetting, of course, because it was far more than a simple prop. Like many of Akalaitis's scenic elements, it became an iconographic, iconoclastic image resonating with psychological value. Other productions have featured equally subversive scenic images. The costume for the prostitute Malika in *The Screens,* for instance, consisted of a fuschia unitard with a huge fabric "black hole" sewn into the garment's crotch, and during *'Tis Pity She's a Whore,* a pair of disembodied mannequin's legs was tossed onstage from the wings just before intermission.

At a 1991 New York Public Library forum entitled "Theater and the World We Live In," Akalaitis pointed out that Shakespeare, too, is subversive when seen from certain points of view. She noted that Shakespeare, while not an advocate for any political position, in his "amazing world wisdom" presents points of view that collide with our experience in extraordinary ways. Akalaitis cited the contemporary resonance of *Henry IV, Part I,* which she views as a play about "white men making war and screwing up again, just as right now white men are making war in the Persian Gulf." She then described the scene in *Henry IV, Part 2,* between the dying King Henry and Prince Hal, "a young handsome Bush-like character about to become the Renaissance political leader." When the King advises his son "to giddy busy minds with foreign quarrels," [IV, v, 213–14][18] Akalaitis, sitting among the audience, would often hear a collective gasp that she describes as "something that actually happens among them."[19] In a single theatrical moment, the past becomes present. A political idea evokes an emotional response. Borders are traversed and connections made. Like Shakespeare, Akalaitis is subversive in the questions she raises and the thought she provokes. Like Genet, she is subversive in her disruption of boundaries and resistance to categorization. Like both of them, she has an obsession with and a passion for the theater.

And, like many artists, Akalaitis views tension as an essential part of the creative endeavor. She appears not only to accept tension, but also to actively seek and encourage its presence. At a 1985 workshop for women directors, Akalaitis cautioned the participants against interpreting Heiner Muller's cryptic text *Quartet* too early in the rehearsal process, pronouncing, "I am always interested in tension. I don't seek harmony or ease."[20] As for her relationship to the New York Shakespeare Festival, Akalaitis stated in February of 1991 that she felt it was important for an institution to have a number of people in its midst who would subvert, demystify, question, perhaps even "terrify" it. She added, however, that there must be more than one person who performs this subversive function for an institution. An "energetic tension" would thus exist between those who questioned the institution and those who "needed to maintain the mechanism of the institution," a tension that Akalaitis described as "potentially interesting."[21] Unfortunately, this tension proved fatal to Akalaitis's relationship with the New York Shakespeare Festival.

The very nature of a rehearsal process entails bringing something to life yet as one of Akalaitis's favorite authors, Samuel Beckett, reminds us, birth contains within it the ultimate darkness.[22] Akalaitis's interest in and tolerance for chaos as a part of the creative process can give way to both productive and problematic tension in rehearsal. Her physical exercises, for example, allow the actors to creatively explore images arising from the dramatic text, the surrounding scenic space, and their own psyches. And because the exercises may prove difficult, embarrassing, or simply a bother to execute, they may provoke resistance on the part of some actors—against the text, against themselves, against the director. Yet, as I observed Akalaitis in rehearsal, I came to realize that the exercises served a crucial function in her directing process. Every director's task involves giving form to amorphous, unruly, at times formally or emotionally overwhelming material, by means of textual analysis, blocking, actor-coaching, and the orchestration of scenographic elements. However, given Akalaitis's predilection for particularly chaotic subjects and processes, her exercises serve not only as a physical warm-up and cast-bonding ritual, but also as concrete, ordered structures that help the actors both express and contain this chaos.

[1] Unless otherwise noted, all quotes attributed to Akalaitis are drawn from the author's rehearsal notes for 'Tis Pity She's a Whore, directed by JoAnne Akalaitis, Goodman Theatre, Chicago, Ill., January–March 1990, and The Mormon Project Workshop, directed by JoAnne Akalaitis, Atlantic Center for the Arts, New Smyrna Beach, Fla., June 1990, as well as from personal interviews and informal conversations.

[2] See Mel Gussow, "The Theater's Avant-Garde Branches Out," New York Times 18 March 1984, nat'l.ed., sec. 2:18, and Don Shewey, "The Many Voices of Mabou Mines," American Theatre June 1984:5.

[3] For responses to Akalaitis's appointment to Artistic Director of the New York Shakespeare Festival, see Mel Gussow, "Other Ways at the Shakespeare Festival," New York Times 17 June 1990, sec. 2:5; Phoebe Hoban, "Going Public: JoAnne Akalaitis Takes Over for Papp," New York Magazine 28 Oct. 1991: 42–47; and Don Shewey, "Rocking the House That Papp Built," Village Voice 25 Sept. 1990: 34–41.

[4] Philip Ausslander quoted in Richard Schechner, interview, "Theory and Practice of the Indeterminate Theatre," by Nick Kaye, New Theatre Quarterly 5 (1989): 355–56.

[5] Alex Witchel, "Papp Names Akalaitis to Step in as Shakespeare Festival Head," New York Times 21 Aug. 1991: C11.

[6] "Stage View," New York Times 1 Feb. 1991, natl. ed.: B2.

[7] Ronn Smith, "Actors, Designers Face Off: Can They Be Partners?" American Theatre April 1992: 49.

[8] JoAnne Akalaitis, jacket notes, Philip Glass and Foday Musa Suso, Music from The Screens, cond. Martin Goldray, Point 432-966-2, 1991.

[9] Emotional geography includes intellectual geography: Ideas as well as feelings have emotional value for the actor.

[10] David Leong, personal interview, 10 June 1992, appended herein.

[11] During an informal conversation with Akalaitis, on 17 Aug. 1990, she suggested, "If you want to talk about influences on my work, you should look at the films of Fassbinder."

[12] See Rainer Werner Fassbinder, "The Kind of Rage I Feel": A Conversation with Joachim von Mengershausen about Love Is Colder Than Death, The Anarchy of the Imagination: Interview, Essay, Notes/Rainer Werner Fassbinder, ed. Michael Töteberg and Leo A. Lensing, trans. Krishna Winston (Baltimore: Johns Hopkins University Press, 1992) xi, 3–4.

[13] JoAnne Akalaitis, "Theater and the World." Performing Arts Forum Series, New York Public Library for the Performing Arts, 28 Feb. 1991.

[14] See Richard Christiansen, "Jean Genet's 'The Screens' a triumph in Guthrie Theater's 4½-hour offering," Chicago Tribune 4 November 1989; Jack Kroll, "Major Doings in Minneapolis: The Genius of Genet," Newsweek, n.d.: N. pag; Don Shewey, "Through the Turds," Village Voice, 12 Dec. 1989: 120; and Lucille

Johnson Stelling, "Genet At the Guthrie: In 1966 *The Screens* provoked riots," *Theater Week* 27 Nov.–3 Dec. 1989: 39.

15 Akalaitis, "Theater and the World."

16 Shewey, "Through the Turds."

17 Akalaitis, "Theater and the World."

18 William Shakespeare, *Henry IV Part 2*, *The Riverside Shakespeare*, ed. G. Blakemore Evans (Boston: Houghton, 1974) 916.

19 Akalaitis, "Theater and the World."

20 Elizabeth M. Osborn, "Directors at Work," *American Theatre* Sept. 1985: 30.

21 Akalaitis, "Theater and the World."

22 See, for example, the Speaker's line, "Birth was the death of him." in Samuel Beckett, "A Piece of Monologue," *The Collected Shorter Plays* (New York: Grove, 1984) 265.

Part One

One

Akalaitis and Mabou Mines, 1970–1984

There is nothing like Mabou Mines any place. . . . They are a
symbol of the highest caliber of theater that exists in this city.
JOSEPH PAPP

Mabou Mines is an artistic collaborative known for its physical and
visual approach to performance, its emphasis on language, and its
interest in the psychological and emotional processes of the actor. The
company has presented numerous performance works that range
from the early theater poems of Lee Breuer to a gender-reversed version of *King Lear,* and include several plays by Samuel Beckett and
Franz Xaver Kroetz, large-scale sociopolitical theatrical collages,
adaptations of historical biographies, radio plays, and holographic
installations. Mabou Mines has no leader, artistic director, or group
aesthetic, but it is instead a collective of individual artists who possess
a wide range of talents and sensibilities. Virtually every member of
Mabou Mines has performed, directed, written, and designed both
inside and outside of the company. At the same time, Mabou Mines
regularly works with an extended circle of associates who are not
formal company members.

While Mabou Mines has been in dire financial straits for years,
and has never had a permanent theater space, it continues to evolve
artistically and to create new work. The company tends to have several

works in development simultaneously over long periods of time, and their production schedule is quirky and erratic. When they do get around to presenting a piece, it is frequently performed in an out-of-the-way space for a limited run, with little advance notice. It is thus likely that many more people have heard of Mabou Mines than have actually seen them perform. Nevertheless, Mabou Mines has been a shaping force in the development of American experimental theater.

Of the individual artists who have either branched out from or left Mabou Mines to pursue independent careers, none has had a greater impact on the American theater than JoAnne Akalaitis. This chapter traces the roots of Mabou Mines in the converging lives and aesthetics of the five founding members, provides an overview of Akalaitis's involvement with the company both as a performer and a director, and discusses the company's unique approaches to performance, staging, and design. It also offers a collection of personal responses to the work of Mabou Mines from company members, associates, and critics.

San Francisco: The Genesis of Mabou Mines

JoAnne Akalaitis was raised in a Lithuanian-Catholic community on Chicago's southwest side, and she graduated from the University of Chicago with an undergraduate degree in philosophy and pre-med. She attended graduate school at Stanford in the early 1960s, intending to get a Ph.D. in philosophy but discovered instead that she really wanted to be an actor. Still supported by her graduate fellowship, Akalaitis moved to San Francisco and began working with Herbert Blau and Jules Irving in their Actor's Workshop, where she met Lee Breuer and Ruth Maleczech.

Breuer was a pre-law student at U.C.L.A. in the late 1950s when he stumbled into the drama department, became fascinated with the writings of Camus, Sartre, Beckett, and Genet, and proceeded to win several campus playwriting awards. He moved to San Francisco with Maleczech in 1959 and made his first foray into directing with a production of Brecht's *Caucasian Chalk Circle* performed by members of the San Francisco Mime Troupe. One of the Mime Troupe actors was Bill Raymond who eventually became a core member of Mabou Mines. Alan Schneider saw the production, was impressed, and suggested that Blau hire Breuer as an assistant director. Breuer was put in charge of the Workshop's experimental wing at the Encore Theatre where his directorial projects included Beckett's *Happy Days* and Genet's *The Maids*.

The Actor's Workshop, which existed from 1952 to 1965, embraced a vision of theater rooted in what Blau considers to be the overall dream of the twentieth century: the marriage of socialism and surrealism. Blau envisioned the Workshop as "a theater of some activist dimension with an audience composed of workers, intellectuals and students." Its theatrical investigations centered around a line of inquiry that Blau defined as "the Brecht-Beckett dialectic," a commitment to the notion of a popular, public, and political theater coupled with an appreciation for the spiritual dimension of the form. A firm believer in Brecht's socialist ideals, Blau nonetheless admitted to being drawn at the level of temperament and taste to Beckett's idea of "writing into the void," the awareness that "there's nobody out there" but somehow you keep working.[1]

It was at the Actor's Workshop that Akalaitis, Breuer, and Maleczech began what was to become for each of them a long and meaningful association with the works of Beckett and Genet. The three also worked together at the San Francisco Tape Music Center along with Morton Subotnick, Ramone Sender, Ann Halprin, and Pauline Oliveros. Akalaitis recalls the excitement of San Francisco's experimental art, music, and theater scene during the early sixties, yet at the same time admits to being ambitious and thinking she had to have "leading ingenue roles in important plays, like [those of] Tennessee Williams and Arthur Miller."[2] In 1962, she left San Francisco to pursue an acting career in New York.

For the next three years, Akalaitis auditioned, acted in showcases, and did summer stock. She studied various Stanislavsky-based acting techniques with teachers such as Herbert Berghof, Bill Hickey, Herbert Machiz, Gene Frankel, and Mira Rostova, but she found the classes "manipulative, Svengali-like and confusing." She became disillusioned with what she perceived to be a complete lack of dialogue in the classes, and an "implicit succession of ambitions" that shaped the way that students and teachers related to each other. According to Akalaitis, the focus of the classes "was not about learning how to work, it was about getting a good scene together, getting out there, and showing it to everybody. It was about presentational acting even when it was theoretically about investigating Method acting."[3] In 1965, disillusioned with her career and the state of the New York theater, Akalaitis moved to Paris with composer Philip Glass whom she had recently married.

PARIS: THE PREHISTORY OF MABOU MINES

Philip Glass had won a Fullbright to study with the renowned composition teacher Nadia Boulanger, and, while in Paris, Akalaitis worked on a LeRoi Jones play. On a trip to Greece, they met Breuer and Maleczech who had been travelling in Turkey, Morocco, and Italy. In San Francisco, Breuer had been unable to talk anybody into doing his own plays and had travelled to Europe with Maleczech in 1964, hoping to "find himself" as a writer. Akalaitis convinced Breuer and Maleczech to join her in Paris, whereupon she introduced them to the actor who was to complete the founding membership of Mabou Mines.

David Warrilow had met Akalaitis in a theater workshop in Paris. At the time, he had acted a bit in student productions but had no formal training. Born in Britain, Warrilow graduated in French from Reading University and then went to Paris where he had been working for eleven years as an editor on the English-language edition of the magazine *Réalités*. Impressed by the originality and daring of the American artists who would eventually form Mabou Mines, Warrilow views his introduction to them as a radical and inevitable turning point in his life:

> They shook me up so. Their way of looking at things and talking about things threw my whole structure of the universe into chaos . . . the way they were able to ask "Why not?" Why not the four of us

work on Samuel Beckett's *Play* for four months in the evening when David is not at the office, and why not just leave it at that? We don't have to perform it; let's just do that. I hadn't come across that kind of thinking. It was new, vital and so compelling that even though it was scary, I decided to go with it. It was the beginning of a very long, difficult, joyful and extraordinary process that is still going on.[4]

The group began work on Beckett's one-act *Play* in 1965. Directed by Breuer, performed by Akalaitis, Maleczech, and Warrilow, with an original score composed by Glass, the piece opened in 1967 for two performances at the American Cultural Center in Paris, and it was subsequently produced by Mabou Mines at New York's Café La Mama. *Play* is a "trialogue" for two women and one man, each of whom are entrapped in a huge urn. Cued by a spotlight, the three characters tell separate but intertwining stories of their romantic triangle. The man, presumably married to one of the women, was discovered having an affair with the other. Confronted by the first woman, the man swore he would end the affair but found he could not do so. As the play draws to a close, each character wonders if the other two are somehow together. The entire play is then repeated verbatim.

Glass's score for *Play* was a one-hour, recorded composition for two soprano saxophones. While studying for several months with Indian sitarist Ravi Shankar, Glass had become intrigued with the way that rhythm determines structure in Indian music. As Glass explains, "In Western music we divide time—as if you were to take a length of time and slice it the way you slice a loaf of bread. In Indian music . . . you take small units, or 'beats,' and string them together to make up larger time values." Exploring this process of rhythmic "induction" in his music for *Play*, Glass composed two saxophone parts each of which consisted of only two notes in the form of an alternating, pulsing interval. When the two saxophone lines were superimposed, they formed a shifting pattern of sounds that stayed within the four pitches of the two intervals. The result was a very static, but rhythmically complex, piece that underscored the entire performance. The score for *Play* was the first of Glass's highly repetitive, minimalist compositions that were to occupy him for years afterward and pave the way for his ensemble music of the early 1970s.[5]

While overseas, the members of the group made frequent pilgrimages to observe and work with theater artists from various countries. Breuer and Maleczech studied with the Berliner Ensemble for a month and were given permission by Helene Weigel to attend several rehearsals. Glass and Akalaitis saw the Living Theatre's seven-hour production of *Frankenstein* at the Avignon Festival in France, after which they travelled to Berlin to see the company's *Antigone* and to talk to them about their work. Glass had first seen the Living Theatre perform during the late 1950s when he was a student in New York City, and he had been enormously affected by their work. Never before had he seen theater that consisted primarily of images and movement, and that radically extended the accepted sense of theatrical time. Glass later saw this same extended time-scale used in the Khathakali dance theater of South India and in the early work of Robert Wilson. In fact, Glass believes he witnessed the prototype for what later came to be called the "theater of images," a description most often applied to Wilson's work, in the performances of the Living Theatre during the early 1960s.[6]

Although the group had discussed the idea of starting a permanent company in Paris, they eventually realized there was not a large enough audience to sustain an English-speaking theater. Akalaitis and Glass left Paris in the fall of 1967, travelling to India and Central Asia before returning to the States. In the summer of 1968, Akalaitis and Maleczech spent a month in Aix-en-Provence working with Polish director and theorist Jerzy Grotowski, hoping to be able to teach his work to others. Akalaitis saw Grotowski's technique as an evolution of the Stanislavsky system, which, at the same time, emphasized the actor's body, personal history, and sense of value as an artist. Of particular importance to her was Grotowski's view that the actor is not merely an interpreter, but as much an artist as a playwright or a painter. Akalaitis's exposure to Grotowski completely changed her ideas about work and solidified the group's interest in a physical and vocal theater that saw the actor as a primary creative force.

Still in Paris, Breuer directed a production of Brecht's *Mother*

Courage in 1968, with Glass returning to Paris to serve as musical director for the original Paul Desau score. Appearing in Breuer's production was Fred Neumann, an American actor who had been doing radio plays, voice-overs, and film dubbing in Europe, and who would later join Mabou Mines. That same year, Breuer completed a first draft of what was eventually to become *The B. Beaver Animation*. Still seeking a venue where he could produce and direct his own work, Breuer left Europe with Maleczech in the winter of 1969.

NEW YORK: THE FOUNDING OF MABOU MINES

Upon returning to the States, Akalaitis attended every theater workshop she heard about. One in particular, led by Joyce Aaron of the Open Theater, had a great influence upon Akalaitis's understanding of the actor's body, its relationship to space and to other bodies, and "the opening of certain areas of physical energy." In 1969, Akalaitis studied again with Grotowski, whose Polish Lab Theatre had come to New York for a series of performances. Akalaitis was frustrated, however, because she was not a part of any ongoing theater group. She was disappointed in most of the plays she saw, even on the so-called "avant-garde" circuit, and failed to see a way that she could function, "as an actor who wanted to be an artist," within the existing structure. Cast in a show that was to be produced at La Mama but was cancelled just before it was scheduled to open, Akalaitis regarded this event as the final nail in the coffin of her professional theater career. She "quit the theater," fixed up a room in her house, and started teaching the work she had learned from Grotowski to a handful of actors, including the then-Performance Group member Spalding Gray.[7]

When Breuer and Maleczech returned to New York, they once again joined forces with Akalaitis and Glass. Warrilow, meanwhile, had been so inspired by his experience working on *Play* that he quit his publishing job at the age of thirty-six and had his passport revised to read "actor" instead of "journalist." He had been trying, in vain, to obtain acting work in London when he received a wire from Maleczech and Breuer inviting him to join them in the States.

Warrilow arrived in New York in December of 1969 and moved into the house that by then was doubling as living and rehearsal space for Akalaitis, Glass, Maleczech, and Breuer. The re-united group began rehearsing its first piece, *The Red Horse Animation,* during Christmas of 1969, and Mabou Mines was officially founded on January 1, 1970.

Earlier that year, Akalaitis and Glass had discovered an abandoned summer camp on a cliff overlooking the sea near the mining town of Mabou, Nova Scotia. They bought it, along with their friend writer Rudolph Wurlitzer, and the company took "Mabou Mines" as its name. According to Bill Raymond, who joined the company shortly after its founding, Mabou Mines was interested in making something of their own that was art but was not part of the traditional "theater bailiwick—that was somehow more real." Raymond suggests that the name "Mabou Mines" may have appealed to the group because it sounded more like a rock band than a theater.[8]

Warrilow confesses that, "at first, living with [Mabou Mines] in an abandoned house on 23rd Street, I wondered what I was doing, but the moment I started to work, it began to feel right. In some way, my double life as editor and amateur actor was over, and I coincided with myself."[9] For Glass, who officially resigned from Mabou Mines in 1973 but remains on their advisory board to this day, "the idea of the company was to eliminate the worst aspects of the commercial theater world. We had the luxury of poverty. We had plenty of time. Pieces evolved from an extended work process. We had first Ellen Stewart and then Joseph Papp as patrons of the company. No one bothered us too much. We collaborated with other artists."[10] For years, Mabou Mines made no money and was continually in debt. Company members, several of whom had young children, supported themselves by working as proofreaders, part-time teachers, waiters, dishwashers, and busboys. Akalaitis worked as a chef at Food Restaurant in SoHo until 1975. Yet the company's sense of artistic reward made up for their financial hardship. As Akalaitis herself sees it, "all the people involved in the group really started their artistic lives—in a sense . . . were reborn—when Mabou Mines began."[11]

The Rehearsal Process of Mabou Mines

Although Mabou Mines's roots lay in performing the scripted works of the European literary avant-garde, the company concentrated on presenting original theater pieces during their early years in New York. While Breuer was clearly the author and director of these pieces, each company member shared responsibility for shaping the overall performance. Breuer would bring in the prose narratives he had written and outline in detail his "concept" for the piece. These ideas served as a springboard for the company's improvisations as they explored actions, movements, gestures, and activities that would eventually evolve into a performance text. Maleczech recalls the Berliner Ensemble's process of "multiple direction" that had a great influence on the Mabou Mines's rehearsal process. At the Berliner Ensemble, every "stage picture" was required to be extremely precise and thus there were always several people watching and commenting upon the rehearsal. There was clearly a head director, but there was also the sense that several people were directing at once, with a number of very up-front conversations going on between the directors and the actors. According to Maleczech, Mabou Mines seized upon this way of working, which they saw as running counter to the American Stanislavsky tradition of privacy between actor and director.[12]

Creating text, staging, and design in a public, collaborative manner took an enormous amount of time and energy. Because all of the actors and designers needed to be present at every rehearsal, Mabou Mines's pieces often took years to develop. Sculptor Jene Highstein created the urns for *Play* and worked on a number of Mabou Mines's early pieces. Describing the company's lengthy and intense rehearsal process, Highstein explains that, "since they work all the time, you go and work with them. . . . They kind-of excruciatingly go through every conceivable option for every conceivable move within the subject, and everybody has a say about what they think that's going to be. So it takes a lot of time to develop a piece."[13]

AKALAITIS PERFORMS WITH MABOU MINES

The Red Horse Animation (1970)

The Red Horse Animation was the first in a series of three Kafkaesque parables that examined man as a "social animal." According to Breuer, *The Red Horse Animation* is about being taken over by romance, about the conflict between freedom and being "taken for a ride"; *The B. Beaver Animation* is about the dam that inhibits creative flow and about speaking through a stutter; and *The Shaggy Dog Animation* is about the master/slave relationship.[14] Breuer looks back on his process of writing the *Animations* as a kind of personal exorcism, a way of exploring and eliminating self-images that were no longer valid. He explains that the word *Animations* refers both to the idea of an animated cartoon and to the Latin animus—to make alive:

> The composite characters presented are essentially psyches—for a while I thought I was talking about metaphors or states of mind, but that was too removed. I now think of the psyches as actual animals, in the sense that you can be in the human world and the animal world—or the world of ghosts—at the same time. They're sort of choral monologues, each one dealing with a different psychological personality.[15]

The Red Horse Animation was performed by Akalaitis, Maleczech, and Warrilow, and had an original score composed by Glass. The piece took nearly a year to develop, with the most concentrated period of work occurring in Nova Scotia during the summer of 1970. New York artist Power Boothe joined the company that summer and designed a special floor for the production. Built in modular wooden units and amplified by contact microphones, the floor functioned as a kind of percussive sounding board on which the actors performed the musical score of the piece. By stamping, tapping, running, sliding, and pounding, the actors could create sounds ranging from galloping hoofbeats to winds sweeping across the Gobi desert. The floor thus enabled the actors to endow movement with sound and sound with shape. The actors also held tiny microphones against their larynxes so they could throw their voices across the stage space. Glass organized these percussive and vocal sounds into a complex arithmetic system, a technique he later referred to as "additive process."[16]

The piece was first performed at the Guggenheim Museum in 1970, and it was subsequently revised and expanded for a presentation at the Whitney Museum in May of 1972. For its presentation at the Guggenheim, the seating in the museum's auditorium was reversed. The audience was seated on the stage and looked down over the performance that took place on the special floor constructed over the auditorium seats. Breuer's program note reads as follows:

> *The Red Horse Animation* is about the process of performing—the building and sustaining of an image. The medium is theater and so the image is one that materializes only in performance.
>
> Three performers play three parts. These parts combine to form and animate the red horse. The red horse, once animated, attempts to create itself. The piece is composed of these processes moving along simultaneously.
>
> The red horse, in its representational form, materializes and falls apart in the course of the performance. It lives in real time. "Lives" in this sense means conveys meaning to its creators and observors. It tries to create its life outside the real performance time. It tries to live in dramatic time.
>
> It is a stage image. It is constructed in mediums of expression available to the performing artist—movement, speech, music and acting. It is not a play. It cannot be read and does not purport to make a literary statement. As a stage piece, it tries to exist in its own terms. Stage time. Stage space. Dramatic structure.[17]

The story of the Red Horse spans huge expanses of time and space, often in a single sentence. The subject matter is presented from the point of view of the three performers who narrate the Horse's tale in the third person, as well as share the interior consciousness of the Horse as they speak its inner monologue in the first person. At the same time, the actors physically illustrate the Horse's body with their own bodies, forming both anthropomorphic and abstract images. The life of the Red Horse is thus dramatized over the course of the performance as a kind of living cartoon, an "animation." Various reviews and descriptions of the piece mention that Mabou Mines used a combination of "internal and external acting techniques," that the actors appeared personally and emotionally connected to the words of the text yet seemed to be *demonstrating* the Horse's story rather than *becoming* the Horse in any traditional sense of creating character.[18]

The Red Horse Animation, while clearly a work of theater, is also painterly, sculptural, photographic, cinematic, and musical. At times, the performance seems to be a living painting with the actors framed against the "canvas" of the floor or the back wall. When the Horse's father Daily Bread, leaps to his death, for example, the actors leap onto the back wall of the performance space, creating a flattened, painterly image of a horse. At other times, the piece appears to be a moving sculpture, the actors' bodies constructing and deconstructing a three-dimensional image of a horse in space. The actors pin photographs of horses on the back wall, many of which are taken from Edweard Muybridge's pioneering study, *Animals in Motion*, which depicts stop-action photographs of horses galloping, trotting, and cantering. Breuer also used the Muybridge sequences as a source for the images of the Horse formed by the actors themselves. Much of the action is organized cinematically by means of "cuts," "dissolves," and "close-ups"; at one point the Horse himself wonders, "Do I owe a debt to the cinema?"[19] The text contains words such as *form, shape, circles,* and *lines* that pertain to the visual arts. And the layout of the printed text reveals an intricate system of visual prosody. Even the documentation of *The Red Horse Animation* is a work of visual art. The first published version of the script was a comic book created by Breuer, a storyboard of thirty-two color plates that alternate between drawings of the actors embodying the Horse in performance, and drawings of the Horse itself.

Ellen Stewart of Café La Mama saw a work-in-progress showing

of *Red Horse* at the Paula Cooper Gallery in New York and was suf-
ficiently impressed to provide Mabou Mines with its the first public
support. Stewart invited the company to be in residence at La Mama
for three years, provided them with rehearsal space on Great Jones
Street, put the five members on a salary of fifty dollars per week, and
paid for the special floor constructed for the piece.

Come and Go (1971)

Come and Go is subtitled a "dramaticule" by its author, Samuel
Beckett. Three women—Vi, Flo, and Ru—sit on a bench and remi-
nisce about their old school days. Over the course of the play, each
woman leaves the stage briefly while the other two whisper an
appalling secret about her into each other's ear. While the secret is
never revealed, it apparently concerns a change that has come over the
absent woman, a change of which she herself is unaware. Finally, the
three women clasp hands, and Flo says, "I can feel the rings." Yet
Beckett specifies in his stage directions that there are no rings apparent.[20] In this play, character is revealed by absence: by what is *not*
seen, by what is *not* said, by silence.

    Come and Go was directed by Lee Breuer and performed by
Akalaitis, Maleczech, and Dawn Gray (later replaced by Ellen
McElduff). The piece was performed as part of the *Brooklyn Bridge
Event* in May of 1971, the actors speaking the text in amplified whis-
pers from underneath the bridge while the audience watched from a
pylon seventy-five yards across the water. Mabou Mines performed
the piece again at La Mama in June of 1971, at the Whitney Museum
in April of 1972, and at the Public Theater in 1974 as part of *Mabou
Mines Performs Beckett: Play, Come and Go, The Lost Ones*. In these
later venues, the audience viewed not the piece itself but its reflection
in a mirror while listening to the disembodied voices of the actors who
were performing from the back of the house.

    Akalaitis recalls that her task as an actress in *Come and Go* was
not to play a character, but to deal with what was actually happening
between herself and the other two women at the particular time they
were performing. She was especially aware of her response to physical

details, such as the way Maleczech's ear looked when she whispered into it, the pattern of the wrinkles around her eyes, or the texture of McElduff's hair. Akalaitis has described performance as "one of the means to enter another state of consciousness. Performance *is* in the present—that's why it's like drugs or meditation—it's one of the few times you're living totally in the moment."[21] This statement is perhaps a key to the particular phenomenology of the Mabou Mines actor, whose work embodies the idea that performance is fundamentally the act, and the art, of *being present*. To suggest that an actor does not lose herself in a character is not to imply that she is emotionally distanced from the work or the audience. Perhaps the actor loses, and finds, herself in something else—the moment itself.

The B. Beaver Animation (1975)

Originally presented at the Museum of Modern Art in 1975, and revived at the Public Theatre in 1990, *The B. Beaver Animation* existed first as a short story that Breuer wrote in 1968. It was then developed over an eighteen-month period into a forty-minute theater piece by the original members of Mabou Mines with the addition of Fred Neumann and Bill Raymond. The central character in the work is B. Beaver, a compulsive and stuttering beaver/architect who "loses the power of damnation."

Recalling his experience on *B. Beaver*, Breuer believes that his script suffered at the expense of the group's performance style which rendered it muddy and destroyed any sense of narrative continuity. He felt he had little control over the production and, for that reason, prefers a single-actor version of the show performed by Fred Neumann on tape. Breuer explains that aspects of the Mabou Mines's collaborative method were at odds with his process and goals as a writer:

> Because we worked it over so much, and had so many high-powered complicated actors who had so much wonderful stuff, ultimately the narrative was overpowered. I got tired of hearing reviews of how great the performing was but that the script was a series of non

sequiturs and fake Beckett. . . . It was made incomprehensible because the emphasis was on the comedy and the performing style. The script was, in a way, trashed.[22]

For Breuer, the beaver's dam and speech impediment are metaphors for writer's block and artistic inhibition. And Akalaitis has stated that the piece was, in part, "a search for the negative aspects of who we were."[23] But because a dam itself is something that inhibits flow, the piece raises the question of whether B. Beaver's inability to build is a blessing or a curse. As the ramshackle set disintegrates over the course of the piece, eventually collapsing into a heap, one wonders if the dam has been roadblock to, or an expression of, B. Beaver's creative powers.

In April of 1975, Mabou Mines brought *The B. Beaver Animation* to the Museum of Contemporary Art in Chicago. They also performed Beckett's *The Lost Ones* at the Space Above the Biograph, and conducted a directing workshop at Northwestern University. An announcement in the *Chicago Tribune* hailed Mabou Mines as a unique theater group that "acts out characters but does not engage in motivational acting." Interestingly, while the article described Mabou Mines's performance style as "very verbal, using words texturally and musically as well as dramatically," Breuer himself emphasized Mabou Mines's position vis à vis theater and the visual arts, explaining that, "We aren't kids you know. . . . All of us had careers before starting this theater. We want to do theater that's art and see if actors can be artists. Some visual artists think acting is corny. Mabou Mines understands this but thinks that [point of view is] too safe, that ultimately standing there and looking subtle is too easy."[24]

The Shaggy Dog Animation (1978)

The Shaggy Dog was the longest and most technically complex of the *Animations,* employing human actors, three-quarter life-size Bunraku-style puppets, amplified speech, and music. Mabou Mines performed a prologue to the piece as a work-in-progress at the Paula Cooper

Gallery in 1974. Breuer then spent 1975 writing Part I and an incomplete version of Part II for another work-in-progress showing while Akalaitis made her Mabou Mines directing debut with Beckett's *Cascando*. Breuer finished writing *Shaggy Dog* in 1977 while the company worked on Akalaitis's next directorial project, *Dressed Like an Egg*.

The protagonist of *Shaggy Dog* is the canine Rose who is in love with her master John, a filmmaker like herself. Unfortunately, John fails to reciprocate Rose's love. As the piece unfolds, Rose gradually achieves liberation from her master/lover, a story told in the form of an extended "Dear John" letter. Rose's voice is electronically amplified, manipulated, and distorted, as well as divided among an eight-member human chorus. The dog's voice is thus disembodied and wrenched from its true "owner." The action takes place in front of a twenty-three-foot-long radio frequency band complete with moveable needle. Over the course of the piece, the performance style varied from rock to jazz to country-western to soap opera depending upon where the needle happened to be located on the tuning band.[25]

Akalaitis describes her process as an actor at that time as more visual, imagistic, and physical than psychological. She would attempt to visualize a "picture" of her character, almost as if she were projecting a slide onto a wall, and then try to to fit herself into that picture by changing her body and voice which in turn began to change the way she felt internally. This process was continually shaped and informed by her fellow company members. At a certain point in the rehearsal process, for instance, Akalaitis was directed by Breuer to explore "mature female warmth and sexuality, working only with the voice." She began to explore her idea of "sincere female sexiness," which reminded another actor of Billie Holiday. Akalaitis then listened to Holiday records and tried to abstract the vocal quality she heard, letting it inform the lines of the text as she worked with the microphone. Someone then threw out the idea of punctuating vocal phrases with physical movement, which Akalaitis tried by thrusting her hip to the side and saying, "Shachoo! Shachoo!" Maleczech approached Akalaitis after the rehearsal and said, "That's great JoAnne, that's S&M." Although Akalaitis felt that her hip movements were simply physical punctuations of a vocal phrases, and had nothing to do with S&M, she began to explore Maleczech's idea, going to porno films and looking at S&M advertisements in magazines. Akalaitis considers it important to have arrived at a character not through her choices alone, but through something that happened in the process of rehearsal with the observation and help of other people.[26]

While Breuer considers *Shaggy* Dog to have been the most well-received of the *Animations,* there were those who felt the four-hour piece to be confusing, inaccessible, or simply too long. *Soho Weekly News* theater critic Gerald Rabkin, for example, suggested that the work confused the thematic metaphor of fragmentation with artistic diffusiveness:

> Is it unreasonable to desire some clear direction through the maze of images? Even accepting Mabou Mines's associative esthetic method, we have to will a cohesive through-line to maintain our attention over the long haul. Author/director Lee Breuer seems to glory in the way the organic structure he has nourished branches and rebranches in all directions. He cherishes each branch, twig, and leaf, rather than taking care that none endanger or obscure the sturdiness of the trunk. Occasional phrases and sentences suggest a thematic overview. . . . But they are not consistently reinforced.[27]

In his essay, "The End of Humanism," Richard Schechner argues that the actions of the performers in *Shaggy Dog* do not illustrate the text; neither does the text tell a story "in that direct kind of way customary to modern theatre." Although the story of Rose's unrequited love can be teased out from the performance, Schechner views *Shaggy Dog* as above all the deconstruction of Breuer's personal experiences with his colleagues (which happen to include his wife and daughter) into bits of information and behavior. Given this scenario, Rose is "a dog a woman a bitch a wife a lover a performer (or two or three) a puppet a concept a way of looking at experience a way of rearranging information to form new experiences a game an artifact." And the piece was flawed, in Schechner's view, because it lacked a crucial final step—the reconstruction after the deconstruction.[28] But was this final step necessary, or even possible? Was it in fact critical for audiences to know, as Schechner wished at the time, what "it all" meant?

The program for *Shaggy Dog* states that the piece was "written and conceived" by Breuer, and "produced and realized" by Mabou Mines, yet the word "director" was nowhere to be found. Interestingly, the fragmented structure of *Shaggy Dog* mirrored that of Mabou Mines itself. Although company members continued to engage in a collaborative investigation of character and text throughout *Shaggy Dog's* extended rehearsal period, working relationships among them had become strained. Citing artistic differences with unspecified company members, David Warrilow quit *Shaggy Dog* during the first year of its development. According to Warrilow, the piece "becomes very difficult for an audience to go on taking in. There's a saturation point. . . . Mabou Mines should be mature enough to reconcile esthetic considerations with the needs of an audience." Akalaitis herself suggested excising the entire second act, as well as several cuts in her own part, yet Breuer felt her advice was reflective of a "painter-sculptor or dance aesthetic" and not in keeping with his "more literary approach."[29]

In an extended interview in the *Village Voice*, Breuer confessed that, although the conceiving and much of the directing in Mabou Mines was in fact collaborative, he always regarded himself as the auteur with the rest of the company as groupies. According to Breuer, " . . . by the time of *Shaggy Dog Animation*, I'm not paying attention to anyone, I'm running roughshod over the company. I get a clean emotional through-line for the piece, but at a price. All the atrociously political stuff finally comes to a head. For one thing, JoAnne and I realize it's the last time we'll ever work together."[30]

AKALAITIS'S THOUGHTS ON ACTING AND DIRECTING: 1976

Shaggy Dog's extended gestation period coincided with Akalaitis's first two directing projects with Mabou Mines. At the same time, her own ideas about the nature of acting and directing were undergoing a transformation. In 1976, Akalaitis considered her personal aesthetic as a performer to be characterized by a commitment to authenticity and honesty, a tendency to underplay rather than overplay, and a resistance to violating or changing a piece in order to please the audience. In Akalaitis's view, the director was a "cartographer" who possessed superior knowledge because he or she was an observer. As a performer, she preferred directorial suggestions about "possibilities, maps and directions," rather than praise, evaluative words, or reactions. She admitted, however, that she was fairly resistant to and cautious about directorial suggestions of any kind because she did not want to feel that she was working for anyone or anything but the piece itself. Her tendency as an actor was to "go with the purity of the situation—the purity being me and my acting and my fellow actors."[31]

For Akalaitis, performance was becoming less and less abut representing a role than about presenting the self. She spoke of no longer working to "lose herself" in the material, as she had done when she was a young actor. She explains that, "It was very important for me to get lost in the piece, or to get lost in character; it seemed 'truer' or more authentic acting, because I could completely eradicate myself. In the last four or five years, [things have] gone a way I would not have expected; I become more myself and less the persona when I perform."[32]

MABOU MINES AS A COLLABORATIVE OF ARTISTIC DIRECTORS: 1975–80

Akalaitis's evolution from performer to director was a natural step in the process of her becoming "more herself" in the theater. In fact, the company's work process over the years has been so collaborative, with actors frequently initiating projects, that virtually every member of Mabou Mines has directed both within and outside the company. Maleczech, for instance, while preferring the immediacy of performance, has directed several projects, beginning with a workshop production of Beckett's *Not I* in 1975 (the year that Akalaitis directed her first play). She has also directed *Vanishing Pictures,* based on an Edgar Allan Poe short story, in 1980; an adaptation of the Jim Strahs's novel *Wrong Guys* in 1981 (in which Breuer made his acting debut); a holographic installation based on Beckett's *Imagination Dead Imagine* in 1984; and in 1989, *Sueños,* a musical theater piece based on the life of the seventeenth-century Mexican nun and poet, Sor Inés de la Cruz. Maleczech views the emergence and encouragement of directors other than Breuer as an extremely important step for Mabou Mines. She argues that "that circling energy has kept us going; [it] is more healthy for art than straight-line energy. It's very important to us to encourage growth in one another, and to keep pushing our work forward."[33]

Akalaitis has repeatedly denied the fact that there was ever a unified aesthetic to Mabou Mines. Breuer, on the other hand, considers the company to have been influenced by two competing aesthetics: his and Akalaitis's. According to Breuer, Mabou Mines had been working with a common minimalist aesthetic, very much influenced by the New York art world of the early seventies, until he "veered off" and began incorporating elements of popular culture into his work.[34] At about the same time, Akalaitis began directing. He sees these two events as leading to a rift in Mabou Mines during the mid-seventies during which the critics and certain company members split into two aesthetic camps. Describing himself as a "pop-head who is interested in low-culture, schlock, garbage and trash," Breuer argues that he was influenced by an "art world aesthetic" only while creating *The Red Horse Animation,* during a time when, in his view, it was fashionable to be involved with minimalism, formalism, and the cool, arch, intellectual style of New York's downtown art scene. He draws an analogy between Akalaitis's theatrical aesthetic and his own: If Akalaitis has been influenced by Jasper Johns, then he himself has been influenced by Andy Warhol.

There are in fact noteworthy differences in the directing styles and methods of Akalaitis and Breuer. Akalaitis is a more visually and compositionally oriented director whose work often has a fragmented, anarchic feel to it. Breuer is more concerned with narrative continuity and what he calls an emotionally "hot" acting style. Akalaitis's sense of humor tends to be ironic while Breuer's is more broad and effusive. Yet there are elements in the work of these two directors that reveal a shared heritage in Mabou Mines. Both are aesthetically indebted to Grotowski, and both have been drawn to and influenced by the works of Beckett and Genet. Dramaturg James Leverett offers the following insight into the aesthetic similarities and differences of the two directors:

> Both are great eclectics. Both are fond of quoting popular culture, fond of breaking up the surface of a thing with a kind of popular vulgarity. But [Breuer's] the one who really generates text. The times that Akalaitis generates text, they are more collages, like *Dead End Kids*. And she's political rather than personal. . . . Akalaitis is much more a director of classic texts, and Breuer is more of a personal poet who occasionally directs classic text.[35]

Interestingly, both Akalaitis and Breuer embrace the notion of a kind of "double-consciousness" on the part of the actor. In Breuer's case, this manifests itself as a concern with the narrative impulse in performance. He explained to the cast of *The Gospel at Colonus* that the actor is always playing two actions simultaneously: the "actor action" that is directed toward the audience, and the "character action" that is directed toward the onstage scene. "Theseus-in-scene," for example, poses as a nice guy at the same time that "Theseus-as-storyteller" shows the audience how tough he is. According to Breuer, the actor playing Theseus must execute these two actions simultaneously rather than sequentially. Akalaitis's notion that the actor is simultaneously in the scene and watching him or herself in the scene, likewise assumes a double-consciousness on the part of the actor. Yet whereas the task for Breuer's actor is simultaneously to embody and *tell* the play, it seems that the task for Akalaitis's actor is simultaneously to embody and *paint* the play. And while both telling and painting involve communication with the audience, the latter is a more ambiguous, subtle, and private activity.

AKALAITIS DIRECTS WITH MABOU MINES

Cascando (1976)

The first piece Akalaitis directed with Mabou Mines was an adaptation of Beckett's radio play *Cascando*. The production won an Obie award for direction in 1976, and enjoyed a successful revival at the Public Theater the following year. "Cascando" is a musical term for a "falling tone": the dying away of sound, volume, or tempo. In Beckett's text, the "character" Opener commands, or directs, the "characters" Voice and Music. Opener tells us that people say Voice and Music are in his head. Opener no longer protests, since other people neither see nor understand him, but insists that Voice and Music bear no resemblance to him. He simply "opens" their performance. Voice, meanwhile, keeps trying and failing to tell the story of Woburn—a huge man who is running through the sand, up and down slopes, falling and getting up, urging himself on despite his exhaustion. With each new telling of the tale, Voice reminds himself to "get it right this time," yet neither he nor Woburn ever finish their tasks. Every now and then, Opener quiets Voice and "opens" Music. At other times, Opener "opens" the two together, encouraging them to perform in harmony. Voice winds down but cannot finish and cannot stop. He is condemned, like so many of Beckett characters, to perpetually recreate his story. Likewise, Woburn is condemned to keep running. Opener simply focuses on his task of opening and closing, hoping to rest after he at last gets the story right.[36]

Akalaitis transformed Beckett's linguistically dense radio play into a visually dense theater piece. She created a set, cluttered with objects from her summer cabin in Nova Scotia, that evoked an old ship's cabin. Opener was a derelict, Voice's words were divided between four men and a woman, and Music was a solo cello score composed by Philip Glass. Akalaitis also invented a prologue in which the seven performers engaged in silent, repetitive activities such as knitting, soap carving, and model ship building, all of which conveyed the delicate nature of the creative process. At one point, the performers collectively assembled a house of cards.

Akalaitis's production of *Cascando*, like all of her directing work to come, was less an elucidation of Beckett's text than a highly personal response to it. Certain critics suggested that the imagistically dense production, though fascinating, ran counter to Beckett's spare text.[37] *Village Voice* theater critic Michael Feingold wrote that Cascando's "images, like the zombie drone of the five overlapping voices, carry the conviction of quietitude. . . . We are all down at the bottom of Beckett's well; in this company we see a group of artists who have made themselves a cozy corner there, the better to remind us of the fact."[38] Akalaitis's idiosyncratic interpretation resonates with something at the core of *Cascando,* a work that dramatizes the creative act and the failure inherent in it. Opener is a derelict "director," surrounded by chaos yet driven to create structure. Voice cannot stop performing stories about subjects who cannot stop performing. Music contributes poetry to the process but cannot express himself in words. In a sense, these three "characters" are all aspects of Akalaitis's creative intelligence.

Dressed Like an Egg (1977)

After *Cascando,* Akalaitis began composing her own texts based on literary, historical, and social issues that captured her imagination. Her sources of inspiration included works of fiction, memoirs, diaries, photographs, even book reviews. *Dressed Like an Egg,* a theater piece based upon the life and writings of the French writer Colette, was one such work. Written and directed by Akalaitis, performed by Akalaitis, Maleczech, McElduff, Raymond, and Warrilow, with music composed by Chopin and Glass, *Dressed Like an Egg* was presented by the New York Shakespeare Festival in May of 1977. The title of the piece came from a dream Akalaitis had in which she saw a beautiful dress covered with a pattern of eggs, an image which Akalaitis felt was a perfect embodiment of Colette's romantic, feminine spirit. The following passage is taken from Akalaitis notes to the published performance script:

> The artistic process—an investigation of romantic form through acting, movement and theatrical conventions. All is heightened and formalized. *Dressed Like an Egg* is an homage to the theatre. The physical production focuses on the movement of light and curtains and the high emotional content that these have in the theatre. It is a proscenium piece. The space is divided vertically by stripes or bands of light that color floor, curtains, and performers, and horizontally by curtains that move from side to side and vertically. There are two unmasked blue lightbulbs on a stand upstage. They are always lit. The footlights are glowing seashells.[39]

The complexity of Colette's femaleness, the interpenetration of her emotional and intellectual life, was evoked not only by the work of the actors but also a scenic environment that was at once luxurious and austere. The production's setting, designed by New York artists Nancy Graves and Ree Morton, recreated objects and environments from Colette's life. On the stage were the aforementioned curtains fashioned in various elegant fabrics, a mylar "rug," an authentic Victorian bathtub that was filled during the piece with hot water from a teakettle, a life-size plaster replica of Colette's pug Toby Chien, and red carnations, which Colette attached to the bodice of her wedding dress. Before each performance, rose perfume was sprinkled on the backs of the chairs in the audience to create an ambience of romance.

Dressed Like an Egg dealt with psychologically volatile material that had everything to do with Colette's femaleness, her independent lifestlye, and nineteenth-century attitudes toward the roles of men and women. The piece consisted of a series of tableaux and images: Colette leaning against parallel bars and performing a trapeze act in her private gymnasium, Colette in an opium den, Colette at the seashore, Colette dancing at her wedding. Colette's words were divided among the male and female performers. Her dress was made out of Celastic (plastic-impregnated felt), and remained empty and disembodied on the stage after each of the three women took their turn wearing it. Dashing men at the seashore wore Celastic scarves that "blew" in the wind. The performance opened with a dance that the audience viewed beneath the bottom edge of a half curtain raised two feet above the stage floor. The dance appeared to be performed by two women wearing high-heeled plastic shoes with lights in the heels. The half curtain rose, however, to reveal two men "dancing" with each other, their hands in the high-heeled shoes.

Sharing her thoughts about Colette in a *Village Voice* interview, Akalaitis confessed that, despite herself, she *does* think women are more emotional and attached than men. Colette made the commitment to living an emotional life, an intense commitment that was personally necessary yet painful. Akalaitis speaks of being attracted to Colette for many reasons, but above all for her combination of uncensored female sensibility and extreme intelligence. According to Akalaitis, Colette is "always talking sense—specifically romantic sense."[40]

New York Times critic Mel Gussow wrote that Akalaitis's direction of *Dressed Like an Egg* was equally imaginative and responsive to its sources. He described the production as "a paradigm of literary adaptation . . . neither a biographical drama nor a compilation of Colette stories, but an impressionistic canvas of visual and verbal imagery inspired by Colette."[41] Scene designer John Arnone considers the production to have opened up his life as an artist, providing him with the inspiration, or courage, to "take a quantum leap" in the area of stage design. Arnone saw *Dressed Like an Egg* at a time when he had been "thinking about these things on stage, but didn't know you could do them—or were allowed to." He eventually wrote Akalaitis a letter asking if he might show her his work. They met, and Akalaitis invited him to work with her on *Red and Blue,* which was presented at the Public Theater in 1982. For *Red and Blue,* Arnone designed a set consisting of nine 2x3 foot cardboard rooms stacked on top of each other. A number of red and blue lightbulbs in the dollhouse-like set were "choreographed" to the amplified voices of three actors sitting backstage. Arnone looks back on *Red and Blue* as "convoluted but very interesting. Audiences were transfixed but the piece got terrible reviews. Many thought it should have been reviewed by art critics."[42]

Southern Exposure (1979)
Inspired by a book review of a biography of explorer, Robert Scott, *Southern Exposure* was directed by Akalaitis and performed by Warrilow and McElduff. The text of the piece was assembled from Scott's *Voyage of the Discovery* and Shackleton's account of his 1914 Antarctic expedition. The set, designed by Akalaitis, was a white bedroom that also functioned as a blank canvas upon which the performers created and subsequently destroyed navigational drawings. The white walls also served as a projection screen for images that demystified the continent. Slides of the explorers' meager rations were projected onto the walls as the actors read Shackleton's description of the men's food fantasies. A movie showed a contemporary couple at Grand Central Station posing underneath a photomural of the Antarctic. The film then followed the couple to the penguin exhibit at the Coney Island Aquarium as a voice-over recounted an explorer's discovery of an Antarctic burial pool filled with frozen, dead penguins. The piece was a collage of text and images that explored the romantic mythology of Antarctica, just as those in the past had explored the harsh reality of the continent itself.

Dead End Kids (1980)
Dead End Kids, a theater piece about the history, uses, and abuses of nuclear power, was conceived and directed by Akalaitis, designed by Robert Israel in collaboration with Akalaitis, and presented at the Public Theatre in November of 1980. Mabou Mines later received funding from the National Endowment for the Arts and ABC Cable to do a screen adaptation of the play that was completed in 1986. The 16-mm film had an expanded script and cast, was scored by David Byrne, and interspersed black-and-white archival footage with color footage shot on location.

Like *Southern Exposure, Dead End Kids* contrasted romantic mythology with hard-core reality. Inspired by the notorious nuclear power plant disaster at Three Mile Island, Pennsylvania, as well as by her own concern about the possibility of nuclear war, the dangers of nuclear reactors, and the safety of the world her children would inherit, Akalaitis set out to create a theater piece that took the history of nuclear power very seriously, beginning with alchemy and continuing through the evolution of modern physics. She was particularly interested in exploring the idea that as man becomes more technological, he becomes increasingly divorced from a world where one is connected to ideas about God, responsibility, and the human or holistic context for being a scientist. Taking science as the subject of her cultural collage, Akalaitis embarked upon an extensive and, in her view, immensely satisfying research process. She accumulated enough information for several theater pieces, and she considers the greatest challenge of *Dead End Kids* to have been cutting and editing the source material.[43]

Akalaitis compiled her script from fragments of found text drawn from sources such as newspaper articles, government speeches, lectures, the memoirs of Marie and Pierre Curie, Goethe's *Faust,* and ancient alchemical treatises. The collage of texts in turn gave rise to images, tableaux, and scenes such as the following: Madame Curie works silently in her laboratory while a Magician, an Alchemist, a Young Woman, and an Announcer recite alchemical recipes and perform an "Alchemical Dance"; a six-headed Mephistopheles transforms into a group of Army generals, scientists, and academics that, after watching Faust make his pact with the Devil, launches into a stirring rendition of The Four Sargents' 1940s pop song "Hubba Hubba"; two actors dressed in contamination suits prepare containers of radioactive isotopes in a glove box and speak poetically about the universe, while a 1950s government propaganda film on nuclear power and weaponry is projected behind them; a sleazy stand-up comic in an equally sleazy nightclub invites a woman from the audience (a plant) onstage, engages her in sexual jokes and repartee, and pulls from his suit a rubber chicken whose skin color, he remarks, is the same as that of Asians. As with all of Mabou Mines work, much of the performance material in *Dead End Kids* was developed collaboratively. And, as Akalaitis observes, given the political nature of the subject matter, lengthy discussions and arguments were frequently a part of rehearsal.[44]

One of Akalaitis's most celebrated works, *Dead End Kids* appealed to both the intellect and the emotions of its audiences. And, as with so much of Akalaitis's work both with and outside of Mabou Mines, the power and energy of the theatrical event derived from the interplay between performance and scenic environment. Applauding the ability of *Dead End Kids* to achieve political impact without offering facile solutions, theater critic Ross Wetzsteon described the piece as "neither dogmatic nor 'moving'" but rather, attempting "to reach a deeper level, where the mind feels and the emotions articulate."[45]

Through the Leaves (1984)

Franz Xaver Kroetz's *Through the Leaves* is a sympathetic yet disturbing examination of post-war Germany's labor class. Akalaitis's 1984 production featured Maleczech as Annette, a desperate, middle-aged specialty butcher, and Neumann as her casual and frequently abusive lover, Victor. *Through the Leaves* was co-produced by Mabou Mines and Women's Interart Theatre, and it won five Obie awards.

Transposing the play from working-class Germany to a blue-collar neighborhood in Queens, Akalaitis once again theatricalized the tension between romantic myth and harsh reality. This tension was present in the exaggerated, "wired" performances of Maleczech and Neumann, as well as in the hyperrealistic stage design. Douglas Stein's set provided simultaneous, unsparing views of Annette's working and living quarters. In her butcher shop, Annette hacked away at actual pieces of meat; in her living room, she engaged in rough, loveless sex with Victor. The play unfolded in a series of fragmentary scenes that were linked by passages from Annette's diary, read aloud or on tape. Most of this action occurred under harsh, flourescent light as if the stage were a scientific laboratory. Sappy romantic Musak underscored the play, functioning as an ironic commentary upon the brutality of the stage action; abrasive German New Wave music was used to punctuate the scenes, yet another example of the director's critical intellience. Everything about the production—actions, voices, bodies, scenery, music, lighting—was jarring, ugly, and unsentimental.

When asked, in a 1984 interview, how she learned to direct, Akalaitis replied that everybody in Mabou Mines is a director, and she surmised that many actors are good directors and either do not realize it or think directing is "a big deal." She said it sickened her that directors were given so much credibility and importance and actors not enough, and she suggested that, even in Mabou Mines, directors had far too much power. Interestingly, she remarked in the same interview that "part of the high of directing is having total responsibility." It appears that, for Akalaitis, this sense of responsibility extends to an awareness of the ways in which directorial power may be both used and abused.

Asserting that "the director is not a kind of god who looks [on] with a total concept in mind while everyone tries to execute it well," Akalaitis spoke of theater as a process of problem solving in which it is useful to have many people involved. She said she had come to be excited by those "truly frightening area[s] of doubt and despair" where there seem to be insoluble problems in a piece. At the same time, she acknowledged that, "Actors don't like it, and as an actor I know I would get very pushy in that situation. Now I like being in that state. Directing has taught me to be patient, to let it be awful for a long time, for really a long time, to let the actors hate me for not being smart enough to solve it."[46]

Akalaitis confessed that she often sees things in a piece very clearly, yet is not able to verbally articulate them. This can be a problem for actors when she is unable to help them, unable to explain their motivation or their inner life:

> I have to say, "trust me" and "find it yourself," and for many actors, especially those not from Mabou Mines, my way of directing seems very technical, external and fragmentary. This can be very frustrating for actors who are used to coming into a situation where there's a reading of the script, the director explains the play, explains the characters, gives everyone their motivation, and gives them a through line. I bounce ideas off them and hope that one of those

ideas, or two or three or four, will catch, and through that process the actor will find his way into my subconscious. I don't think it works all the time.[47]

1 Herbert Blau, "The Play of Thought," interview, *Performing Arts Journal* 14.3 (1992): 2–21.

2 Sally R. Sommer, "JoAnne Akalaitis of Mabou Mines," *The Drama Review* 20.3 (1976): 5.

3 Sommer, 5.

4 Laurie Lassiter, "David Warrilow: Creating Symbol and Cypher," *The Drama Review* 29.4 (1984) : 3.

5 Philip Glass, *Music By Philip Glass,* ed. Robert T. Jones, (New York: Harper, 1987) 6–7.

6 Glass 17–19.

7 See Sommer, 5–6.

8 Bill Raymond, interview, *Fresh Air,* by Lee Ann Hansen, Natl. Public Radio, WHYY, Philadephia, 12 Aug. 1987.

9 Rosette C. Lamont, "Interpreting a Russian Poet's Comic Language," *New York Times* 22 Nov. 1987, natl. ed., sect. 2: 20.

10 Alexis Greene, "Mabou Mines Turns Twenty," *Theater Week* 29 Jan.–5 Feb. 1990: 10.

11 Sommer, 15.

12 Ruth Maleczech and Elizabeth LeCompte, interview, "Two Women Creating Their Own Worlds," by Wanda Phipps, *High Performance* 13.1 (1990): 34.

13 Jene Highstein, *Mabou Mines: The First Twenty Years,* Grey Galler, New York University, New York. Jan. 1991.

14 David Savran, *In Their Own Words: Contemporary American Playwrights* (New York: TCG, 1988) 4.

15 Robb Baker, "Mabou Mines: Animating Art," *Soho Weekly News* 12 Dec. 1974.

16 Glass, 8.

17 Lee Breuer, Program Notes for *The Red Horse Animation,* Mabou Mines: The First Twenty Years.

18 See Bonnie Marranca, *The Theatre of Images* (New York: PAJ, 1977) 113–18; and *Theatrewritings* (New York: PAJ, 1984) 42–59.

19 Lee Breuer, *Animations: A Trilogy for Mabou Mines* (New York: PAJ, 1979) 40.

20 Samuel Beckett, *Come and Go, The Collected Shorter Plays* (New York: Grove, 1984) 196.

21 Sommer, 7.

22 Savran, 10–11.

23 Sommer, 5.

24 Linda Winer, "Art & Fun," *Chicago Tribune* 20 April 1975: N. pag.

25 For a detailed account of *The Shaggy Dog Animation* in performance, see Ingrid Nyboe, "The Shaggy Dog Animation," *The Drama Review* 22.3 (1978): 46–54.

26 Sommer, 8–9.

27 Gerald Rabkin, "Mirror of a Master's Eye," *Soho Weekly News* 9 Feb. 1978: 27.

28 Richard Schechner, "The End of Humanism," *The End of Humanism: Writings on Performance* (New York: PAJ, 1982) 100.

29 For a discussion of the artistic conflicts surrounding *Shaggy Dog*, see Tish Dace, "Mabou Mines Collaborative Creation," *Soho Weekly News* 18 May 1978: N. pag.

30 Ross Wetzsteon, "Wild Man of the American Theater: Lee Breuer in the Middle of Life's Passage," *Village Voice* 26 May 1987: 33.

31 Sommer, 6.

32 Sommer, 8.

33 Misha Berson, "Keeping Company: Against Economic Odds, Ensembles Keep Trouping Along." *American Theatre* April 1990: 22.

34 Unless otherwise noted, all quotes attributed to Lee Breuer are drawn from the author's rehearsal notes for *The Gospel at Colonus,* directed by Lee Breuer, Goodman Theatre, Chicago 26 May 1990; and personal interview, 26 May 1990.

35 Greene, 12.

36 Beckett, *Cascando, Collected Shorter Plays* 135-44.

37 See Gerald Rabkin, review of *Cascando, Soho Weekly News* 19 May 1977: N. pag; and review of *Cascando, New York Times* 5 Nov. 1976: N. pag.

38 Michael Feingold, quoted. in Greene, 12.

39 JoAnne Akalaitis, *Dressed Like an Egg, Word Plays 4: New American Drama* (New York: PAJ, 1984): 193.

40 Terry Curtis Fox, "The Quiet Explosions of JoAnne Akalaitis," *Village Voice* May 1977: N. pag.

41 Mel Gussow, "Other Ways at the Shakespeare Festival," *New York Times* natl. ed., sect. 2, 17 June 1990: 5.

42 John Arnone, interview, *American Set Design 2,* by Ronn Smith (New York: TCG, 1991) 28–29.

43 JoAnne Akalaitis, interview, *Theater,* by Jonathan Kalb, 15.2 (1984): 10.

44 Akalaitis, *Theater* 10.

45 Ross Wetzsteon, "Mabou Mines," *New York Magazine* 23 Feb. 1981: 30.

46 See Shewey, *The Many Voices* 9, and Akalaitis, *Theater* 10.

47 Akalaitis, *Theater* 13.

two

The Legacy of
Mabou Mines

Mutate or face your fate.
LEE BREUER, *THE B. BEAVER ANIMATION*

Since 1980, Mabou Mines has functioned primarily as a producing collective, with members working outside as much as with the company. Additionally, there is a large group of colleagues who work with the company on a regular basis as acting or design associates. Breuer suggests that few American experimental theater groups have stayed together for as long a period as Mabou Mines: Elizabeth LeCompte, for example, left Schechner's Performance Group to found the Wooster Group, Joyce Aaron split off from Chaikin's Open Theatre, Lola Pashalinski and Black-eyed Susan resigned from the Ridiculous Theatre after Charles Ludlam died. From its beginnings, Mabou Mines has valued the freedom and autonomy of its individual members over a single guiding spirit or a kind of "group mind." This has prolonged the life of the company, but also it has contributed to the development of, and conflict between, strong artistic egos. In April of 1990, Mabou Mines reached a point where it could no longer find an organizational structure that would suit its core members, and Akalaitis, Bill Raymond, Ellen McElduff, and Greg Mehrten resigned from the company.

Akalaitis believes that Mabou Mines's uniqueness lies in the fact that it has never been an institution. Rather, it has been a collective, a group of people with very different interests and opinions not only about theater but also about many other things. Akalaitis considers this "difference" to be the very thing that has kept the company together for so long. She herself was a part of Mabou Mines for twenty years, and the company, in reduced form, has continued to create and produce theater. Mabou Mines has neither an artistic director nor any kind of hierarchical structure, and its members have always been free to come and go as they pleased. Moreover, they have encouraged each other to initiate, develop, and collaborate on whatever project interests them—whether that involves working with people outside the company, or working in film or television—for whatever reason they see fit. Akalaitis is quick to add that this atmosphere of freedom and democracy has its disadvantages. The company deliberates over decisions and has endless fights about everything. Finally, Akalaitis thinks it significant that, for Mabou Mines, "there was no place." Aside from its early residency at La Mama and a small studio at P.S. 122 in the East Village, the company has had no artistic home, no permanent stage on which to perform. For a while, they were in residence at the Public which, according to Akaliaitis, was "exciting, but then Joe Papp got tired of us and that was exciting, too, because we had to solve the problem of finding another place."[1]

Maleczech suggests that Mabou Mines passed the ten-year mark that is the dissolution point for so many theater groups by resisting the tendency on the part of the public, the press, and the funding community "to isolate people in their various labels." She emphasizes the fact that Mabou Mines is a company created by artists for artists, and its members are free at any time to "change their job description," to move from actor to writer to designer to director to technician.[2] Maleczech herself, for example, has always been interested in the visual elements of theater (an area generally considered to be the province of the director and designers), and considers it natural to have moved from acting into directing.

The qualities valued, if not always exhibited, in the organizational structure of Mabou Mines—individuality, autonomy, equality—also informed Akalaitis's adminstrative style at the New York Shakespeare Festival. She asked Joseph Papp for the title of Artistic Associate rather than Associate Artistic Director because it was less formal and more in keeping with her vision of the job as "a key artistic force in the institution with decision-making autonomy."[3] Furthermore, Akalaitis stated that she preferred to see herself as a peer, rather than a supervisor, of the Public's three young resident directors who were invited by Papp to shape their own artistic seasons. She considers *supervise* and *oversee* to be loaded words that "describe a certain kind of activity that has been abhorrent to her in the theater."[4]

EMPOWERING THE ACTORS

The "genius of Mabou Mines," in Akalaitis's view, was that a group of people was empowered to think creatively about all aspects of the theater including text, staging, and design. Although this way of working was not always successful, an important "methodology of saying what you think" developed in the company. Akalaitis points out, however, that a misconception exists regarding the type of collaboration that took place among the members of Mabou Mines. While many people believe that the company's pieces were entirely group-created, there was always a director present who was responsible for the concept and structure of a piece, and who had the final say about everything in rehearsal. Even so, Akalaitis argues, Mabou Mines's work process was unique in that actors and designers were empowered to think creatively about a piece and not just execute the "divine artistic vision" of what the director thinks a play means or needs.

Akalaitis has said that she enjoys working with actors who are intellectual, spiritual, flexible, and collaborative—actors who are able to "be in the flow," who are willing to try things and then toss them out if they fail to work. She is distressed that actors are frequently treated like talented infants who possess no authentic thoughts. For Akalaitis, to "empower" actors is to be interested in what they are interested in and who they are as people, and to refuse to condescend to or infantilize them. In Mabou Mines, for example, actors were "empowered" to direct other actors or direct themselves, even on the very practical level of refusing to participate in something that held no interest for them.[5] Director Anne Bogart, who staged Mabou Mines's 1991 production of Brecht's *In the Jungle of Cities,* described the longtime company members as "voracious, open, intelligent and truthful. It's not about their careers. They've been through so much hell together, they're large human beings."[6]

Mabou Mines's perception of the actor as an autonomous, intelligent being able to function creatively both onstage and off has contributed to what Akalaitis describes as the "strong sense of performance" that permeates the company's work. It is not surprising that the members of Mabou Mines more often refer to themselves as "performers" than as "actors," particularly when speaking about their work within the company. Asked whether she thought there was a difference between a performer and an actor, Maleczech replied that she thought most people who call themselves actors tend to think of themselves as interpreters. In her view, performance is a kind of active, public meditation in which the performer moves out of self into the performance of self. "Every once in a while," says Maleczech, "it does happen that you are only performing the performance. That's the ideal."[7]

The Influence of Grotowski

Mabou Mines's philosophy of performance was informed by the work of Polish theater director and theorist Jerzy Grotowski as well as by the ideas, strategies, and techniques of the New York art world of the early to mid-seventies. Both Grotowski's system of training and art world performance emphasized the importance of bringing one's *self* to the performance, of shrinking the gap between who you are and what you play. As noted above, Akalaitis regards her training with

Grotowski's Polish Laboratory Theatre as a turning point in her career, one that radically altered her ideas about acting and directing.

In the classes and workshops Akalaitis attended, Grotowski would speak about his theories and actor Ryszard Cieslak would teach the physical technique. From Cieslak, Akalaitis learned what she regards as the single most important fact about acting—that it happens in the body. Grotowski's technique focuses on the body of the actor as both the source of and the medium for performance. In contrast to American methods of actor training which tend to emphasize spontaneity over disciplined technique, Grotowski stresses the importance of rigorous and lengthy physical training. In his manifesto *Towards a Poor Theatre*, he asserts:

> There is no contradiction between inner technique and artifice (articulation of a role by signs). We believe that a personal process which is not supported and expressed by formal articulation and disciplined structuring of the role is not a release and will collapse in shapelessness. We find that artificial composition not only does not limit the spiritual but actually leads to it. . . . The forms of common "natural" behavior obscure the truth.[8]

Grotowski's ideas inspired Mabou Mines to investigate the "inner" emotional values inherent in "outer," often stylized, physical expression, as well as in the formal elements of stage design.

Particularly significant for Mabou Mines was Grotowski's idea that the actor is not just an interpreter of texts but is as much a creator as a painter, writer, or any generative artist. For Mabou Mines, the act of performance consisted less in fulfilling the supposed intentions of the author than in bringing oneself to the work. The impetus for performance was the encounter between the life of the individual artist and a text, rather than the attempt to fit oneself into an idea of character or somehow match the perceived attributes of a role. Maleczech recalls that, at a certain point, it was no longer interesting for her to play parts in other's people's plays, just as it was no longer interesting for directors to do new interpretations of often-done works. In Maleczech's view, this alternative vision of performance had its roots in Grotowski's idea that "it was no longer necessary for the actor to realize the author's intention when he wrote the part. Once that became clear, then a piece becomes the story of the lives of the performers. . . . We're really not working with any material except ourselves."[9]

Art critic Henry Sayre argues that the "personal" in performance is anything that disrupts the naturalism of the stage, interferes with character and [paradoxically] announces the presence of acting. The personal need not assert itself overtly, but may "exist, as it always has in art, as a kind of *tache,* a gestural mark that indicates the presence of a controlling, artistic, often ironical point of view, one that disrupts the scenic event."[10] As Sayre suggests, artworks cannot help but manifest the subjectivity of their creators. Yet Mabou Mines's overt exploration of the personal in performance, especially when viewed against the backdrop of the company's intellectual sophistication, was aesthetically progressive for its time. Audiences, particularly in New York, were becoming familiar with the autobiographical, physical, and temporal explorations of the performance art movement. But Mabou Mines was clearly a *theater* company—a group of actors investigating the intersection between self and text, self and body, self and form.

In 1985, David Warrilow described the meeting ground of self and structure in another way, remarking that "improvisation" had become increasingly important for him, even within highly choreographed pieces: "Improvisation only means that which is not foreseen, that which appears at the moment. Something is always appearing at the moment. The point is how much attention do you pay to it. I now pay great attention to what happens in the moment, and it's part of the flow of each performance. It is what brings to life the structure."[11]

PERSONAL TASKS, PERSONAL IMAGES

Related to Mabou Mines's philosophy of performing the self, was their investigation in rehearsal of personal physical and vocal tasks. Grotowski's technique emphasizes the actor's involvement in one or more highly personal and specific tasks as a way to approach character. While these tasks need not have anything to do with the character, they must come from and belong to the actor alone—as opposed to being somehow connected with the author, director, or audience. Ideally, a complete and total involvement with the personal task leads the actor to an experience of being "in the moment," of being connected to fellow actors and the audience. For Akalaitis, this sense of connection is experienced in the body which, in turn, activates the emotional life of the performer.

For the actors in Mabou Mines, the idea of personal task extends to the activity of visualizing images. Akalaitis illustrates this with an example from Beckett's *Come and Go*. The final line in the play is "I can feel the rings." And, as Beckett states in his stage directions, no rings are visible. As a performer, Akalaitis had no sense of the line's meaning other than that it seemed to negate the piece in some way. She also felt that she had no "psychological character" to fall back on. Akalaitis discovered, however, that when she engaged in the personal task of imagining, or imaging, her daughter Juliet as she delivered the final line, her performance was emotionally very full.[12]

As a director, Akalaitis suggests that actors "store" any images that arise from particular words in the text, which may be connected with personal memories, feelings, dreams, or fantasies. She also advises the actors to pay attention to any physical or emotional responses triggered by the images. The physical exercises that Akalaitis uses in rehearsal are a means by which the actor can then physically release and explore these images, incorporating them into the body and voice of their character. Maleczech's description of her creative process while working on Breuer's gender-reversed *Lear* (1989) is another example of the performer using personal images which in turn may generate physical, vocal, and emotional energy:

> . . . there are these words, these wonderful, wonderful words. When I say them, they bring forth certain ideas that come from the language itself—visual images, pictures—and then I play out the pictures that I see. . . . When you have an idea a certain energy starts generating. It's a physical energy and a vocal energy. Then of course

you want to try it, see how it flies, so you do. If the performer is having ideas then you're all in the same ballgame; the director is having one kind of idea and the performer's having another kind of idea and you put those conflicting ideas on the table.[13]

Mabou Mines and the New York Art World

Akalaitis asserts that, despite Mabou Mines's reputation for creating highly visual theater, their work in design *per se* has not been as strong as their sense of performance. Yet this very sense of performance has been influenced by the company's collaborations with visual artists, as well as by their interest in exploring the emotional values of form. Mabou Mines has continually sought and supported collaborations with artists from other disciplines, many of whom had not previously worked in theater. Visual artists such as Power Boothe, Jene Highstein, Suzanne Harris, Keith Sonnier, Ree Morton, Nancy Graves, Tina Girouard, and Gordon Matta Clark have worked as designers with Mabou Mines. The company also has a rich collaborative history with composers such as Philip Glass, David Byrne, John Zorn, and Bob Telson. According to Philip Glass, "Of all the theaters then developing in New York, I think Mabou Mines made the firmest commitment to extending the range of its work by means of extratheater collaborations. . . ."[14]

The experimental theater movement of the early 1970s was part of a larger, extremely vital artistic community that existed at the time in lower Manhattan. A hotbed of collaborative activity, this community included numerous SoHo artists and gallery owners, the "new dance" companies of Lucinda Childs, Yvonne Rainer, the Judson Church Group, and the Grand Union dance cooperative; and Jonas Mekas's Film-Makers Cinematheque, a combination archive, museum, and theater.

This flurry of activity in the visual and performing arts, occcurred on the heels of a decade in which formalism reigned supreme in the American art world. In the early seventies, conceptual artists such as Vito Acconci, Laurie Anderson, Julia Heyward, and Stuart Sherman began investigating the boundary between art and the performance of art. Yet while the art world was experimenting with theatricality, theater itself was more reluctant to approach the visual arts. The non-commercial theater movement was, at the time, largely concerned with political ideology, agitprop activism, and the aesthetics of audience participation.

Mabou Mines, however, was one of the few theater groups, even in the aesthetically progressive climate of 1970s downtown Manhattan, to be influenced by the techniques and strategies of the art world, to be interested in the articulation and theatricalization of form, and to collaborate with visual artists in the making of their theater pieces. Gallery collectives such as 112 Greene Street and The Kitchen, as well as individual spaces such as the galleries owned by Leo Castelli and Paula Cooper, presented not only visual art but also music, dance, and theater events, and they were particularly supportive of collaborative work. Initially, the audiences for these music, dance theater events were largely comprised of artists themselves. Mabou Mines's first New York appearance, *The Red Horse Animation,* was at the Guggenheim Museum. Much of the company's early work was performed in museums and galleries because visual artists and musicians proved to be a more responsive audience than the theatergoing public.

After viewing *The Red Horse Animation* at the Whitney Museum in 1972, art critic Barbara Rose praised New York museums for recognizing that the performance arts possessed the quality and authenticity lacking in the visual art of the day. Rose saw the work of Mabou Mines as ushering in "an extraodinary renaissance of experimental theater. That this burst of energy should come as the energy level of the visual arts declines is no surprise; for those involved in 'poor theater' have the discipline, integrity and conviction that arte povera— ephemeral heaps of cheap materials decoratively enshrined in galleries—lacks simply because it must remain a commodity in a context of bad faith."[15]

Art world audiences at times complained that Mabou Mines's work was too actorly, expressive, and emotional. Yet when the company sought greater exposure and began playing primarily in theaters during the mid-seventies, audiences often found their work too abstract, pictorial, and metaphorical. According to Breuer, the difficulty Mabou Mines experienced working with "the dialectic between theater and visual art" was largely due to the aesthetic traditions of the two art forms that "peer at each other as over a Gaza Strip. What's 'good' in one is 'bad' in the other. Good performance is bad acting. Good acting is bad performance. 'Dramatic' time is cornball art. Abstract imagery is 'arty' theater. Psychology is too personal for art. The conceptualizing art intellect is too 'minimal' for theater."[16] Mabou Mines's unusual predicament was a function of their attempt to challenge established disciplinary boundaries by synthesizing the ideas and techniques of theater and visual art. Too "hot" for a certain faction of the art world, too "cool" for mainstream theatergoers, Mabou Mines nevertheless enjoyed an enthusiastic and devoted following.

PERFORMER AS IMAGE, IMAGE AS PERFORMER

The members of Mabou Mines have traditionally referred to themselves not only as "performers" but also as "artists." The term "artist" is frequently invoked in order to confer a sense of seriousness or "weight" upon the actor. Yet in the case of Mabou Mines, it perfectly describes the unique nature of the performer's endeavor. Founding member Warrilow remarked that, somewhere in him "is the ability to visualize and then actualize line—line like [sic] painterly, sculptural, dancerly line, and shape. And to use the body as a way of creating symbol and cypher and of depicting energy in action and in space."[17] The Mabou Mines actor has always been, in a sense, a visual artist whose primary imagistic medium is the body.

If, in the work of Mabou Mines, there is a sense in which the performer creates and embodies images, there is also a sense in which stage design conveys aspects of character. The company has long interacted with and thought about visual elements in the theater. Maleczech suggests that, in the work of Mabou Mines, "Objects on stage are another performer. They're both real and magical. They create the weather on stage—the snowstorms and the desert. They evoke for me an emotional resonance that enables me to invest a line or gesture with meaning." Contrasting the scenic objects in Mabou Mines's 1990 retrospective at New York University with those in the concurrent exhibit of Robert Wilson's set designs at Boston's Museum of Fine Arts, Maleczech suggests that "Wilson's objects and our objects are different because we start from different points. He's a visual artist interested in the geometry of architecture. We're theatre people interested in the geography of the heart. Our objects are three dimensional representations of inner states. His are explorations of form."[18]

For Stanislavsky, motivation is associated with the psychology of realism: The actor first allows himself to be motivated internally and then imposes style. Of greater interest to Mabou Mines, however, have been Grotowski's ideas about motivating abstractions and style itself. Like Grotowski, Mabou Mines believes that there is an emotional truth to every formal idea, and that theatrical styles such as Classicism, Surrealism, Expressionism, and Absurdism spring from a deeper place in the human psyche than does realism. Citing the example of a bag lady spinning and dancing in the middle of the street, whose behavior appears sylized yet is in fact completely "real," Breuer argues that realism is not the foundation upon which style is imposed but is rather one particular way of viewing the universe.[19]

Mabou Mines's Twenty-Year Retrospective: Psychology and Form

"Mabou Mines: The First Twenty Years," sponsored by New York University's Grey Art Gallery & Study Center, was a retrospective exhibit marking the end of Mabou Mines's twentieth anniversary. The exhibit reconstructed aspects of the physical environments and objects from thirteen of Mabou Mines's productions, and it included extensive audiovisual documentation of the company's history. While Akalaitis was appreciative of and moved by the hundreds of people who attended the exhibit's opening, she objected to what she viewed as the "museumification of Mabou Mines." Ironically, even Akalaitis's dissent was "museumified." A wall text stated that Akalaitis's protest "speaks directly to the group's power," and reproduced her disclaimer as follows: "I don't want to have a twentieth anniversary celebration. When you say, 'Now we're going to have this retrospective,' you close the doors. It's my job personally to resist . . . sanctifying Mabou Mines. What interests me is what's unknown, in doubt, what's in chaos, what's terrifying."

It is interesting to reflect upon the many questions the exhibit raises. Was Akalaitis's statement simply included in or co-opted by the exhibit? Did her protest argue with and thus invigorate the exhibit, or did the exhibit somehow de-fang the protest? Have these theatrical objects, which were at one time "three-dimensional representations of inner states," become static and lifeless when presented within the context of a gallery retrospective? Did the exhibit attempt to impose ideas of order and continuity upon Mabou Mines, a group of artists notoriously resistant to being inscribed, or even described?

It is nevertheless possible to discern the presence of certain overarching aesthetic ideas, and ideals, in the work of Mabou Mines. These include the notion that performance is physical, that the physical triggers the emotional, that the actor is a generative as well as interpretive artist, that performance is an expression of the self and of personal history, that making theater is a collaborative endeavor, and that the formal aspects of theater such as structure, architecture, composition, space, objects, music, and light convey emotional values.

Maleczech suggests that the combination of psychology and form is a hallmark of Mabou Mines's style:

The emphasis has been very heavily on language, not necessarily poetic language, sometimes documentary language, but language and the places language can take you technologically in terms of movement and vocal choices. On the other hand, there's a pretty firm grounding in psychology. It's a formal theater but it engages in an awful lot of psychology for a formal theater. Maybe that's the combination people recognize . . . that it's very formal but it has internal things that are not, and when you knock those two things together it gets interesting.[20]

Looking back over Mabou Mines's evolution from their early work on the *Animations* and Beckett to their 1988 gender-reversed *Lear*, Breuer points out that "the link is very clear, largely because there is still the blend of formalism and emotion that the group aimed to achieve from the start. . . . What we forged was a concentration on a formal statement of the body, and a formal statement of imagery, linked with emotional and psychological truth."[21]

Thinking about Mabou Mines, it seems as if the only thing for the mind to grab hold of is the presence of paradox. And one of the more powerful paradoxes evoked by the company's work is this: Despite Mabou Mines's interest in formal experimentation—their investigations of "high" culture, pop culture, film, music, dance, comic books, detective novels, painting, sculpture, laser technology—their work remains grounded in a concern for the psychological processes, the emotional life, the creativity, and the power of the individual actor. As Akalaitis herself often says in rehearsal, "The work is very technical, but nothing in the theater is just technical because it's done by a human being and it comes from the inside."

[1] JoAnne Akalaitis, "Theater and the World." Performing Arts Forum Series, New York Public Library for the Performing Arts, 28 Feb. 1991.

[2] Ruth Maleczech and Elizabeth LeCompte, interview, "Two Women Creating Their Own Worlds," by Wanda Phipps, *High Performance* 13.1 (1990): 35.

[3] "Joseph Papp Reorganizes the Shakespeare Festival to Add 'Creative Blood,'" *New York Times* 29 May 1990, ntl. ed.: B3.

[4] Don Shewey, "Rocking the House That Papp Built," *Village Voice* 25 Sept. 1990: 36-41.

[5] JoAnne Akalaitis, lecture, University of Florida, Gainesville, Fla., 21 June 1990.

[6] Anne Bogart, lecture, "Seminars for Working Directors, Drama League of New York, 13 Nov. 1991.

[7] Maleczech and LeCompte, interview, "Two Women Creating Their Own Worlds," 35.

[8] Jerzy Grotowski, *Towards a Poor Theatre* (New York: Touchstone-Simon, 1968) 17.

[9] Ruth Maleczech, interview, "Acting/Non-Acting" by John Howell, *Performance Art* 2 (1976): 11.

10 Henry M. Sayre, *The Object of Performance: The American Avant-Garde Since 1970* (Chicago: University of Chicago Press, 1989) 79.

11 Laurie Lassiter, "David Warrilow: Creating Symbol and Cypher," *The Drama Review* 29.4 (1984): 9.

12 Sally R. Sommer, "JoAnne Akalaitis of Mabou Mines," *The Drama Review* 20.3 (1976): 10.

13 Maleczech and LeCompte, interview, "Two Women Creating Their Own Worlds," 35.

14 Philip Glass, *Music by Philip Glass,* ed. Robert T. Jones, (New York: Harper, 1987) 9.

15 Barbara Rose, "Museum as Theater," *New York Magazine* 15 May 1972: 76.

16 Lee Breuer, "The Avant-Garde is Alive and Well and Living in Women," *Soho News* 2 Feb. 1982: N. pag.

17 Lassiter, 10.

18 Arthur Holmberg, "Objects Speak Volumes in Two Design Exhibits," *American Theatre* April 1991: 55.

19 David Savran, *In Their Own Words: Contemporary American Playwrights* (New York: TCG, 1988) 9.

20 Maleczech, interview, *Two Women* 35.

21 Lee Breuer, quoted in Alexis Greene, "Mabou Mines Turns Twenty," *Theater Week* 29 Jan.–5 Feb. 1990: 10–14.

three

The Physical Exercises

Whatever [the actor] represents in the play,
in the order of time he is representing nobody but himself.
How could he? That's his body, doing time.
HERBERT BLAU

Improvisation must be a research activity conducted by someone
who is trying to break out of their own passivity . . .
PETER BROOK

When Ryszard Cieslak, a core actor in Grotowski's Polish Laboratory Theater, was asked what he was attempting to teach his acting students at New York University, he gave the following response:

How to be true in performance, that above all. I struggle to plant in them the principle that Grotowksi handed on to me: we act so much in our daily lives that to make theatre what we need to do is to stop acting. Another very important thing to understand is that an actor must concentrate on his own body. The actor's instrument is not [simply] his voice or his diction, it's his whole body. Theatre can be a combination of all the arts—music, dance, painting, writing—but above all it is moving visual art.[1]

Cieslak, who died of lung cancer in 1990, was an important influence on Akalaitis. In the Grotowski workshops and classes she attended during the early seventies, it was Cieslak who taught the actual physical technique while Grotowski himself put forth his theories. And it was Cieslak who taught Akalaitis what she regards as her most important lesson about the theater: that acting happens in the body.

Akalaitis, like Cieslak, is interested in the "truth" of the body in performance. It makes sense then, that her approach to directing is first and foremost a physical one. When casting a show, she seeks out actors who "live" easily and expressively in their bodies, who possess the habit of being emotional but who also like to work physically. And in her rehearsals, a large part of the actor's work involves developing a physical connection to the text, to fellow actors, and to the space itself. Even first-time audience members sense, on some level, that the in-the-flesh presence of the actor's body is vital to any theatrical event: The text is spoken by the voice that comes out of the body, costumes go on the body, scenery exists in relation to the body, sweat and spit are excreted by the body. In Akalaitis's work, the actor's body is the central nervous system of the production.

During the first few days of a rehearsal process, Akalaitis spends very little time "at the table," reading and discussing the text. The actors are almost immediately up on their feet or down on the floor, engaging in a complex series of physical exercises that last anywhere from 20 minutes to several hours per day and serve as preparation for work on the text itself. As the actors perform these exercises, Akalaitis either watches attentively, goes through the exercises herself in her imagination, or allows her mind to wander freely. At times, she asks the actors to improvise on their own while she jots down ideas and images. Akalaitis emphasizes, however, that the exercises are for the actors' benefit, referring to them in fact as "pure actor-research."

Akalaitis compares the actor's sense of energy to that of a team athlete whose reflexes are automatic and consistently oriented toward the physical task of moving.[2] The actor, like the athlete, uses peripheral vision to sense another player's approach, to sense the energy coming from the spectators, to sense how to shape the rhythm and dynamics of the moment. The physical exercises condition the actors to use their minds practically and spontaneously, focusing on the tasks of movement, actions, and speech. Akalaitis has said that she dislikes "people standing in front of scenery, talking to each other," and therefore considers it crucial that the actors become super-sensitized to the theatrical space around them, a space that contains other bodies and scenery. The physical exercises she uses in rehearsal help the actor develop this sensitivity to the here and now of theatrical space.

While each exercise has its own purpose and set of instructions, most of them require the actor to move about the rehearsal space to music that Akalaitis associates—thematically, emotionally, or structurally—with the particular text on which she is working. She reminds the actors to be aware of and to "use" the music, even if what they happen to be doing physically is occurring in opposition to it (for example, moving in slow motion to music with a frenetic beat). The actors are not to choreograph their actions to the music; rather, they are to be conscious of the music's emotional qualities, to "let the music in." The music thus facilitates the actor's investigation of images arising from his or her personal history, from the text, from the director's suggestions, or from design elements in the physical space. What follows is a discussion of four basic exercises, along with their variations, used by Akalaitis in rehearsal. These exercises encourage the actors to physicalize, and consequently emotionalize, images and structural principles within the work.

The Warm-Up

The actors begin the daily physical session with an individual warm-up to music that lasts about 15 minutes. The warm-up is highly personal and private; the actor is free to spend the time simply lying on the floor and breathing, shaking out the body, moving around the space, or vocalizing. The purpose of the individual warm-up is to allow the actor to release physical and mental tension in order to arrive at a state of relaxed alertness. This is also a time during which the actor may investigate his or her physical and emotional responses to the particular music Akalaitis happens to be playing.

In preparation for the series of physical exercises to follow, the actors close their eyes and walk freely about the space. Their task is to sense, without opening their eyes, when they are approaching a wall or another actor. Akalaitis informs the actors that there is nothing violent about this exercise and that they will not get hurt if they proceed slowly and sensitively. As the actors work to awaken their literal feeling of the space around them, Akalaitis reminds them to listen to everything in the room, including the sound of their own breath and the breath of the others. She lets the actors know that they may bump into or pass someone with whom they have a relationship in the play and asks them to be open to the possibility that this physical encounter may inform that relationship. This exercise is usually performed only once during a rehearsal period, to emphasize the importance of being super-sensitized to the space and to the physicality of one's fellow actors.

EXERCISE #1: DANCING TO KNOW THE SPACE

Akalaitis introduced the physical work in the two rehearsal processes I witnessed with an exercise that deals, in the simplest of terms, with the relationship of the body to space. She begins by asking the actors to "dance," or simply move, to the music in order to "know" both the space they are in and the other people in that space. The actors are not to dance solipsistically. They are instead to keep their eyes open and dance in relationship to, but not touching, the other people in the space. Once the actors appear to be moving through the space spontaneously and easily, Akalaitis asks them to "work with" the physical sensation of the air on their bodies, as well as the air between their bodies and the bodies of the other people moving through the space. The actors visualize themselves carving the air with their bodies. They imagine that the air is dead until they move through it, at which point the air becomes charged because they are charged; the others in the space become ignited because they are ignited. As Akalaitis puts it, the air "becomes something, and that 'something' is community, energy, and color. It is intense and life-affirming. It exalts, elevates, and gives power. You are giving 'it' to each other. You are making super-color, super-environment, super-air."

Variation: Investing the Space with Emotional Qualities

In a variation on the above exercise, the actors concentrate on walking, rather than dancing, through the space. They investigate different speeds, rhythms, and styles of walking, sensing the air on and inside their bodies, as well as the air between their bodies and the other bodies in the space. In yet another variation, Akalaitis instructs the actors to "let the air be the thing that resists, oppresses, pushes, limits, and hurts." It is important to note that while Akalaitis's imagination is frequently drawn to theatrical texts that portray menacing worlds, she always begins the physical work by having the actors investigate the supportive and energizing aspects of the space around them. Only after the actors have become physically attuned to the space and to one another, does she ask them to infuse the space with negative emotional qualities.

The physical exercises are not about creating improvisational situations. Neither are they about the deliberate invention of images associated with the text, although this may be a by-product of the exercise. Rather, the exercises are designed to allow the actors to experience a kind of "pre-narrative" physical state that both precedes and transcends the specific physicality of his or her character. According to Akalaitis, to exist in this primal, unconscious, or at times hyperconscious, state is to be open to the world, or worlds, of the play.

EXERCISE #2: SLAM-DANCING WITHOUT TOUCHING

In this exercise, Akalaitis instructs the actors to move through the space to the music, as if they were "slam-dancing" with, but never actually touching, one another. The actors investigate the idea of attraction and repulsion on a purely physical, rather than a psychological, level. While doing so, they must accomplish two tasks: 1. to begin to know each other as physical human beings, and 2. to avoid bumping into each other. The actors engage in brief moments of non-touching "contact" with each other, which must be acknowledged by both parties. They then "bounce off" each other and continue to move through the space. Akalaitis reminds the actors, as she did in the previous exercise, to keep their eyes open, to be aware of the actual physical sensation of the air on and between their bodies, and to work with the image of carving through and energizing the space.

Again, Akalaitis informs the actors that this exercise is not to be executed in a solipsistic manner. They are to keep their eyes open, focused and alert, and use their peripheral vision to see the others in the space as well as themselves. As the actors move through the space, Akalaitis side-coaches them to pay particular attention to the feel of the surface of their bodies, including the surface of the face and the back of the head. She cautions against generating their movement from their arms, as though they were doing "interpretive dance" or the moving-through-peanut-butter-type exercises common to beginning acting classes. Neither should their arms hang like deadweights, but rather they should follow or resonate from the body, which always moves from its center.

Akalaitis suggests to the actors, "if you want to think about character or if something about character occurs to you, work on it." The exercise, however, is less about the overt exploration of character than about the actors paying scrupulous attention to the way the body is moving through space, to the way it activates and is activated by the other bodies around them. Throughout the exercise, Akalaitis reminds the actors that they should be "interested in what every part of their body is doing and the way it is being done." This suggestion brings to mind director Anne Bogart's notion that the actor must continually strive to work "with interest," as if they are carying on a lively conversation, or even argument, with their own gestures, movements, or actions.[3] In this way, the formal work releases rather than inhibits the actor's inner life.

Variation: Slam-Dancing in a Personal Architecture

In later rehearsals, Akalaitis instructs the actors to work with the added information that they are slam-dancing within a piece of architecture. The architecture might consist of a building, a room, or a corridor from the actor's actual life; it might also be a place that exists in a work of art. The architecture may change as the exercise progresses:

for example, from a bank to a hospital to a theater. The only stipulation is that the place, or places, must somehow be "real" to the actor. At the same time that the actors are investigating this specific architecture, they must not ignore the present time, the present space, the other people in the space, the music, even Akalaitis's voice. The actors' task is to stay rooted in the here and now while referencing personal images.

As the exercise unfolds, the actors vary the tempo of their movements, allowing their bodies to inform them when to change speeds. They then work with the additional information so that the architecture they happen to be in becomes infused with a particular emotional quality. Akalaitis specifies whether the architecture is, for example, joyous, exhalting, threatening, or oppressive. Again, the architecture must be real, though not necessarily *realistic,* for the actor. It may be remembered, for example, from childhood, from a dream, or from a painting. Finally, the actors work with the idea that the architecture inside which they are all moving is a shared, rather than private, one.

EXERCISE # 3: STOPPING-AND-STARTING

Akalaitis introduces the next exercise with the statement that, for quite some time, she has been interested in exploring a "stopping-and-starting type of movement" in her work. She observes that, in addition to portraying this specific quality of movement, her work also has "a kind of stopping-and-starting feel to it." Akalaitis is not interested in "an aesthetic of curves," but one in which actions, scenes, and even characters come to a complete stop, and then something entirely new begins with a sharp attack. She emphasizes the importance of the idea that "I'm in a scene, the scene is over, a door slams, a new door opens," and shares a passage by Genet, which has inspired her thinking on the subject. In a letter to director Roger Blin, Genet writes:

> [E]ach scene, and each section with a scene, must be perfected and performed as rigorously and with as much discipline as if it were a short play, complete in itself. Without any smudges. And without

there being the slightest suggestion that another scene, or section within a scene, is to follow those that have gone before.[4]

The stopping-and-starting exercise encourages the actors to make physical "sense" of the idea that every action onstage is comprised of a clearly articulated departure, execution, and arrival. The actors begin by moving to the music, investigating the idea of stopping and then starting up again with a deliberate attack. Akalaitis asks them to notice which specific part of their body initiates the starting-up movement. She also points out that the "stop" is not an exaggerated or theatrical "freeze" in which the body goes dead. It involves simply stopping, remaining motionless but energized, while at the same time allowing one's physical being to "understand" what it means to stop.

Akalaitis asks the actors to imagine they are travelling along vectors in space, with bold, sharp, jagged movements that stop and then start up again. The actors work with the idea that their bodies are carving extremely direct, linear paths through space. They move in order to "understand" what it means to travel upstage, downstage, or along a diagonal; to "understand" what it means to change direction or tempo and which part of their body initiates the change. They also move in order to "understand" what it means to stop or to start up again because another body is perhaps nearby or blocking their path. And, as alway, they move in order to "understand" their own bodies, the bodies of their fellow actors, and the space itself.

Variation: Stopping-and-Starting in a Shared Architecture

Once the actors' have become accustomed to the idea of stopping-and-starting, Akalaitis adds the instruction that they are now moving within a communal architecture. She specifies the emotional quality of the architecture and asks the actors to continue their physical exploration of stopping-and-starting, as well as the idea of communicating physically without actually touching. Akalaitis may change the emotional aspect of the architecture several times within a single exercise. She may also ask the actors to change from stopping-and-starting to slow motion while remaining in a single architecture.

The Influence of Oliver Sacks's *Awakenings*

Oliver Sacks's book *Awakenings*(1973) provided the spark for much of Akalaitis's thinking about the idea of stopping-and-starting. In his book, Sacks documents the lives of patients who survived the great 1917 to 1927 epidemic of viral sleeping sickness. Although these patients had been frozen in decades-long trances, several of them experienced radical "awakenings" when adminstered the drug L-DOPA. Sacks interviews a patient named Rose R. who describes her entranced state as one in which whatever she does and whatever she thinks leads deeper and deeper into itself:

> [. . .] I think of a map; then a map of that map; than a map of that map of that map, and each map perfect, though smaller and smaller . . . Worlds within worlds within worlds within worlds . . . Once I get going, I can't possibly stop. It's like being caught between mirrors, or echoes, or something. Or being caught on a merry-go-round which won't come to a stop.

Yet after Rose has been "awakened" for about a month, her physical behavior becomes blocked, or "jammed." She is impelled to rush forward four or five steps and then suddenly come to a halt and freeze without warning. And as Rose becomes increasingly excited and frustrated, the jamming gets worse.[5]

In Sacks's unique view, it is insufficient to consider disease in purely chemical or mechanical terms; disease may also be viewed in terms of its organization and design. And interestingly, it was the image of Sacks's patients running toward something, suddenly getting stopped as if paralyzed, and trying endlessly to become unlocked that captured Akalaitis's directorial imagination. Akalaitis explains that the stopping-and-starting exercise is an embodiment of the external, kinesthetic aspect of that image. It is a way for the actors to understand what it means for the body to "stop," yet at the same time to feel as if one were somehow "moving forward" through space in mind and spirit. Akalaitis repeatedly emphasizes that the actors must not "go dead" when they stop. Their energy must continue outward through the space, just as the energy of Rosie R. continues outward as it tries to unlock her jammed body. There is also, for Akalaitis, an "inner aspect" to the image, a condition of the mind or spirit that involves the idea of hurtling toward something, getting caught or transfixed, then becoming released again only to find onself hurtling toward something new.

Akalaitis first experimented with the idea of stopping-and-starting during her production of Beckett's *Endgame,* a work for which, she points out, the dynamic of stopping and starting is thematically relevant. She later refined her ideas when she worked on Büchner's *Leon and Lena (and lenz).* Akalaitis believes that the idea of stopping-and-starting, while not necessarily relevant to all dramatic works, is nonetheless an important subject for physical investigation inasmuch as it facilitates the actor's understanding of danger and chaos.

INTERNALIZING THE STRUCTURE OF MONTAGE

Montage is a compositional approach whereby a written or perform-ance text is pieced together from various sources in a kind of cut-and-paste structure. The term "montage" was first used by Russian film director Sergei Eisenstein to describe the technique of editing together adjacent camera shots or pieces of film in such a way that their rela-tionship produced an entirely new meaning. This process was exem-plified during the the 1930s and 1940s by the work of visual artists such as John Heartfield, an artistic collaborator of Bertolt Brecht. Heartfield created photomontages of Nazi Germany by juxtaposing popular images from the news media of the day with bits of photog-raphy culled from various other sources: a dove impaled on sword, for example, or a swastika fashioned out of four axheads bound together with rope. These composite images urged the German public to question the meaning of symbols commonly taken for granted. The art of montage makes no attempt to create the illusion of a seamless, organic whole. Neither is montage characterized by narrative conti-nuity or logic; rather, each individual reader/viewer is presented with the obligation, or privilege, of making her own sense out of a juxta-posed series of juxtaposed images or, as Roland Barthes puts it, "a contiguity of episodes."[6]

A more recent, and waggish, practitioner of verbal montage, writer Donald Barthelme, describes the practice as one "in which unlikely things are stuck together to make, in the best case, a new real-ity" that "may be or imply a comment on the other reality from which it came, and may also be much else. It's an itself if it's successful [. . .]"[7] And Eugenio Barba suggests that "montage" not only characterizes compositions of words, images, or relationships; it may also describe a composition of rhythm that not only represents or reproduces movement, but actually constructs meaning. El Greco, for example, assembling the individual "frames" of his paintings, not only repre-sented ecstatic characters, but also created "an ecstatic construction of the paintings."[8]

Likewise, stopping-and-starting, aside from appearing as a par-ticular quality of movement in Akalaitis's productions, also charac-terizes the very soul of the works to which she is drawn. In other words, the medium is the message, and stopping-and-starting is the kinesthetic equivalent of montage. The effect that montage produces in the eye of the viewer is not unlike the effect that Akalaitis's work produces in both her actors and audience members. Just as the cut-and-paste rhythm of montage is marked by an absence of visual tran-sitions, the stopping-and-starting rhythm of Akalaitis's theatrical work is marked by an absence of both geographic transitions in the form of exits and entrances, and psychological transitions in the form of continuous "realistic" behavior.

As Akalaitis herself has observed, stopping-and-starting is more than just a specific style of movement, but it is also manifested in the structure of the work itself. The stopping-and-starting exercise is thus a way for Akalaitis's actors to "put the structure inside," to internal-ize the fractured, jumpy, edgy rhythm of the work. In doing so, the actors open themselves intellectually and emotionally to structure, shape, and image. In a sense, they engage in and expand upon the directorial work that Akalaitis has begun.

EXERCISE #4: MOVING THROUGH THE SPACE IN SLOW MOTION

In this final group of exercises, the actors are instructed to move through the space in slow motion. At times this slow-motion series is done to music, at other times it is executed in silence. The actors are instructed to begin moving from any image that is "clear" to them: For example, the way they walked into rehearsal that particular morning. They continue moving in slow motion, in order to understand what every part of their body is doing. Akalaitis emphasizes the fact that, although the actors are moving extremely slowly, they must not behave like "zombies from *Night of the Living Dead*." Rather, they must be alive and energized as they investigate what every part of their body is doing and the way it is being done. According to Akalaitis, this exercise is about technique, control and observation. She emphatically side-coaches, "Control, control, control! Be clear! Keep it slow!"

During this exercise, the actors may either engage in "their own work" or character work. They are free to think consciously about their character, or to explore anything that happens to pop into their heads about their character. Again, Akalaitis reminds the actors not to shut out anything having to do with the here and now of the exercise, including the sound of her own voice. The actors investigate the way that their clothes, their shoes, and the air, or lack thereof, feel on their bodies. They envision their bodies pushing through the air and leaving a mark in space, allowing whatever is "charged" in the environment, or in their fellow actors, to inform their movement. Akalaitis reminds the actors that this work should be interesting to them because they are constantly exploring not only their own bodies, but also the other bodies around them and the space itself.

Variation: Group Composition in Slow Motion
In a variation on the above exercise, the actors move in slow motion through the space, working with the idea that they are moving within a group composition, or "painting." This composition may contain any number of people and is continually changing in order to become

more and more "perfect." Everything the actors do occurs in relationship to the other people in the space, yet, as Akalaitis points out, these relationships are spatial rather than psychological. The actors are immersed in the process of constantly adjusting these spatial relationships, "millisecond by millisecond," in order to make the composition more and more perfect. Every part, every cell, of the actor's body is actively involved in creating the composition. While Akalaitis overtly dissuades the actors from approaching this exercise psychologically, she does so only as a means of encouraging them to focus on their bodies. She suggests that actors cannot help psychologizing everything they do and thus need to be reminded to work physically. She informs the actors that the work is very technical, but the composition will be perfect—that is, both emotionally and formally powerful—as long as they are extremely clear and sincere in their choices. It will be perfect as long as they are working, investigating, and discovering. The actors must know exactly "where they are" and what painting they are in. And if for some reason they do not know where they are, it is important that they are aware of this. In other words, Akalaitis prefers that the actors acknowledge their confusion rather than pretend to know what they are doing. In her theatrical universe, it is fine to "not know," as long as one approaches one's work with clarity and sincerity.

Akalaitis reminds the actors that the exercise should be extremely interesting to them because it is never static, and because they are continually working to make the composition more perfect and to understand everything their bodies are doing. They must work to understand, for example, the exact way that they place their foot on the floor; for example, if they place their toe down first, they must work to understand why. They must also work to understand exactly where their breath originates in their bodies, and where that breath is headed when exhaled.

Just as the composition itself is becoming more and more perfect, the actors are to envision their technique becoming more and more perfect as well. Akalaitis tells them that they are "involved in total control," that they must see both themselves and the entire group, from "the outside," at the same time that they are working from "the inside." She compares this type of awareness to being in performance and seeing "the entire stage, not only with your eyes but with your body. For example, if you pick up a teacup down-right, you are aware of making a perfect composition with someone up-left that you may not even see." This statement contains an important clue to Akalaitis's directorial method: She is giving her actors compositional responsibility, encouraging them to think visually as well as psychologically.

Variation: Slow-Motion Composition in a Shared Architecture

In this variation, the actors are instructed to put all of the information from the above exercises into the creation of another group painting, with the added information that the painting now takes place within a shared architecture. This exercise is most often performed silently, rather than to music. The entire group understands exactly what this painting is and works together to make it more and more perfect. The nature of the architecture, as well as the movement dynamic, is determined by the group; either a single person or the group as a whole may initiate a change in the architecture at any time during the exercise. The exact moment of change, often barely detectable by an observer, occurs when a change in physical behavior is effected by one or more of the actors. If the group is truly functioning as an ensemble, however, the entire "painting" undergoes a noticeable shift in mood, tone, rhythm, or dynamic. Akalaitis also suggests that, if an individual does not want the architecture to change, they may use their "energy and will" to resist. However, even if the individual succeeds in keeping the architecture the same, he or she must still allow the composition to adjust itself as it becomes increasingly more perfect and beautiful. As Akalaitis suggests, "Let *it* take *it* where *it* needs to go."

As the actors investigate the shared painting, they are free to explore any ideas about character that may occur to them. They remain aware of their breathing and keep their eyes open, never losing sight of their present surroundings. They block nothing out: each other, the air on their faces and bodies, their clothing, the sound of Akalaitis's voice. The actors work to know exactly where they are, and what they are doing; if they are uncertain of either of these, though, they must acknowledge that fact and continue to work with clarity and sincerity.

Akalaitis suggests to the actors that:

> Everything is controlled, slow, and beautiful. You are working on your technique, yet you are open to everything and anything around you. You are utterly alert and sensitized; every molecule in your body is alive and responsive to the other bodies in the painting. You are not only doing it for the group, though; you are doing it for yourself. You are making these tiny, perfect adjustments for yourself. You are working from both the inside and outside.

Variation: Slow-Motion Composition with Character Movement

In this variation, the actors investigate character movement while working in slow motion. At the same time, they allow the exercise to become a composition that they are constantly adjusting, millisecond by millisecond, in order to make it more and more perfect. Akalaitis instructs the actors to listen, to look, and to breathe—to take in everything around them; she refers to the composition as "super-sensitized, super-electrified and, above all, *real.*"

Although Akalaitis frequently stages slow-motion sequences, her work is not characterized by the presence of calm surfaces. The theatrical world of a work directed by Akalaitis is quite unlike the world of a Robert Wilson piece, for example, that moves almost entirely at reduced speeds. While it is possible to detect an inner agitation in Wilson's repetitive gestures, the surface of his work conveys a sense of tranquility. In his *Einstein on the Beach* (1984), there is something calming, hypnotic, even intoxicating about the enormous elevators perpetually ascending and descending onstage, or Lucinda Childs dancing endlessly along the same diagonal path with arms akimbo. Akalaitis, on the other hand, has included slow motion in her productions as pageantlike introductions (to the congregation of Mormons in *The Mormon Project*) or farewells (to the company of *The Screens* as they pass into the Land of the Dead), or at moments of extreme violence such as Woyzeck's stabbing of his girlfriend Marie or Soranzo's poisoning of his mistress Hippolita in *'Tis Pity She's a Whore.*

As Akalaitis points out, this exercise is not simply about working on one's individual character; it is rather about investigating one's character in a composition peopled with others who are also investigating their characters. No single person in the composition is superior to the group; no single person understands the composition better than the rest. Akalaitis remarks that, in this respect, the exercise is "just like being onstage" because everyone is equal, and "makes a contract" to support and sustain, rather than compete. And just as the stage is a place where everything is always new despite the fact that the lines have been said before, this exercise is an investigation in which every moment is a new discovery,

The Actor as Image-Maker

Akalaitis emphasizes that the actors must at once "be in it and see themselves in it," whether they are performing a physical exercise or a scripted scene. The type of presence that Akalaitis asks her actors to investigate brings to mind the kind of dual-consciousness that some people experience while dreaming or recollecting their dreams. While dreaming, there is at times a feeling that one is existing as two distinct "selves." There is the "self" that is the protagonist of the dream, experiencing it, going through it, doing it—the self that the dream happens to. And there is also the "self" that is the observer of the dream, witnessing it, evaluating it, perhaps narrating it—the self that sees the dream happen. Just as one is both the architect ("I dream") and agent ("I am dreamed") of one's own dreams, Akalaitis's actors are both architects ("I perform") and agents ("I am performed") of theatrical space. The images of the onstage "dream" are transformed not only into the emotions of the spectator, but also into the emotions of the actor. And the site where this alchemical transformation takes place—where image and emotion collide—is the actor's body.

Akalaitis's notion that the actor is both "in it and sees him or herself in it," suggests that the actor is, ideally, responsive to and responsible for something larger than his or her own role. The actor not only is, but also casts, the image, knowing exactly what he or she is contributing to the totality of the onstage composition. Furthermore, the actor must commit equally to the *fictive* scene or composition and character, and to the *actual* "where" and "who" that actor is—a body moving in space, investigating a structure with clarity and sincerity. According to Akalaitis, the actors must be open to everything around them yet never "lost in the emotion"; they must always know where they are in the physical and emotional geography of the work.

The idea of seeing oneself as image has induced resistance in some actors, causing them to feel like dehumanized *übermarionettes,* or simply part of the scenery. Joan Elizabeth, an actress who appeared in both the Chicago and New York productions of *'Tis Pity She's a Whore,* addresses the notion that Akalaitis's actors are at times viewed as "pawns" existing only to serve the director's vision:

> [That idea] always struck me as a huge irony. Because this style of theater demands so much more of you as an actor. So much more of your imagination, your intelligence, your physical and emotional commitment. You can't slack off or you'll look really bad. Because you're serving a very specific master. You're really trying to carry out someone's idea. And so, consequently, if you do it really well, you can end up looking like a lackey to the master. When in reality you're working ten times harder than you have in any kind of conventional play.[9]

Akalaitis encourages her actors to both physicalize and personalize the formal elements of theater. If they succeed, the stage becomes a maelstrom in which image, emotion, and the body whirl together. If the actors are willing to commit to Akalaitis's exercises and have faith in her approach, they open themselves to the possibility of experiencing an unusual degree of spontaneity, individuality, and emotion onstage.

Akalaitis offers the following insight into the imagistic base of her directorial approach: "I get most of my ideas from pictures. In fact, all images in the theater are visual, even language—it's impossible to read without making pictures in your mind. The crucial thing for me is always to remain true to your images."[10] She has developed these exercises to help her actors explore, within a shared space, connections between their physicality and the pictures in *their* minds, to encourage them to be true to *their* images. It is ironic that while Akalaitis is often referred to as a designer's rather than an actor's director, she is in fact interested in giving her actors an unusual degree of imagistic responsibility. Particularly during the early stages of rehearsal, Akalaitis encourages her actors to think directorially, inventing images that may eventually find their way into the staged production. She is empowering them to become, in Barthes's phrase, "masters of meaning."[11] The dynamic between actor and image is featured in the following two exercises, in which the actor evokes personal images in order to inform his or her relationship to the present theatrical environment.

IMAGING PERSONAL HISTORY: "WALK THROUGH YOUR LIFE"

"Walk Through Your Life" is an exercise that Akalaitis introduces early in the rehearsal process; it is performed only once rather than repeated on a daily basis. The exercise was invented by Lee Breuer, and it is designed to allow actors access to a flow of personal images. However, unlike a Stanislavskian emotional memory exercise, which tends to remove the actor from the experience of the here and now, "Walk Through Your Life" encourages the actor to live in the duality of personal history and the present moment.

The object of the exercise is to "be in the room," while at the same time allowing personal images to "pass through you." The actors walk randomly around the space, spending a minute "working with" each year of their lives. As Akalaitis calls out each age change, the actors simply "drop" the year they are working with and go on to the next year in their lives. Aklalaitis cautions them that what they are doing is not "pantomime" (i.e., silently acting out moments from their lives), but an investigation of images. They are not to relive their pasts nor attempt to reexperience past emotions. Moreover, the images they investigate need not be monumental; any image that presents itself is important because it is belongs to them. Akalaitis suggests that an image may be as specific, or as seemingly inconsequential, as "a pencil, a brother, a teacher's face, a piece of pizza, a tree, something that happened at school, something that happened to your family, something that hurt you or that you're ashamed of, something funny, or something stupid."

Akalaitis lets the actors know that while the exercise is *always* physical, it is emotional only if it *happens* to be so. The only two requirements are that the actors keep moving and "stay in the room." They are to allow any images that arise to inform their bodies and, if they wish, their voices. It is fine if they draw a blank, as long as they acknowledge they have done so and stay open to any images that may appear to them. They neither touch each other physically nor shut each other out. They work with whatever is actually happening in the moment; for example, the feeling that the exercise is stupid or that they are superior to it. As Akalaitis coaches:

> It is all happening now. You are here now, in the present, in an associative flow of images from your personal history. You are alert, seeing and listening to everything that is happening around you, and, at the same time, perhaps you are seeing something inside.

Upon completion of the exercise, the actors stand in place with their eyes closed and focus their attention on their breath. They select a single image from the exercise that interests them and that they would like to investigate more fully. For the next five minutes, they are free to move around the space or to interact with the image in any way they wish. Akalaitis reminds the actors that "this is all an investigation for yourself. It may also be an investigation about the play, as long as you continue to work for yourself."

Imaging the Audience: The "Partner in Security"

Akalaitis frequently refers in rehearsal to Grotowski's idea of the "partner in security."[12] It is an idea that she herself has found valuable both as a director and as an actress. In this exercise, the actor envisions saying their words to someone with whom they are absolutely comfortable and relaxed. This may be a friend, a lover, a family member, or even a pet; it is someone for whom the actor can do no wrong, someone who never judges or criticizes, someone who is completely trustworthy. Akalaitis asks the actors to envision their partner in security while working on group composition exercises, exploring specific character relationships in the play, or engaging in direct address to the audience. The exercise thus allows the actors to imagine their various "auditors" as open, supportive presences. It is not surprising that, given Akalaitis's interest in disturbing and chaotic subjects, she may also ask an actor to envision what she refers to as their "partner in insecurity." Turning Grotowki's exercise on its head, the actor now imagines speaking to the person with whom he or she feels "the most uncomfortable, angst-ridden or rejected."

The Cool-Down

At the end of the physical session, Akalaitis leads the actors through one of two "cool-down" exercises. In the first of these exercises, the actors lie on their backs with their eyes closed and their arms and legs extended. If individuals experiences any lower back pain, they may bend their knees and put the soles of their feet flat on the floor. The actors focus on their breath, inhaling through the nose and exhaling through the mouth. They allow their minds to review what they just experienced during the physical session. As Akalaitis puts it, the actors let themselves "study those events." She then talks the actors "through their bodies." Beginning with the soles of the feet, the actors use the breath to become conscious of and release each part of their body. Throughout the exercise, Akalaitis reminds the actors to stay conscious and awake. When the actors have completed moving through their bodies, she asks them to "let the exercise go" and to visualize their breath, perhaps as a color, for a few minutes prior to opening their eyes.

In the second cool-down exercise, the actors stand in a relaxed posture with eyes closed and feet planted firmly on the floor, shoulder-width apart, in parallel position. The knees are unlocked, the pelvis is slightly tucked, the shoulders are relaxed with the arms hanging loosely by the actor's side, and the head is resting on the neck in an aligned and alert position. Akalaitis suggests that the actors visualize a pole, perpendicular to the ground, that passes through the top of the head, down through the center of the body, and emerges out from between the legs. The actors concentrate on breathing through the nose into a place in the middle of the stomach.

After a few minutes of breathing, Akalaitis asks the actors to "think about what you just did, but don't think too hard. Think about whether this means anything to you." She then asks the actors to "think about a color that is the color of what you just did: the color of your character, the color of your love or the color of your hate." She instructs the actors to envision placing the color on the soles of the feet as if it were pigment or paint, and letting it "tingle" until the feet become inflamed, ignited, and energized as they rest on the floor. As the color washes over their toes and ankles, the actors envision it as "electric, life-giving, vital, specific and intense." The color washes up over the entire body (Akalaitis talks through each body part), washes over the shoulders, runs down the arms, and emanates from the fingertips. It washes up over the face and across the forehead, dripping over the scalp, hair, eyebrows, eyelids, and eyeballs. It washes over the entire face, flowing into the nose and and the mouth and over the tongue and teeth. It drips down the entire body, part by part, finally washing back over the soles of the feet.

The color then washes up the backside of the body, over the calves, the back of the thighs, and the buttocks. It flows into the spine, electrifying and illuminating it. It floods inside the bones and organs, igniting the lungs, heart, kidneys, sex organs, muscles, tissue, mucous, and blood. The actors envision themselves, from their very insides, as "color—electrified, ignited, and alive." And not only their bodies but also their breath is infused with energized color. Just before opening their eyes, the actors envision exhaling this "aura of color and energy" to anyplace they desire, inside or outside of their bodies.

It is fitting that Akalaitis ends the physical session by leaving the actors with an image of themselves as energized, electrified color. The actors are now ready to use this image of color and light to infuse their work on the text, just as they have done with the physical exercise. As Genet, one of Akalaitis's favorite authors, has observed:

> [I]t will be a good idea if each actor, by his performance, casts light on the other or others who, in turn, will cast their light on him. The stage will therefore be a site not where reflections spend themselves but where bursts of light meet and collide.13

THE FUNCTION OF THE PHYSICAL EXERCISES

Mark Bly, who served as dramaturg on Akalaitis's production of *Leon and Lena (and lenz)* and her workshop of *The Screens* at the Guthrie Theatre, offers the following insight into Akalaitis's directorial method:

> JoAnne's process is a shared one. It is an event in space, always. First and foremost, an event in space. I thought those exercises in rehearsal for *Leon and Lena (& lenz)* were wonderful. . . . But it wasn't until I saw [the show] get up on the stage . . . and saw people moving in space, that I understood how she had somehow created some very invisible threads between the actors. So that everyone was spatially connected in a way I had never seen on [the Guthrie] stage. And it was the exercises that did that. The actors' awareness of the other actors around them, and your sensing that the actors literally knew that someone was in back of them, and how many feet and how many inches—it's very rare to see that and sense that.14

Akalaitis's physical exercises encourage the actors to connect with the space and with one another and to internalize the various images around them. The actors "put inside," or emotionally engage, images from their own lives, as well as images supplied by the director and designers. At the same time, the actors see themselves "from the outside," as part of an entire stage composition. Through the repeated performance of these exercises, the actors become familiar with the dual process of being emotionally activated by scenic images at the same time that they are seeing themselves as images in that scenic space. The actors are thus endowed with responsibility for shaping the overall scenic composition; in a sense, they are allowed a hand in fashioning the visual design of the production. The actor translates outer images into inner responses, which are then retranslated into outer behavior.

Thus, form goes in and form comes out. Form locates itself in the body, and the body becomes form. In Akalaitis's work, form always reflects an inner condition. And theatrical space is much more than a place to act. It is an image-filled atmosphere within which and by which one is possessed. Acting and design are intertwined not only because the actor's body and the stage space exist in the same imagistic realm, but also because the actor enters into an intimate and mutually affective relationship with scenic space itself. Theater critic Ross Wetzsteon suggests that, as a result of Akalaitis's gift for conceptual structure, and of her visual, architectural, and compositional use of the stage, she has "the greatest sense of atmosphere" of any director now working in the American theater. As Wetzsteon observes, "even the shadows become characters."[15]

[1] Ryszard Cieslak, interview, "Running to Touch the Horizon," by Marzena Torzecka, *New Theatre Quarterly* 8 (1992): 261.

[2] Sally Sommer, "JoAnne Akalaitis of Mabou Mines," *The Drama Review* 20.3 (Sept. 1976): 8.

[3] Anne Bogart, "Performance Composition Workshop," Movement Research, New York, 1989.

[4] Jean Genet, *Letters to Roger Blin: Reflections on the Theater*, trans. Richard Seaver (New York: Grove, 1969) 29.

[5] Oliver Sacks, *Awakenings* (1973: New York: Harper-Perennial, 1990) 76–84.

6 Roland Barthes, "Diderot, Brecht, Eisenstein," *Image-Music—Text,* ed. and trans. Stephen Heath (New York: Hill-Farrar, 1977) 72.

7 Quoted by Joseph Coates, "Modern Arthur: Donald Barthelme Relocates the Round Table," review of *The King,* by Donald Barthelme, *Chicago Tribune* 10 June 1990, sect. 14:5.

8 Eugenio Barba and Nicola Savarese, *A Dictionary of Theatre Anthropology: The Secret Art of the Performer,* trans. Richard Fowler (New York: Routledge, 1991) 158.

9 Joan Elizabeth, interview with author, Chicago, 21 October 1992, appended herein.

10 Ross Wetzsteon, "Mabou Mines," *New York Magazine* 23 Feb. 1981: 30.

11 See Barthes's description of the epic actor, who demonstrates a "knowledge" that goes beyond both "human knowledge" (an awareness of a character's emotional state—the ability to become an other) and "knowledge as an actor" (virtuousity): "The actor must prove that he is not enslaved to the spectator (bogged down in 'reality,' in 'humanity'), that he guides meaning toward its ideality—a sovereignty of the actor, master of meaning [...]" 74–75.

12 Grotowski himself uses the term "secure partner" to refer to an image of someone in the actor's life with whom that actor feels completely at ease. When imaginatively invoked by the actor in performance, this "secure partner" may help the actor to enter into a direct and intimate relationship with the audience. Although Akalaitis uses the variation "partner in security," her use of the term correlates with Grotowski's idea of the "secure partner."

13 Genet, 40.

14 Mark Bly, interview with author, Seattle, 6 April 1992.

15 Wetzsteon, 30.

four

'Tis Pity She's
a Whore

The crimes of which a people is ashamed constitute its
real history, and the same is true of man.
JEAN GENET

My principal job has been to help the performers get
in touch with extremely disturbing, very deep emotions.
JOANNE AKALAITIS

John Ford's Jacobean revenge tragedy, *'Tis Pity She's a Whore,* was
written in 1633. Set in Parma, Italy, the play tells the story of an inces-
tuous love affair between the young student Giovanni and his sister
Annabella. Because Annabella loves her brother, she hesitates to
choose among her three suitors: the lord Soranzo, the soldier
Grimaldi, and the fool Berghetto. Soranzo, Annabella's leading suitor,
has been having an affair with Hippolita, and swears he will marry
her if she becomes widowed. Yet when news arrives that Hippolita's
husband, Ricardetto, has been lost at sea, Soranzo breaks his promise
and continues to pursue Annabella. Annabella, finding herself pregnant by her brother, at last gives in to Soranzo's marriage proposal.
Hippolita intends to poison Soranzo at his wedding but is double-
crossed by Soranzo's loyal servant Vasques and mistakenly drinks the
poison herself. Ricardetto, meanwhile, has returned to Parma in dis-
guise in order to spy on his wife and Soranzo. Ricardetto and the

spurned Grimaldi plot to kill Soranzo but murder the fool Berghetto by mistake. Soranzo learns that Annabella is already pregnant and beats the name of her lover out of her; he then plots to expose and murder Giovanni at a banquet held for the notables of Parma. Giovanni kills Annabella to save her honor, rushes to the banquet with her heart on his dagger, stabs Soranzo, and is killed by Soranzo's followers.

Akalaitis staged *'Tis Pity She's a Whore* at Chicago's Goodman Theatre during the winter of 1990. The production was revived by the New York Shakespeare Festival in the spring of 1992, winning an Obie Award Special Citation for Conception and Design. I begin this chapter by discussing several ideas and images that inspired Akalaitis's Goodman Theatre staging of the play, after which I describe the specific physical exercises performed by the cast throughout the rehearsal period. Suggesting that the Akalaitis's exercises are explorations of both form and content, I conclude the chapter by reflecting upon the means by which they strengthen the actors' connection to the world of the play.

The World of 'Tis Pity She's a Whore

Addressing the assembled company of *'Tis Pity She's a Whore* on the first day of rehearsal, Akalaitis remarks that she has been thinking about the title of Raymond Carver's short story anthology, *What We Talk About When We Talk About Love.* She believes that all theater, even a classical comedy such as Molière's *School for Wives,* is about things that are forbidden, and she herself is particularly interested in the things that are forbidden to talk about when we talk about love. Many of these taboo subjects, including incest and wife beating, appear throughout *'Tis Pity She's a Whore.*

Akalaitis speaks about her decision to set the production in 1930s Italy, a decade that witnessed the rise of that nation's Fascist political party under the leadership of Benito Mussolini who, according to D. C. Watts, "united public works, the politics of theatre and a relentless search for glory abroad (providing the risks were strictly limited), which was expressed in alternating bouts of vainglorious unilateral aggression and in posing as Mussolini the peacemaker."[1] Akalaitis feels that Fascism had frighteningly widespread appeal among Italian citizens, its allies being not only the Vatican, the King, and the army but also the bourgeoisie. She points out to the company of *'Tis Pity She's a Whore* that the Fascist movement was patriotic, aggressive, and anti-intellectual to its core.

Akalaitis goes on to describe the philosophical basis and justification Fascism found in Futurism, an aesthetic movement launched by the Italian writer and painter Emilio Fillippo Tomaso Marinetti during the first decade of the twentieth century. Both Fascism and Futurism were obsessed with youth, action, athleticism, and power. Both movements celebrated chaos, irrationality, and extreme subjectivity. Both were adversarial and antagonistic, calling for the destruction of what they perceived as the canonized culture. Marinetti himself was referred to as "the caffeine of Europe" because of his ability to annoy, disturb, and live at a fevered pitch. Marinetti's Futurist *Manifestos,* published from 1909 onwards, called upon artists to turn their backs on the past, celebrate the present in all its forms—including war ("the world's only hygiene") and machinery—and to emancipate themselves from any formal, linguistic, or prosodic restraints, using "words in liberty."[2] Marinetti's first *Manifesto* includes the following tenets:

> We intend to sing the love of danger, the habit of energy and fearlessness.

> Except in struggle, there is no more beauty. No work without an aggressive character can be a masterpiece.

> We will destroy the museums, libraries, academies of every kind, we will fight moralism, feminism, every opportunistic or utilitarian cowardice.

> We hurl ourselves against you, holding our hearts in our fingers like revolvers, our hearts burdened with hate and courage.

> Museums; cemeteries![3]

Akalaitis tells the company that she is particularly interested in, and envisions the play embracing in its very acting style, the Futurist mandate of speed. She is also intrigued by the idea of confusion, or, as the Jacobeans called it, "ruin." The world of *'Tis Pity She's a Whore* is filled with chaos, wreck, decadence, and disaster. It is a world gone bad, a world out-of-synch, a world that both terrifies and exalts. Characters find themselves trapped in a dangerous confusion of sex and power. They do not evolve in the direction of reconciliation, realization, or redemption; rather, they hurtle toward personal tragedy and political collapse. Yet the play, for Akalaitis, is also an unusual love story, whose poignancy lies in witnessing characters as young as the two lovers, particularly Annabella, who is female, caught in a cascade of horrifying events. In the end, it is Annabella's beloved brother Giovanni, as much as society, who is responsible for her death.

'Tis Pity She's a Whore is a bloody play. Much of the text either depicts or suggests acts of brutality. Akalaitis's imagination is especially captured by the fact that so much of the play's violence is perpetrated against women. She has remarked in casual conversation that a woman's vulnerabilty is both her triumph and her downfall; it is, unfortunately, the very quality that allows her to be hurt, abused, or objectified. Each of the play's four female characters are vulnerable to physical and psychological violence. The young maiden Philotis witnesses the murder of her lover Berghetto, after which she is sent away to a convent. Hippolita, regarded by those in power as a jealous maniac, is poisoned. Putana, as the name Ford gave her allows, is called a "slut" and has her eyes put out. And Annabella is stabbed to death by the person who loves her most. As Akalaitis informs an interviewer, "This is not a feminist play."[4]

Yet Akalaitis is attracted to *'Tis Pity She's a Whore* for what it reveals about the misogyny of contemporary society, particulary in its treatment of sexual and domestic violence. She points out that the "very intense, hideous wife-beating scene" between Soranzo and the pregnant Annabella, for example, "could have happened behind closed doors in the suburbs today."[5] And Akalaitis's staging of this scene reflects her view that it displays a horrifying combination of eroticism and physical violence: The more Soranzo physically and verbally abuses his wife, the more he becomes sexually aroused.

In Akalaitis's opinion, *'Tis Pity She's a Whore* is both stylistically modern in the terseness and directness of its language, and thematically modern in its startling examination of unbridled subjectivity and selfishness. At the same time, she considers the play to have more in common with late nineteenth-century romanticism than with the work of Ford's contemporaries, including Shakespeare. Akalaitis envisions Giovanni as an intellectual who pursues a completely solipsistic ideal to its limit. Also, she believes that, with Annabella, Ford appears to be writing about a kind of "new woman" who is willing to do anything, including sacrifice herself, for love. For Akalaitis, these two characters are extremely "modern" in the nineteenth-century sense of the word, and they embody Romantic ideals moreso than they do Elizabethan or Jacobean ones.

Akalaitis explains to the company that she is directing *'Tis Pity She's a Whore* "in order to find something out about the sexual politics and psychosexual attitudes of the period." She finds it fascinating, for example, that each character in the play gets "aroused" in his own particular manner: the Friar from metaphysics, Grimaldi from being a soldier, Soranzo from beating his wife. Akalaitis is also directing this play in order to discover the ways in which these attitudes resonate in our contemporary lives:

> [. . .] I think you do a play like this simply to find out what you feel and what it all means. What happens in it is horrible, but to a large extent, it reflects what I see today in government, and out on the streets and in homes. Look at that guy in Boston who shot and killed his pregnant wife. I think we live in a society that is eroticized, bourgeois and violent, [a society which is] not so different from the one that Ford describes.[6]

Akalaitis has a clear sense of what intrigues her about Ford's text, and she conveys her enthusiasm and sense of adventure to the company. She admits that she "suspects things" about the play, but does not know all the answers. She approaches her directorial work as an investigation and encourages the actors to do the same.

The Physical Exercises

Akalaitis spends the first two days of rehearsal "at the table," reading and discussing the text. On the third day, she introduces the company to the physical and vocal exercises they will perform throughout the rehearsal period. Discussing her work process with Chicago theater critic Richard Christiansen, Akalaitis explains that it is crucial for actors to be able to "electrify their bodies and see themselves in space," and has designed the exercises with this goal in mind. She wants "to get [the play] up on its feet as soon as possible, and [wants] the actors to start working deep inside their bodies. A lot of people don't know how to do that, but it's very important in establishing working relationships and in forming a group of people into a company."[7]

The Warm-Up

While the actors prepare for each day's physical session by doing individual warm-ups, Akalaitis shares thoughts and questions regarding the text, the characters, or the rehearsal process itself. Rather than seeking immediate answers from the actors, she wants instead to get certain ideas "boiling" in their minds and bodies. Ideally, the actors will allow these ideas to inform the group exercises that follow. During both the individual warm-up session and the group exercises, Akalaitis plays music ranging from Mozart to reggae to "world music" from Africa, the Caribbean, Latin America, Cambodia, and Bulgaria.

On the first day of the physical work, the actors warm-up to the haunting music of "Le Mystère des Voix Bulgares." Akalaitis asks them to think about the question, "What does my character talk about when he or she talks about love?" Cautioning the actors against judging their characters, she suggests that the actors should nonetheless be able to see their characters clearly for what they are, even if they happen to be manipulative or evil. She then reads aloud the following passage by Jean Genet:

> [. . .] the patron saint of actors is Tiresias, because of his dual nature. Legend has it that he retained the male sex for seven years, and for seven more the other. For seven year's a man's clothing, for seven a woman's. In a certain way, at certain moments—or perhaps always—his femininity followed in close pursuit of his virility, the one or the other being constantly asserted, with the result that he never had any rest, I mean any specific place where he could rest. Like him, the actors are neither this nor that, and they must be aware that they are a presence constantly beset by femininity or its opposite, but ready to play to the point of abasement that which, be it virility or its opposite, is in any case predetermined.[8]

Finally, Akalaitis reminds the actors that they are the character, but they are also themselves. They should therefore think about specific times in their lives when they themselves were in love, or were the recipient of love; the specific times when they were in pain, exalted, sexy, or eroticized. And like Genet's ideal actor, they must be willing to "play to the point of abasement" whatever they happen to be investigating at the moment.

About a week later, as the actors warm-up to Mozart's *Requiem*, Akalaitis suggests that the play has the feel of a 1930s movie. She asks the actors to keep this image in mind as they think about love, elitism, speed, and Italy. During another warm-up, to Jimmy Cliff's reggae tune "By the Rivers of Babylon," Akalaitis asks the actors to think about the physical condition of their characters, particularly their bodily "humours" and any diseases they might have. The actors are to think specifically about allergies, cancers, conditions of the skin, spinal fluid, sexual fluids, menstrual blood, urine, and excrement.

Dancing in the Architecture of Danger

On the first day of physical work, the actors begin the slam-dancing exercise, imagining that they are in an architecture of their own choice that is somehow "real" to them. Akalaitis then overlays the information that this architecture defines a place that is "bad, negative, and threatening." It may be a place from their childhood, their dreams, or a work of art, as long as that, too, is "real" to them. Even if the place is fictive, the actors must be able to see it clearly in their mind's eye. Akalaitis encourages the actors to "use" the music, and to allow the place to transform as needed. She then asks them to work with the idea that they are all in the same dangerous place together.

As the rehearsals progress, the slam-dancing exercise becomes more and more intense. The actors hurtle through the space, all the while investigating their bodies and the bodies of their fellow actors. At times, they work with the idea that air is charged with positive, supportive, life-affirming energy. At other times, they allow the air to become the thing that resists, oppresses, pushes, limits, and hurts them. Akalaitis observes that each character in the play is in an extremely difficult situation through which they must push. It is as if the characters are forever thinking to themselves, "I am here. I have to get there." Yet, as Akalaitis points out, "moving from A to B" in this play is extremely difficult. The characters do not simply walk or stroll, but rather, surge, thrust, hurtle, and throw themselves through their environment.

Akalaitis suggests that, ideally, the audience will feel ill at ease because the onstage environment is one of danger. In fact, the moment the audience enters the theater, they should sense a world gone bad, a world out-of-synch even for the few good people who inhabit it. In the world of *'Tis Pity She's a Whore,* one is rewarded neither for being good nor for being evil. And in order to convincingly inhabit this world as an actor, Akalaitis argues, one must commit to a feeling of entrapment. In this respect, she suggests, acting Ford is far more difficult than acting Shakespeare who is "so generous in his genius." Perhaps to compensate for this absence of generosity in the Jacobean worldview, Akalaitis works with the actors to "empty everything— body, mind, heart, and soul" in order to create the architecture of support, community, aliveness, and inspiration. Only after a sense of group energy and connection is achieved, do the actors construct "the architecture of the dangerous place"—in other words, the architecture of Ford's play.

Akalaitis calls attention to the fact that the play is direct, speedy, and linear, that its events "cascade" with such force that none of the characters is able to control them. On more than one occasion, the actors construct the dangerous architecture to the music of Peter Tosh's "Stepping Razor." Tosh's lyrics begin:

> If you wanna live, treat me good. (Repeat)
> I'm like a walking razor, don't you watch my sides, I'm dangerous.
>   I'm dangerous. (Repeat)
> If you are a bully, you better treat me good. (Repeat)
> I'm like a stepping razor, don't you watch my sides, I'm dangerous
>   I'm dangerous. (Repeat)"[9]

As the actors move through the space to the throbbing reggae beat, Akalaitis coaches them to keep their eyes open and really see their fellow actors. Even as they work with the idea of being entrapped, they must remember they are creating the architecture of "a place where everyone is in it together." Above all, they must keep in mind that there is energy in danger and repression.

At times, Akalaitis does not specify the emotional quality of the architecture, but instead asks the group to determine its nature. Even so, the actors work daily to create an architecture of danger and exaltation. Akalaitis directs the actors to "build, together, a place that is dangerous and exalting—whatever that means to you. You are near death, but this place awakens and energizes you. Look at one another and see one another. You are not at work alone; you are doing it together."

STOPPING-AND-STARTING IN THE ARCHITECTURE OF DANGER

According to Akalaitis, 'Tis Pity She's a Whore is not a "curvy" play; there is nothing leisurely about it. The play is extremely direct. Although the characters are "twisted" in the sense of being conspiratorial and vengeful, they behave in a straightforward and "in the moment" manner. Akalaitis suggests that the play is marked by a very powerful sense of stopping-and-starting, and that Ford's writing has "the feel of a jagged, intended, attacked, committed, vortex." In the text, there are few entrances and exits; many of the scenes begin with the characters in mid-action. Akalaitis advises the actors to heed Genet's advice that every scene should be played as if it were a play in itself,[10] or, as she puts it, "I'm in a scene, the scene is over, a door slams, and a new door opens." She does not envision 'Tis Pity She's a Whore as a beautiful, meditative European play, and reminds the company that they are Americans perfoming "a jagged play" with a great deal of intention.

Keeping this in mind, the actors explore stopping-and-starting, imagining that they are moving along sharp, jagged vectors in space. While doing so, they work together to create a shared, dangerous architecture. At times, Akalaitis asks the actors to work with the idea that "things are curved, rather than direct and upright." They construct the architecture of pleasure, happiness, and support, eventually allowing it to transform into a place of danger, paranoia, and negativity. On one particular day, the actors switch back and forth between stopping-and-starting and slow motion, all the while working within an architecture of danger. Akalaitis urges the actors to be daring in their investigation of this "bad place," and to "go as deeply and as far" as they are able.

INTERNALIZING THE IMAGES AND THE RHYTHM OF VIOLENCE

As the rehearsal period unfolds, the actors continue to investigate both the technical and the emotional aspects of stopping-and-starting. They envision themselves travelling through space with extreme speed (even if they are not actually doing so), just as the Futurists did. They work with the idea of "changing direction" in whatever way makes sense to them: physically, psychologically, or spiritually. They work to create an "architecture of adventure" that, according to Akalaitis, is very dangerous but also energizing. As the actors perform the various exercises, Akalaitis encourages them to be open to discovering things not only about their characters but also about themselves.

'Tis Pity She's a Whore is unrelenting in its harshness of subject and style. While the physical exercises allow the actors to investigate images of violence suggested by the text, there is also something violent in the very nature of the exercises themselves. Slam-dancing and stopping-and-starting, for example, are not simply movement forms that explore and express violent content. The sharp, jagged rhythm of the exercises is in fact the rhythm of violence. Also, the exercises' protracted length and use of repetitive gestures that persist but do not dramatically progress, add to this sense of violence. Once again, the medium is the message. The exercises are not simply *explorations* of violence, chaos, obsession, and compulsion; they are themselves violent, chaotic, obsessive, and compulsive.

CONSTRUCTING THE ARCHITECTURE OF DANGER IN SLOW MOTION

Akalaitis begins the slow-motion composition work by asking the actors to create a group painting that takes place in a dangerous architecture. She explains that the entire group understands exactly what the painting is about and is all the while working to make it more perfect. The actors then allow the composition to change from the painting of "The Dangerous Architecture" to the painting of "The Destruction of The Dangerous Architecture." Akalaitis informs the group that, again, they have a perfect understanding of this second painting that, in its slowness, becomes increasingly dynamic and monumental. The actors also work with the idea that they themselves determine the nature of the architecture portrayed in the painting; for example, a "good person" in the painting may initiate a "positive architecture." The architecture may undergo several transformations, or contain more than a single composition.

While the actors investigate both the shared architecture and the way their bodies are moving through the space, they are free to explore any ideas, gestures, or movements associated with their character. Akalaitis reassures the actors that the character work "may take place on the simplest of terms," that it is fine if their knowledge of the character is incomplete. She emphasizes that the composition work is very technical, but if entered into with "heart and sincerity," the actors may discover something about the inner life of their character. She reminds them that they are working within the context of the play; if they are aware of the costume that has been designed for their character, for instance, they may imagine those particular clothes on their body. Akalaitis points out that *'Tis Pity She's a Whore* is a microcosm of society, inhabited by servants, bougeoisie, clergy, alchemists, virgins, fools, and sophisticated young men. These people all know, or at least have seen, one another; some of them hate each other, some of them love each other. If the actors wish, therefore, they may relate to other characters in the space, as long as they do so without talking.

The actors investigate the body, health, and metabolism of their characters: their heart, lungs, diaphragm, intestines, brains, genitals, skin, bones, blood, mucous, seminal or menstrual fluids, sex life or lack thereof, muscle tone or lack thereof, obesity, injuries, cancers, ulcers, and heart attacks. Akalaitis reminds the actors that even nuns, soldiers, and bandits have bodies that contain fluids and diseases. The actors then put what they have gleaned from the above investigation "inside" as they create, in slow motion, the architecture of danger. The actors are aware of their bodies and the place they are constructing as a group. At the same time, they are attuned to the sights and the sounds of the room they are in at the present moment. Of all these sounds, that of their own breath is the most important. They listen to their breath as the entire composition becomes increasingly perfect with each passing millisecond. They think about control, but not with their brains. They "think" with their bodies. Nothing in the space escapes their awareness.

As the slow-motion work for each day draws to a close, Akalaitis will occasionally ask the actors to put whatever they've "caught" from the exercises into their bodies. The actors then embark upon a slow-motion investigation that involves five minutes of moving through the space, exploring their character, working from both the inside and the outside. Coaching the actors to be bold and not censor themselves, Akalaitis refers to this work as an investigative opportunity for them rather than for her, as "pure actor research."

STAGING STOPPING-AND-STARTING AND SLOW MOTION

One of the ways in which Akalaitis incorporates the rhythm of stopping-and-starting into her staging is by using a kind of theatrical jump-cut effect between scenes. There are few entrances and exits in the production. More often, a scene ends in an abrupt blackout (stopping), and the lights just as abruptly come up (starting) on the following scene that appears to be in progress. Even more jarring, the lights at times come up to reveal a scene "frozen" for several seconds before snapping into action, as if the scene has a mind of its own and will begin when it pleases. It is possible, when viewing a scene that terminates abruptly or "refrains" from starting, to experience a strange sense of deprivation. It is as if one were experiencing only a slice of the action rather than the entire scenic pie. Yet what one loses in narrative continuity, one gains in sensory intensity.

Act II, scene vi, for example, begins with what Akalaitis refers to as a "family portrait" tableau that, she suggests, resembles an old photograph of the Mussolini family. The lights come up on the "portrait," frozen for about five counts before the characters animate each other in a kind of domino effect: Florio and Annabella "click" into action; this triggers Vasques and Putana who "click" into action; this triggers Giovanni who "clicks" into action. The "click" takes the form of a penetrating stare that each pair of characters gives the next; the spoken text begins only after the entire "portrait" is activated.

Act III, scene iii begins as the lights come up on Giovanni and Putana, frozen in place; they hold for about four counts, then suddenly launch into a frantic discussion of Annabella's pregnancy. Act

III, scene iv, in which Giovanni argues with the Friar about his love for Annabella, is physically static and contains virtually no movement. Akalaitis incorporates a "freeze-frame" effect at various points in the scene, which interrupts what she describes as "urgent talk talk talk talk talk." After Giovanni's line, "Her sickness is a fullness of her blood (Annabella is pregnant) [55]," [11] for example, he and the Friar lock gazes with each other for several seconds. The final line of the scene is the Friar's, "Gentle sir./ All this I'll say, that Heaven may prosper her." Rather than exiting after the line, as Ford's stage direction instructs, the Friar and Giovanni once again lock gazes for about three counts, whereupon the lights abruptly black out.

Giovanni's final line in Act III, "I fear this Friar's falsehood." [62] sets off a slow-motion composition in miniature. As Giovanni exits offstage, the Friar and Annabella travel downstage for the confession scene that follows. At the same time, Florio enters from up-left, and Soranzo and Vasques enter from down-left. The characters move simultaneously and continuously, as if they were creeping, until the marriage promise between Annabella and Soranzo is sealed, at which point there is an abrupt blackout. The staging physicalizes both the tangled web of relationships and the converging, cascading forces of destruction in the play.

Akalaitis incorporates both stopping-and-starting and slow motion into the wedding scene that opens Act IV. At various points throughout the scene, the ensemble responds to the principal characters by laughing hysterically in unison for a predetermined count, ending with what Akalaitis describes as a "surgical cut-off." There is a sense in which this laughter, which begin as abruptly as they end, is a vocal manifestation of stopping-and-starting.

As part of the "entertainment" for Soranzo's wedding to Annabella, Akalaitis stages a scene in which a young woman sings a beautiful Italian aria as the stage lights dim and the rest of the characters strike stylized "frozen" poses, creating the impression that each of them is lost in his or her own thoughts. Akalaitis's work on this section was inspired by a soap-opera technique whereby a scene goes into soft-focus as the camera travels "inside the head" of someone remembering his or her past. At the moment the aria is over, the stage lights abruptly bump up and the action becomes completely natura-listic—a stylistic manifestation of stopping-and-starting. The poison-ing of Hippolita is then enacted in slow motion while the onlookers remain frozen until their unison line, "Ha, wonderful justice!" Akalaitis asks the actors to internalize the rhythm and feeling of this line, suggesting that it should feel "hushed and lilting, like a piece by Mozart."

INTERNALIZING THE DRAMATIC STRUCTURE

Akalaitis mentions one day in rehearsal that the director's job is to find the structure of the play whereas the actor's job is to articulate the "beats," or individual units of action, that comprise each scene or speech. She points out that the actor must always know exactly where he or she is, and is headed, in the overall physical and emotional geog-raphy of the play. Moreover, the actor's intention must be directed not only toward his or her fellow actors, but also toward making the story of the play absolutely clear to the audience. The majority of Akalaitis's early rehearsals are thus spent marking the beats and clar-ifying the rhythm of each scene. She also devotes time to any extended speeches an individual actor may have in the play, working with the actor to answer questions such as: When is there the feeling of a period? When are the thoughts separate or connected? When does a thought "top" a previous thought? When is a thought subordinate to a previous thought? When does the speech tumble out? Where does each new beat occur within the speech? What is the effect of "con-necting words" such as *but, and,* and *therefore* located either within or between beats?

Akalaitis reminds the cast that Jacobean tragedy is stylized—that is, expressing grand human passions by means of heightened language and imagery—rather than naturalistic. She tells the cast that while it is important not to indulge in overacting, the beats must not only be articulated but must also be firmly and clearly attacked; there is no sense of leisure, no sense of running out of steam, in this play. This forward-driving movement of sharply articulated beats is yet another manifestation of the rhythm of stopping-and-starting. It is a rhythm that must be experienced in the body as well as the mind.

VOCAL WORK

'Tis Pity She a Whore vocal coach Catherine Fitzmaurice had worked with Akalaitis on the Guthrie Theatre production of The Screens. Fitzmaurice is unable to join the company until the third week of rehearsal so, in the meantime, Akalaitis conducts a simple vocal warm-up at the end of each day's physical session. She asks the actors to "open your mouth and make a sound which is the sound of your body. Now play with that sound." She then instructs the actors to continue thinking about their character as they play with the various vocal resonators in their face, chest, abdomen, and groin. The actors do this for about five minutes, exploring any sounds or words that they feel belong to their character. They also explore the various place in their body that might give rise to their character's voice. Throughout this vocal warm-up, Akalaitis reminds the actors that they are always "doing it physically," even as they imagine their character saying and playing with words.

Akalaitis suggests that each character speaks differently, and that the way in which a character uses language defines who he or she is. The actors must therefore work to discover their character's unique manner of talking and "internalize it." Akalaitis points out that certain scenes in the play alternate between "a kind of Maria Callas operatic feel" and the feel of a 1930s movie. She asks the actors to listen not only to the "music" that their character speaks but also to the "song" each scene is singing.

INTERNALIZING PERSONAL IMAGES

Akalaitis believes that the actor must always visualize something as he or she speaks. Working on the final banquet and fight (Act V, scene vi), for example, Akalaitis instructs each actor in the scene to "place inside" of himself a very specific image of death. Rehearsing the speech in which Hippolita begs Soranzo to marry her, Akalaitis suggests to actress Barbara Robertson that Hippolita's speech becomes "internal" as she approaches the line, "And shall the conquest of my lawful bed!" At the same time, however, Akalaitis instructs the actress to "locate" this internal image "out," in the direction of the audience.

The wedding of Annabella and Soranzo (Act IV, scene i), opens with the entire company, clad in masks, travelling downstage, one abreast, in excrutiatingly slow motion. To help prepare the actors for their work on this "surrealist pageant," Akalaitis reads aloud another passage by Genet:

> Don't allow an actor to forget himself unless he carries this forgetfulness to the point of pissing squarely in front of the public. You should force them to dream—those who have no lines—to dream about the death of their son or the death of their beloved mother, or they should imagine that a thug is robbing them or that the public sees them naked.[12]

Akalaitis then asks each actor to internalize the image of a humiliating sexual act. She instructs the actors to:

> Work with a private moment: something that happened to your body that you were ashamed of. Now, add to that a social mask that is extraordinarily bright. So, this horrible thing has happened to you at the same time that you're in a room with a crowd of people trying to look *great*.

The actors practice their slow motion procession downstage, working first with facial "masks" of sexuality, cruelty, and humiliation, and then with those of a hermetic, disaster-ridden world. Akalaitis reminds the actors that they cannot create a "mask" simply by showing emotion on the face but rather they must first internalize a specific image of that emotion. Although the actors eventually carry constructed masks depicting animal faces and surrealist objects, the experience of humiliation remains in their bodies.

Akalaitis believes it is the actor's responsibility to be aware of and responsive to not only the physical space but also to the scenic images contained in that space. Thus, the actors work to internalize images arising from the scenic world around them, as they do with images arising from their own psyche or from the text. Obversely, there are scenic images in 'Tis Pity She's a Whore that seem uncannily aware of, and even responsive to, the action. While the play is full of secrets, plots, and conspiracies, there is almost always a witness, spy, or eavesdropper privy to the action. Often, however, this witness is not a flesh-and-blood character but a "scenic presence" such as the baby's face painted on the backdrop, the bleeding classical busts on top of the arcade, the twine-bound statues in Soranzo's study, or the cartoonish cut-out of Man Ray cruising by in his streamlined automobile. It is as if these scenic objects are actually watching, listening, and even moving of their own volition. In 'Tis Pity She's a Whore, as in all of Akalaitis's work, the scenic elements take on aspects of character just as the actor takes on aspects of image.

Set designer John Conklin has suggested that the visual artifacts surrounding a work may be investigated not only as a source for images that eventually find their way onstage, but also as a way of understanding one's personal relationship to the work itself. In the case of 'Tis Pity She's a Whore, the visual "artifacts" surrounding the (transposed) work were the paintings and photographs of the Surrealists. For Akalaitis and Conklin, the work of artists such as Dali, Tanguy, and Man Ray portrays the same strange, hostile terrain that Ford evokes in his play.

As part of their visual research for 'Tis Pity She's a Whore, Conklin and Akalaitis looked at photographs of a homoerotic sports palace built by Mussolini, the work of the Spanish architect Gaudi, and of course, the photographs of Man Ray. They were particularly inspired by the paintings of Giorgio de Chirico whose deserted arcades and town squares radiate a sense of oppressive sadness and alienation. Surrealist images were incorporated into the production's design in the form of an ochre-colored cyclorama covered with odd, whimsical designs such as clouds, disembodied limbs, and a baby's face, as well as entirely abstract shapes: tiny windows where eaves-dropping heads appeared throughout the production; a pair of man-nequin's legs tossed onstage by a stagehand stationed in the wings; a gigantic, red-toenailed foot that accompanied the fool Berghetto wherever he went; and the image of a headless, rope-bound female torso that appeared on the production's program, poster, and press materials.

Surrealism's depiction of the repressed and forgotten material of the unconscious meshed perfectly with Akalaitis's interest in the for-bidden aspects of romance and sex such as violence, humiliation, and the abuse of power. She found it particularly intriguing and disturb-ing that so many Surrealist works portrayed women as faceless objects. Discussing her design concept for the production in a *Chicago Sun-Times* interview, she explains that:

> Surrealism operates in a very psychosexual terrain that celebrates chaos, so it seemed right [for the production], as did the way women and sexuality were treated by the Surrealists. Man Ray was particu-larly brilliant in the way he made women into objects in a very kinky, twisted, slightly sadomasochistic, titillating, erotic way. He understood that area of sexuality very well.[13]

THE SCENIC SPACE

From the moment the audience enters the theater, before the play even begins, they are bombarded with scenic images that evoke this "psy-chosexual" landscape. At center-stage is an enormous blowup of Man Ray's 1930 photograph entitled *"La Prière."* The photograph depicts a naked woman, crouching, her hands curled around her buttocks that rest on the soles of her feet. The woman's buttocks fill the frame of the photograph yet her head cannot be seen. One wonders whether she is offering or protecting herself. One also cannot help thinking that she has merely been arranged into a composition that pleases the photographer. The image is sensual and disturbing. As the play nears its conclusion, the photograph will reappear along with several smaller versions of itself, almost as if it had given birth.

The stage floor is draped with black cloth so that the photograph appears to float in a dark void. Hauntingly sad, sweet music fills the unusually dark house. Created by Jan A. P. Kaczmarek, a Polish-born composer with several film scores to his credit, the synthesized music has the feel of an eerie, melodramatic 1930s sound track. Suddenly, a row of bright white lights along the top of the proscenium comes up full, nearly blinding the audience. These "eye lights" are focused directly into the house and will be used throughout the play during scene changes. The harsh light seems to scream "WAKE UP," forcing the audience into an encounter with the photograph. Like the naked female model, the audience is "exposed." One feels an odd mixture of relief (the woman disappears) and anxiety (we remain in the light) as the stage goes to black. Then there is a sudden, loud "sting" of music as the eye lights go out and the house comes up full. The pre-set is gone, and in its place is a wide open space set against a sickly yellow sky. A soccer ball is thrown onstage, followed by the Friar and Giovanni who likewise "throw" themselves into a metaphysical argument. The play has barely begun, yet the audience is already uneasy with the experience of witnessing, and perhaps feeling incriminated in, this not-quite-right world.

Akalaitis believes that actors have a responsibility to be aware not only of the physical space that surrounds them, but also of the entire theatrical composition that occurs in that space. The physical exercises she uses in rehearsal are designed to strengthen this awareness, encouraging the actors to see the world onstage as a "painting" that must be both physically and emotionally filled. The exercises also provide the actors with a sense of what it means to "listen" with their bodies—to actually "listen" rather than merely indicate they are doing so. Finally, the exercises are a means by which both actor and director may investigate images that may ultimately find their way into the performance.

Akalaitis remarks one day in rehearsal that the plays of ancient Greece are written in a very formal style yet are full of passion. The same may be said of her exercises that are extremely technical yet are designed to open the door to, rather than inhibit, emotion. Because the exercises themselves are violent, chaotic, obsessive, repetitive, and dreamlike, they provide the actors in 'Tis Pity She's a Whore with an opportunity to explore not only the thematic content of the work but also its sharp, jagged rhythm and structure. The stopping-and-starting exercise, in particular, allow the actors to physicalize the violent, cascading feel of Ford's world, as well as the sensation of intense speed mandated by the Futurists. The exercises thus help the actors forge a connection to both the chaotic, ruined world of the Jacobeans and to the disturbing scenic world created by Akalaitis and her designers.

On the afternoon before the opening performance of 'Tis Pity She's a Whore, Akalaitis explains to the cast that, for her, the most challenging aspect of doing theater is to be able to work simultaneously from the inside, while seeing yourself from the outside as part of an entire stage picture or composition—to both be in it and to watch yourself in it. In so doing, the actor is never "lost in the emotion," but always knows where he or she is in the work as a whole. Above all, Akalaitis reminds them, they must never forget that they are in a *place*.

1 D. C. Watt, "Benito Mussolini," *Twentieth Century Culture: A Biographical Companion,* ed. Alan Bullock, R.W. Woodings and John Cumming (New York: Harper, 1983) 541–42.

2 Judy Rawson, "Italian Futurism," *The Avant-Garde Tradition in Literature,* ed. Richard Kostelanetz (Buffalo, N.Y.: Prometheus, 1982) 151.

3 Emilio Fillippo Tomas Marinetti, "The Foundation Manifesto of Futurism," *Le Figaro,* trans. R. W. Flint, 20 Feb. 1909.

4 Hedy Weiss, "In 'Pity,' JoAnne Akalaitis Examines the Last Taboo," *Chicago Sun-Times,* 4 March 1990: 4.

5 Richard Christiansen, "Setting 'Pity': JoAnne Akalaitis Lights the Fuse on a 1633 Drama," *Chicago Tribune* 11 Marh 1990, sect. 13: 10.

6 Weiss, 4.

7 Christiansen, 10.

8 Jean Genet, *Letters to Roger Blin: Reflections on the Theater,* trans. Richard Seaver (New York: Brove, 1969) 63–63.

9 Peter Tosh, "Stepping Razor," *Equal Rights,* audiotape, Columbia, PCT 34670, 1977.

[10] Genet, 29.

[11] All textual references cited in this chapter are to John Ford, *'Tis Pity She's a Whore,* rehearsal script (Chicago: Goodman Theatre, 1990). In order to "help the audience understand" a text that she regarded as intellectually and verbally dense, Akalaitis added, cut, or rewrote textual information she felt to be confusing. She arrived at her editorial decisions independently or with the assistance of dramaturg Tom Creamer. A few examples: Akalaitis cut Berghetto's reference to a fight with his "elder brother that was a coxcomb" [7] because she believed it to be a "red herring" that would be distracting upon first meeting the character. She considered Berghetto's reference to Philotis's gift of a "cod-piece point" [45] to be confusing within the context of 1930s Italy, and accordingly changed the name of the object to "jock strap." She also added the word *Annabella* to the end of Berghetto's line, "I'll have the wench." [8] so as not to confuse Annabella with Philotis.

[12] Genet, 13.

[13] Weiss, 4.

five

The Mormon Project
Workshop

... of course Mormonism is not exotic, it is indigenous—
it is perhaps the only indigenous American religion.
DIANE JOHNSON, *THE LOST WORLD OF THE MORMONS*

I'm looking for something insane and tormented, not cool and dry.
JOANNE AKALAITIS

The Atlantic Center for the Arts, in New Smyrna Beach, Florida, is an interdisciplinary arts facility that sponsors a number of annual workshops, bringing together established artists from diverse disciplines to work in-residence on collaborative projects. Each of these residencies culminates in a weekend of open rehearsals attended by members of the local community and invited guests. In June of 1990, the Atlantic Center sponsored a three-week workshop designed to continue an ongoing investigation, begun by Akalaitis in 1987, aimed at developing a music-theater work about the Mormon experience in America. The workshop was led by Akalaitis, in collaboration with playwright Eric Overmyer, designer Kristi Zea, and a company of "associate" actors, designers, and composers. Overmyer's plays include *On the Verge, Native Speech, In Perpetuity Throughout the Universe, In a Pig's Valise, The Heliotrope Bouquet by Scott Joplin and Louis Chauvin, Dark Rapture,* and *Alki;* he has also also written for the television series *St. Elsewhere, The Days and Nights of Molly Dodd,* and

Sisters. Zea has been the production designer for several feature films including *Lorenzo's Oil, The Silence of the Lambs, Married to the Mob, Good Fellas,* and *New York Stories.* She designed the costumes for Akalaitis's production of *The Balcony,* as well as for numerous films including *Dead End Kids* (directed by Akalaitis), *Birdy, Terms of Endearment, Shoot the Moon, Fame,* and *Dead Man Walking.* The associates, which included myself, were drawn from both the professional and academic theater communities.

The Mormon Project was an ongoing series of workshops cocommissioned by Mabou Mines, The New York Shakespeare Festival, The Walker Art Center in Minneapolis, Center Arts at California's Humbolt State University, and the Atlantic Center for the Arts. The various developmental workshops funded by these organizations endeavored to explore, develop, and present images of both the Mormon pioneer past and its "suburban, political/cultural/missionary present" through the use of text, movement, music, video, and visual design.[1] While focusing on the history of the Mormon religion, *The Mormon Project* sought also to be a theatrical investigation of the fascination, power, and potential danger of religious fanaticism and spiritual cults in America.

Akalaitis began the 1990 Atlantic Center workshop intending to work with both original text written by Overmyer and found text culled from various, mostly Mormon, sources. As the workshop progressed, however, Overmyer found the primary sources to be of such interest that he decided to let them speak for themselves. He consulted histories by both Mormon and non-Mormon writers, compiling the text not so much from the historians' words but from the quoted speeches of Mormon leaders such as Joseph Smith and Brigham Young. At the end of each rehearsal, Overmyer provided us with "Mormon texts" to take away and look over, and encouraged us to bring to rehearsal any texts we discovered in our own reading. Overmyer thus functioned in more of a dramaturgical than authorial capacity and described his role in the workshop not as the playwright but as the "designer of text."

On the morning of our first rehearsal, we sit around a table and discuss our goals for the following three weeks. Akalaitis says that she would like the workshop to be loose, open, collaborative, noncompetitive, and nonhierarchical. She envisions the environment as one in which the actors will feel free to draw and the designers to act. She tells us that the workshop is about "playing." Akalaitis approaches *The Mormon Project* workshop as a personal investigation, just as she does a lengthy and technically complex rehearsal process in a major regional theater. She informs us that she is directing the project not only to learn about the Mormons, and to discover what the Mormon experience has to say about contemporary American society, but also to find out more about her own response to the subject. As she later explains to a local reporter:

> One of the great things about the theater is that you can do many things at one time. You don't need to have an agenda or a position. Investigating the Mormons allows one to examine one's own feelings about religion, religious expression, God, and spiritual events.[2]

We watch a video documentary about the Mormons, as well as a *Sixty-Minutes* segment about a a group of contemporary polygamists in Utah who are being persecuted by other, more "mainstream," Mormons. We then discuss our responses to the videotapes, to the world of the Mormons, and to the subject of religion, in general. Many of us are intrigued by the fact that the while the Mormons we saw on tape are no doubt complex people, they seem to have an air of innocence about them. Akalaitis remarks that this innocence is rather alien to those of us "who live in urban environments fraught with neurosis, anxiety, and cynicism, and who work in the theater, which is very corrupt in some ways."

Akalaitis tells us that she became interested in the Mormons by chance, after reading an essay in the *New York Review of Books*. She is particularly interested in Mormonism as a distinctly American phenomenon, a powerful religion that survived persecution and flourished in the American West. She feels that the subject matter is important for several reasons, the first being that it centers around a time in America's history when there was great religious fervor. Akalaitis observes that, although this fervor was misled, it was at the same time energizing and "pure." She suggests to the cast that, today as well, we are living in an age of religious fervor, fanaticism, and resurgent fundamentalism as witnessed in the radical practitioners of Islam in the Middle East, the inflexible anti-abortion position espoused by the Roman Catholic Church, and the Branch Davidians of Waco, Texas.

America has always been, almost despite itself, a religious country. Both the New England and Virginia colonists were fueled by a sense of religious mission and an intense desire to receive redemption in the New World. One of America's first mass revival movements was born during the 1820s in upstate New York when, according to Mormon history, the Angel Moroni appeared to Joseph Smith and enabled him to transcribe the Book of Mormon. According to Roger Rosenblatt, these early citizens sought something in American religion that was far more personal and emotional than the religion they had practiced in Europe. Rosenblatt suggests that while, officially, America is an a-religious country, its very separation of church and state has in fact "created and intensified a hidden national feeling about faith and God, a sort of secret, undercurrent religion, which, perhaps because of its subterranean nature, is often more deeply felt and more volatile than that of countries with official state religions."[3]

In Utah, Mormonism is anything but underground; it is the *de facto* official state religion. Seventy percent of the state's population are members of the Mormon Church, also known as The Church of Jesus Christ of Latter Day Saints, or "LDS." Salt Lake City is a virtual theocracy whose holdings included CBS's Salt Lake City television and radio affiliates, several major corporations, and Brigham Young University. The majority of Mormons are deeply devout and regard the Church as the ultimate authority. It is the rare Mormon who feels free to question his or her faith from within the structure of the Church.

For Akalaitis, *The Mormon Project* is also about the evolution of America's only surviving indigenous religion, and the way in which this religion reflects "the delusion of our time." She considers Mormonism to be "very American—like our dream religion" in that it is politically conservative, racist, sexist, homophobic, materialistic, and expansionist, with its membership increasing steadily at an annual rate of six percent. Yet, at the same time, Akalaitis believes there are genuinely positive aspects of Mormonism. She considers the Mormon emphasis on community and family, for example, to embody traditional American values, in the best sense, and admits these are "things that . . . New York artists do not have much of in their lives." Confessing that she feels like an anthropologist whenever she travels to Utah, she observes that "if it weren't for all the 1950s hairdos, I might as well be in New Guinea standing around with a bunch of people covered with mud."[4]

Akalaitis also calls our attention to the spirit of optimism that seems to characterize the Mormon world, and that she believes may reflect a more widespread national *ethos*. At the New York Public Library's "Theater and the World We Live In" forum, she discussed with playwright John Guare the strange phenomenon that in America "All news is happy news." To illustrate her point, Akalaitis described an advertisement for HIV testing that was, at the time, posted on New York City bus stops. Below a caption reading, "It's better to know" are two photographs. The "before" photo, shot in black-and-white, portrays a man with a glum face. The "after" photo, shot in color, shows the same man smiling. Akalaitis finds this type of naive and insensitive "optimism" to be a truly disturbing aspect of American culture.[5]

Finally, Akalaitis is intrigued by what she regards as the "fascinating stories" associated with Mormon history, such as the tradition of polygamy that began in the nineteenth century and continues to this day. Diane Johnson, reviewing a collection of books written by and about members of the Mormon church, notes that more than 30,000 people still live in polygamy, mostly in Utah and Arizona:

> Not only is the practice ongoing, it seems to be tolerated by the larger community, perhaps because at one time or another it touched most Mormon families, or perhaps they just don't see it as that odd.

If something can be said for it, one legacy of polygamy seems to be a more straightforward and cheerful, though conservative, attitude to sex among Mormons than one finds in religions dominated by hellfire or the virtues of celibacy.[6]

In a 1984 interview, Akalaitis discussed the fact that both her upcoming opera about Charles Darwin's *Voyage of the Beagle* and her production of *The Photographer*, based on the stop-action photography of Eadweard Muybridge, deal with the Victorian *ethos*. She explained that she had a long-standing interest in the late nineteenth century, an era of intense sexual repression during which men were free to be "scientific adventurers" and "intellectual spirits" while women were, for the most part, regarded as objects.[7] Interestingly, the contemporary Mormon world is one in which sexual repression and inequity continue to thrive, at least from the perspective of Akalaitis's critical eye. It is a world that, in Akalaitis's view, seems to have wrenched itself free from the nineteenth century only to land in the 1950s.

The Mark Hoffman forgery incident is another Mormon "story" full of intrigue and sensationalism. In the mid-eighties, two letters were discovered that challenged Joseph Smith's account of how the Angel Moroni had appeared and led him to the golden tablets containing the Book of Mormon. One of the letters made no mention of angels or other divine beings, but instead referred to a figure that "transfigured himself from a white salamander." Initially suspected by some fundamentalist Mormons to be fakes, the letters were subjected to expert scrutiny and proved to be "almost certainly authentic." The "Salamander Letter," as it became known, implied that Mormonism had its origins in the popular folk magic of the late nineteenth century, and thus became an embarrassment to the Church.

In October of 1985, two months after Yale historian David Brion Davis's essay about the letters appeared in the *New York Review of Books*, the original purchaser of one of the letters, who had by then donated it to the Church, was murdered by a pipe bomb. Shortly after this incident, the wife of another prominent Mormon was murdered by a bomb most likely intended for her husband. Mark Hoffman, a

Salt Lake City dealer in rare documents, was eventually convicted of the two murders, and he was also discovered to have forged hundreds of documents relating to, and twisting, Mormon history. Hoffman had either sold these documents to the Church or to wealthy businessmen who had donated them to the Church that, in turn, placed the documents in their secret archives. As if unable to believe that a good Mormon could be capable of such evil, the Church initially refused to cooperate in Hoffman's prosecution. Hoffman was allowed to plead guilty in return for a sentence of manslaughter, and he was eventually sentenced to life in prison by a renegade Board of Pardons.[8]

Akalaitis is both intrigued and disturbed by these stories which reveal the violence, chaos, and obsession lying below the tidy, middle-class surface of Mormon life. The Hoffman incident, as well as both the practice and the persecution of polygamy depict what Diane Johnson refers to as "the darker side of Mormonism—the petty tyrannies, rigidity and lack of clarity, the rivalries that creep into all the hierarchies, the internal spying, and the generally subservient role women are expected to play."[9] Akalaitis does not, however, indulge in facile "Mormon-bashing." Instead, Mormon history functions as a lens through which she examines the terrain where religion, power, sex, and politics meet. Working on 'Tis Pity She's a Whore, Akalaitis used the multiple "lenses" of Jacobean England, Fascist Italy, Futurism, and Surrealism to examine the very same terrain. Yet whereas the cultural landscape of Ford's play is European, intellectual, and decadent, that of the Mormons is American, suburban, and sterile. Akalaitis's production of 'Tis Pity She's a Whore was appropriately characterized by a lushness, even a surfeit, of images drawn from the history of art; it was just as fitting that the public performance of The Mormon Project workshop took place in a bare, wood-panelled room completely devoid of scenic imagery.

THE PHYSICAL EXERCISES

Before introducing us to the physical exercises we will perform over the course of the workshop, Akalaitis speaks about her belief that the primal element of theater is bodies moving in space, and that everything onstage either comes out of, or exists in relation to, the actor's body. For Akalaitis, the Mormon world evokes images of automatic, mechanical behavior that in turn give rise to feelings of emotional numbness and emptiness. The Mormon women, in particular, bring to her mind images of the mannequin-like women in the film *The Stepford Wives,* whose pathologically cheerful behavior emphasizes the dullness and repetitive superficiality of their modern suburban lives.

Early in the rehearsal period, Akalaitis guides us through the "Walk Through Your Life" exercise. We spend a minute "walking through" each year of our lives up to age twenty-nine, recalling images from our past while staying attuned to the theatrical present. After the exercise is complete, we spend five minutes with our eyes closed, "working with" any image of a spiritual experience that may have come to us during the exercise. Akalaitis then gives us large sheets of paper and colored pencils, and asks us to draw an image of ourselves at a time in rehearsal when we felt at our most awkward, embarrassed or, as Akalaitis puts it, our "most stupid." This image may come from our memory, or from seeing ourselves on the video "documentary" that the designers are shooting as the workshop progresses.

Each day, after a fifteen-minute personal warm-up, we "dance" to Akalaitis's musical selections, many of which are the same reggae and Afro-pop compositions she used during rehearsals for *'Tis Pity She's a Whore.* We dance, or simply move, through the rehearsal room in order to "know" the space and the other bodies moving in the space. On more than one occasion, we perform a "Dance of Exaltation" to the Talking Heads song "Burning Down the House." As we move to this music, Akalaitis asks us to "work with the idea of auras," and to keep in mind that our dancing is positive and celebratory. We also perform the "Slam-Dancing without Touching" exercise, working with the idea of attraction and repulsion on a purely physical level.

On the third day of rehearsal, Akalaitis introduces the stopping-and-starting exercise. She explains, as she did during rehearsals for *'Tis Pity She's a Whore,* that she is interested not only in a specific type of physical movement that stops and starts but also in a more general "feeling of dropping one thing and starting something entirely new"—the feeling of clearly defined gestures, actions, and scenes. She informs us that Oliver Sacks's *Awakenings,* a book about "people who were in comas and woke up too much," has greatly influenced her ideas about acting. We keep this image of "waking up too much" in mind as we investigate stopping-and-starting, visualizing ourselves moving boldly and directly along vectors in space. Akalaitis reminds us that "stopping" is simply an alive, energized cessation of movement rather than an exaggerated "freeze."

We also perform the "Slow-Motion Composition" exercise, making "paintings" of Danger, Exaltation, God, The Devil, The Angel Moroni, Joseph Smith Receiving the Golden Tablets, and The Procession Westward. On one particular day, Akalaitis gives us strips of white cloth and asks us to tie each other or ourselves up as we perform a slow-motion "Aura Dance." She then asks us to repeat the dance, working with the idea that we are tying the strips of cloth with the objective of inflicting pain upon others and ourselves.

For the first few days of the workshop, the designers as well as the actors participate in the physical exercises. At the end of our daily physical session, or at the conclusion of the day as a whole, we discuss our visual responses to the work—in particular, any intriguing images we happened to see either onstage or "in our minds"—with Zea and the associate designers.

CREATING MORMON *MUDRAS*

Much of our physical exploration is devoted to working with character *mudras.* The word *mudra* comes from the Kathakali, an Indian dance/drama form in which episodes from the Hindu epics are acted out by means of an elaborately codified system of stylized physical gestures. *Mudras* are hand gestures that are part abstraction, part representation: A particular gesture might at the same time symbolize and actually look like a bird in flight.

Akalaitis decribes *mudras* as "formalizations of psychological gestures"—archetypal physical gestures, emanating from the character, that are stylized yet somehow "true." An important part of Akalaitis's pre-production work entails reading the play to discover a few basic iconographic gestures or images that characterize the work as a whole. By asking actors to investigate character *mudras*, Akalaitis is in effect asking them to undertake the same activity *vis à vis* their individual roles—to distill the whole into a physical icon. The *mudra* is, in this sense, similar to the Brechtian *gestus*, emblematic physical behavior that reveals both the personal and the social attitudes of a character.

Akalaitis frequently asks her actors to work with the *mudras* of a particular world or society: for example the bourgeois, corporate Sun Belt world in which she set *Leon and Lena (and lenz),* or the mad, drunken world of the the tavern-goers in Shakespeare's *Henry IV.* In the case of this workshop, we invent *mudras* that express both the violent, chaotic "fringe" and the rigidly ordered center of Mormon life. These stylized gestures at once create the image of a unified, mechanized world and allow us access into the inner life of our characters. Like the Brechtian *gestus, mudras* are crystallizations of personal and thematic imagery.

Akalaitis teaches us the following Mormon *mudras:* 1. We bend forward from the waist, bringing our hands together, as if in prayer. Akalaitis sugggests to us that there should something tortured about this gesture, almost as if we were doubling over with a stomach cramp; 2. We extend both arms straight out to our sides, vocalizing a breathy "aaaahhhh," as if we were "receiving the spirit"; 3. We extend both arms straight up to the sky and, silently, "speak in tongues"; 4. In pairs, we perform Mormon-style baptisms: Partner A supports partner B, who leans back and holds her nose as she is dipped into "the water."

As we practice these *mudras*, Akalaitis encourages us to "find the soul of the cliché and go beyond it, as if you are gods and goddesses." She also encourages us to "find the resistance in the gesture." Once we are comfortable executing the Mormon *mudras,* we incorporate them into our various physical exercises. We work with the stopping-and-starting exercise, executing one of our four *mudras* with a clean, sharp attack each time that we stop. We also perform a "*Mudra Dance*" that is celebratory and exalting.

The *mudras* are both representational and abstract physical gestures. They may be "read" by the audience as actual behavior exhibited during religious rituals or as distillations of mad religious fervor. The *mudra* work brings to mind Lee Breuer's notion that every formal idea has its own emotional truth, that what we might consider stylized, clichéd behavior often comes closer to the truth than "realism." Perhaps Genet was thinking in a similar vein when he cautioned Roger Blin, who staged the original production of *The Screens,* against allowing the actors to "slip back into the movements and gestures that are theirs off-stage, or that they resort to in other plays."[10] Genet knew that it was normal for actors to seek gestures appropriate both to their character and to their own personality. Yet naturalness and spontaneity onstage mattered far less to him than behavior that, however stylized, captured the psychological truth of his work.

NOTES TO THE ACTORS

A few hours before our first open dress rehearsal, Akalaitis holds a final note session. She suggests that we must, above all, find a way to "internalize stopping-and-starting" as we go through the performance. In other words, she is telling us that we must learn to put the structure of the piece inside our bodies. Secondly, we must be able to visualize both the physical and emotional geography that we travel through during the piece. As Akalaitis explains, "You are in it but you also see yourself in it, as if from above. You see yourself there before you get there. You are no longer negotiating how and when to get there." Finally, she urges us not to be "closed and hermetic" when we perform, but to be generous and open, to "give the performance to the audience."

Akalaitis leaves us, as usual, with a few of her favorite passages from Genet's *Letters to Roger Blin.* After informing us that the passage she is about to read is, in her opinion, the single best piece of advice to actors, she reads Genet's admonition to play each scene as rigorously as if it were a play in itself.[11] She then reads the passage in which Genet demands that the actor be able to play virility or femininity to the point of abasement.[12] Finally, she reads the following:

> If we maintain that life and the stage are opposites, it is because we strongly suspect that the stage is a site closely akin to death, a place where all liberties are possible.[13]

> If I wanted the stage to be bathed in bright light, it was to keep each actor from covering up his errors, his fleeting mistakes, his fatigue, or his indifference, in a redeeming darkness.[14]

THE PERFORMANCE MONTAGE

The Mormon Project workshop culminated in a weekend of open dress rehearsals attended by members of the local community and invited guests. This public "performance event" was a work-in-progress in the roughest sense. There was little dramatic structure or narrative logic to the evening; in fact, we had barely memorized our lines because the roughly assembled script was in a constant state of flux. The performance was less a coherent theater piece than a loosely constructed montage of scenes and tableaux woven together with music, dance, and song. Both actors and audience were called upon to supply their own psychological transitions between texts, actions, and scenes. Each participant in this theatrical event was required to literally "make sense" out of the evening.

In a similar spirit, I offer the following moment-by-moment description of *The Mormon Project* in performance. It is neither a definitive analysis nor critique but rather a chronicle of selected images, tableaux, and scenes that found their way into our work-in-progress showing. It is an insider's account, detailing the idiosyncratic images, rhythms, and movement styles we explored in rehearsal. I prevail upon the reader to supply his or her own transitions in order to make imaginative sense of the performance.

The evening begins as the cast, stationed in the woods surrounding the rehearsal hall, files into the theater singing "Born Free." Because the performance space is surrounded by enormous glass windows and sliding doors, the audience is able to see us emerging from the darkness, our faces are illuminated by tiny flashlights held under our chins. We sing beautifully and reverently in four-part harmony. We sound like a cross between the Mormon Tabernacle Choir and a chorus of weird angels. By the time we reach the final chorus, we are all assembled inside; we stand in formation and sing directly to the audience.

When the song is over, two of us unfurl an enormous "scroll" of blank newsprint paper diagonally across the stage floor. The entire cast drops to the floor and begins furiously writing upon the scroll, an image that I associate both with Joseph Smith transcribing the *Book of Mormon* and with the Mormon propensity for rewriting history. Each of us is engrossed in his or her own personal writing project. I lie on the floor, writing tiny hieroglyphics rather than words. Upon standing, I feel dizzy—the perfect mental and physical state in which to perform our next song-and-dance number.

Rinde Eckert, one of the actors and an established performance artist from San Francisco, begins singing his version of the spiritual "I Never Been To Heaven." A large, bald man with a beautiful tenor voice, Eckert is at once seductive and frightening. He sings forcefully yet his attention is directed "inward," giving him an ecstatic and tortured appearance. As Eckert alternately sings and blows into a huge lead pipe that looks as if it had been taken from a Mormon church organ, the rest of us writhe through a slow-motion "*Mudra* Dance," turning our flashlights on and off at random intervals. Akalaitis has suggested to us that, in this section, we "are possessed by the spirit."

When Eckert's song is over, we begin walking backward in slow motion toward the audience as electronic, Twilight Zone–type music fills the room. Every now and then, still walking backward in extremely slow motion, we turn our upper bodies to face the audience wearing facial "masks" of extreme paranoia that we illuminate with our tiny flashlights. We slowly pass among us a stuffed dove impaled on a tall stick, creating the illusion that the dove is circling above our heads. We arrive about three-quarters of the way downstage, slowly turn to face the audience, and continue our "paranoid walk" directly toward them. We stop within inches of the audience, whereupon we all speak different passages of Mormon text simultaneously in a mass babble. I rattle through the following text: "Emma [one of the plural wives of Joseph Smith] knocked Eliza [Emma's sister, and another of the plural wives of Joseph Smith] down the stairs with her broom. Eliza lay in a pool of blood. She had miscarried, and her hopes of giving birth to the prophet's son were crushed." We sound as if we are speaking in tongues.

One of the men stands center stage and performs a passage from Mark Hoffman's autobiography in which Hoffman "retells" the story of Joseph Smith and the Golden Tablets. The rest of us set up folding chairs onstage in church-like formation. When the Hoffman speech is finished, we break into the Anglican hymn "Abide with Me." As we sing, we drape the chairs with heavy brocade fabric and slowly "ooze" into position for a very formal Mormon family portrait. The hymn ends, and we "inflate" the portrait on a ten-count inhalation, as if we are pumping ourselves up for the camera. A flash goes off in the audience, and we snap out of slow motion. We return to our onstage seats, talking, as Akalaitis has suggested, "about potato salad."

Sitting in our chairs, we take turns reading solo passages from the *Book of Mormon* (which, Overmyer has informed us, Mark Twain described as "chloroform in print"). As each actor reads, the rest of us respond in various unison behaviors, as directed by Akalaitis; these include playing absently with the aforementioned strips of white cloth, performing assorted Mormon *mudras* with our hands and faces, making "barnyard noises," and erupting into violent fits of coughing.

Brigham Young, played in this section of the performance by actor Erik Avari, reads a lengthy passage justifying the fact that it is "right for a man to have several wives and children in heaven at the same time." Throughout his entire speech, the rest of us bob our heads in response, as if to say "Oh, I get it." Brigham Young then poses a series of questions such as, "Do you believe in the Bible? Are you a believer in the Old Testament? The New Testament? Do you believe in the Resurrection? Do you believe parents and children, wives and husbands, will recognize one another in the Resurrection?"

During this litany, we move around the space, stopping-and-starting. Akalaitis has suggested that we move as if we are "looking for a thought." Each time Brigham Young poses a question, we stop and respond with a unison "I do" or "I am."

Joseph Smith urges a Mormon woman, Martha Brotherton, to become one of the plural wives of Brigham Young. Smith reassures her that, if she does not "like it after a month or two," she may return to him and he will make her "free again" to become one of his own wives. Brotherton replies, "I want time to think first." Smith and the Mormon men try to win her over with a vaudeville-style song-and-dance routine entitled "Nothing Ventured Nothing Gained." Brotherton leaves the men to their hijinks and exits with the rest of the women through the glass doors to the porch that runs around the periphery of the performance space. The women, viewed by the audience through the windows, embark upon "the long journey westward." We pull enormous swaths of white cloth from an outside "clothesline," winding ourselves up in them as we travel "across the prairie." We become both entirely invisible and hopelessly tangled up in the cloth.

The entire company performs an elaborate tap dance to the 1960s top-ten hit "Finger-Poppin' Time" by Hank Ballard and the Midnighters. The number begins with the Mormon men sitting self-importantly in their chairs, as if attending a for-men-only Church business meeting. Upon hearing the music, they begin snapping their fingers in a somewhat goofy and hesitant manner; they appear rather dazed and confused. All of a sudden, the men are up on their feet, whirling about the stage as if they have been dancing their entire lives. The illogic of the men's behavior is disconcerting but for only a moment; their enthusiasm is contagious. The women, bearing silver trays laden with enormous, multicolored "live" jello molds, sashay across the stage and join in the tap dance; the journey westward has apparrently transformed us into lively sock-hoppers. Akalaitis has described the tap dance as a "1950s production number," and has advised us that it should be a "gift to the audience. It it is indeed a "showstopper," in the bright and snappy tradition of American musical comedy.

The applause from "Finger-Poppin' Time" dies out, and we once again hear the strange "Twilight-Zone" music. We very slowly pull strips of white cloth from "secret places" on our person, and begin a slow-motion "Aura Dance," tying ourselves and each other up with the strips of cloth. The music segués into a strange, dissonant version of the "Leave It to Beaver" theme as we sink down onto the floor, still bound with the cloth, and arrange ourselves into a rapt TV-watching tableau. Suddenly, one of us catches sight of a large, bald man who has been stalking us from outside the glass windows. The man, played by Eckert who now uses his "organ pipe" as a machine gun, enters the theater, and guns us down in a slow-motion mass murder.

For the final scene, the entire company is resurrected in a "celestial supermarket." We walk back and forth in slow motion across the stage, pushing imaginary shopping carts up and down long aisles. We sing the reggae song "By the Rivers of Babylon" with vacant smiles on our faces as we reach for groceries and drop them into our shopping carts. One by one, we stop shopping, turn to face the audience, and very naturally and directly, describe a "spiritual moment" we have experienced in our personal lives.

When the performance is over, audience members and local journalists crowd around Akalaitis. They are anxious to know exactly what *The Mormon Project* is: a play? a performance piece? Akalaitis explains to a reporter that, "The bottom line is: it is good or bad? If it's a true voice, it cannot be labeled."[15]

The Mormon Project workshop was for all of us a challenging theatrical investigation into an intriguing and disturbing subject. Akalaitis informed us at the beginning of the workshop that it was fine with her if our final performance lasted only fifteen minutes; she had, in fact, agreed to the public showing only because it was an Atlantic Center for the Arts tradition. As it turned out, we performed approximately one hour's worth of material, filled with images of exaltation, oppression, bondage, pain, power, control, zeal, and terror all of which had been developed in the physical exercise sessions.

Even over the course of an informal, three-week workshop, the exercises had helped us to become increasingly attuned to the physicality of the rehearsal space and to our fellow actors. Just as Akalaitis used the workshop to investigate her personal response to Mormonism, religion, and spiritual events, we used the exercises to investigate our own physical and emotional responses to these same subjects. We came away knowing more about the Mormons and perhaps a bit more about ourselves.

1 Eric Overmyer, *About the Mormon Project,* (New Smyrna Beach, Fla.: Atlantic Center for the Arts, June 1990) N. pag.

2 John Wirt, "Mormon Intrigue Takes Center Stage at Atlantic Center for the Arts," *Daytona Beach Sunday News-Journal,* 24 June 1990: H1.

3 Roger Rosenblatt, "How to End the Abortion War," *New York Times* 19 Jan. 1992, sect. 6: 41.

4 Don Shewey, "Rocking the House that Papp Built," *Village Voice* 25 Sept. 1990: 41.

5 Akalaitis, "Theater and the World."

6 Diane Johnson, "The Lost World of the Mormons," *New York Review of Books* 15 March 1990: 29.

7 JoAnne Akalaitis, interview, *Theater,* by Jonathan Kalb, 15.2 (1984): 9–10.

8 See David Brion Davis, "Secrets of the Mormons," *New York Review of Books* 15 Aug. 1985: N. pag; Steven Naifeh and Gregory White Smith, *The Mormon Murders: A True Story of Greed, Forgery, Deceit and Death* (New York: New American Library, 1990); and Linda Sillitoe and Allen Roberts, *Salamander: The Story of the Mormon Forgery Murders* (New York: Signature, 1990).

9 Johnson, 30.

10 Jean Genet, *Letter to Roger Blin: Reflections On the Theater,* trans. Richard Seaver (New York: Grove, 1969) 20.

11 Genet, 29.

12 Genet, 62–63.

13 Genet, 12.

14 Genet, 48.

15 Elizabeth Maupin, "*Mormon Project* Defies Theatrical Conventions," *Orlando Sentinel* 24 June 1990: F1.

six

Akalaitis and the New York Shakespeare Festival

At first no one knows anything. The actors have little knowledge, but the man who is teaching them must know nothing and learn everything, about himself and his art, as he teaches them. It will be a discovery for them but also for him.

JEAN GENET, LETTERS TO ROGER BLIN

On Thursday, March 11, 1993, the executive committee of the New York Shakespeare Festival's board of directors informed Akalaitis that they were recommending her dismissal as the theater's Artistic Director, and that they expected agreement from the full board. When Akalaitis arrived at the theater on Monday, March 15, she received a memo instructing her to vacate her office by the end of the next day. As *Village Voice* theater critic Alisa Solomon explains, "the memo offered no 'Thank you for your twenty months of dedication,' no 'We appreciate the sincere care and guidance you gave this institution.' Politely, it just gave orders: Please cooperate, and do not talk to the press in the name of the theater."[1] Akalaitis had served as Artistic Director of the Festival since August of 1991, when Joseph Papp named her to succeed him. She had been associated with the theater for seventeen years.

The executive committee offered the stewardship of the Festival,

American Repertory Theatre's 1984–85 production of Samuel Beckett's *Endgame*. Above: Shirley Wilber (Nell). Below left to right: Ben Halley Jr. (Hamm) and John Bottoms (Clov). Photos by Richard Feldman.

American Repertory Theatre's 1984–85 production of Samuel Beckett's *Endgame*.
Above left to right: John Bottoms (Clov) and Ben Halley, Jr. (Hamm).
Below left to right: Ben Halley Jr. (Hamm) and John Bottoms (Clov).
Photos by Richard Feldman.

American Repertory Theatre's 1985–86 production of Jean Genet's
The Balcony. Above: The acting company. Below left to right:
Eric C. Menyuk (The Executioner Arthur), Rodney Hudson (The Judge),
and Mary McCue (The Thief). Photos by Richard Feldman.

American Repertory Theatre's 1985–86 production of Jean Genet's *The Balcony*. Above left to right: Ben Halley Jr. (The General), and Rima Miller (The Horse Girl). Below left to right: Ben Halley Jr., John Bottoms, Rodney S. Hudson, and Harry S. Murphy. Photos by Richard Feldman.

The Guthrie Theater's 1987 production of *Leon & Lena (and lenz)*.
Above: The acting company (Finale). Below: Jesse Borrego (Prince
Leon) and Mimi Lieber (Rosetta) dance in the corporate kingdom as
Val (Don Cheadle) watches. Photos by Joe Giannetti.

The Guthrie Theater's 1987 production of *Leon & Lena (and lenz)*.
Above: Jo Ellen Allen (Governess) tries to convince Lauren Tom
(Princess Lena) of the importance of her future marriage.
Below: Don Cheadle (Val) discusses the meaning of life with
Jesse Borrego (Prince Leon). Photos by Joe Giannetti.

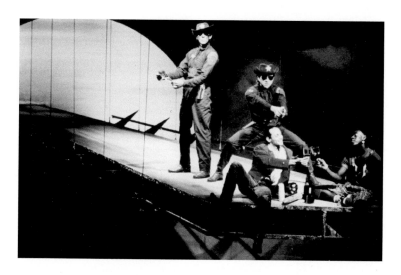

The Guthrie Theater's 1987 production of *Leon & Lena (and lenz)*.
Above: Jesse Borrego (Prince Leon) and Don Cheadle (Val) enjoy a meal as
Texas Rangers Richard Ooms and Charles Janasz watch over them.
Below: Lauren Tom (Princess Lena). Photos by Joe Giannetti.

The Guthrie Theater's 1987 production of *Leon & Lena (and lenz).*
Above: Jesse Borrego (Prince Leon) and Don Cheadle (Val). Below: Don
Cheadle (Val) and Jesse Borrego (Prince Leon). Photos by Joe Giannetti.

The Guthrie Theater's 1989 production of Jean Genet's *The Screens*. Above: The acting company. Below: Ruth Maleczech (The Mother) and Jesse Borrego (Said). Photos by Joe Gianetti.

The Guthrie Theater's 1989 production of Jean Genet's *The Screens*.
Above: Jesse Borrego (Said) in foreground. Below: The acting company.
Photos by Joe Gianetti.

The Guthrie Theater's 1989 production of Jean Genet's *The Screens*.
Above: Richard S. Iglewski (Mr. Blankensee) and Erick Avari (Sir Harold).
Photo by Joe Gianetti.

The Goodman Theatre's 1990 production of John Ford's *'Tis Pity She's a Whore*. Don Cheadle (Soranzo) and Lauren Tom (Annabella) in rehearsal. Photos by Lisa Ebright.

The Goodman Theatre's 1990 production of John Ford's *'Tis Pity She's a Whore*. Above: Jesse Borrego (Giovanni) standing on platform, center. Below: Jesse Borrego (Giovanni) forground. Photos by Liz Lauren.

The Atlantic Center for the Arts' 1990 production of
The Mormon Project Workshop. Above and below: The acting company.
Photos courtesy of Atlantic Center for the Arts.

The Guthrie Theater's 1994–95 production of Aphra Behn's *The Rover*.
The acting company. Photo by Michal Daniel.

The Shakespeare Theatre's 1999 production of Euripides' *The Trojan Women*. The trojan women left to right: Jennifer Mendenhall, Kathryn McGlynn, Rachel Leslie, Leighann Niles, Holly Brown, Maia DeSanti, Shannon Parks, and Wydetta Carter. Photo by Carol Rosegg.

The Shakespeare Theatre's 1999 production of Euripides' *The Trojan Women*. Elizabeth Long (Helen) and Jonathan Fried (Menelaus). Photo by Carol Rosegg.

The Shakespeare Theatre's 1999 production of Euripides' *The Trojan Women*. Petronia Paley (Hecuba) holding Opal Alladin (Cassandra). Photo by Carol Rosegg.

with the revised title of "Producer," to George C. Wolfe, the then thirty-eight-year-old playwright and director of *The Colored Museum, Spunk,* and the Broadway hit *Jelly's Last Jam.* Wolfe also staged Tony Kushner's *Angels in America* that enjoyed a lengthy and critically acclaimed Broadway run. Like Akalaitis, Wolfe had neither administrative nor fund-raising experience. Nor did he have producing credits to his name other than the two series of original performance pieces he curated at the Public. Yet the board was convinced that Wolfe would restore the Festival's vibrancy and reputation that they felt had dissipated during Akalaitis's tenure. Perhaps the board's hopes lay in the fact that Wolfe, unlike Akalaitis, had roots in both the "uptown" and "downtown" New York theater communities and was at the time enjoying great commercial success. Wolfe had "box-office" appeal, as did actor Kevin Kline who was invited to join the theater's staff as Artistic Associate.

Executive committee president Harry Condon asserted that the board's only motivation in firing Akalaitis was alleviating the theater's bifurcated leadership, an administrative structure that the board felt was responsible for tensions that had been developing throughout the organization. As Condon explained, the board first determined that they preferred a single producer who would have complete artistic and managerial authority, in the style of Papp, rather than an Artistic Director and a co-equal Producing Director. The board then asked themselves who would be the best producer, and chose George Wolfe. Under Akalaitis, the management and administration of the theater was presided over by Jason Steven Cohen who would remain in his position but now report to Wolfe. Cohen himself referred to Wolfe as "the most emerging and emerged writer-director the theatrical scene has to offer," while Broadway producer Margo Lion suggested that Wolfe was "going to bring the theater into the 90s."[2]

Although Condon stated that the board was "not trying to turn the Public into a commercial theater," Solomon pointed out that various board members who spoke to the press after Akalaitis's firing called for "more popular" work at the Public.[3] And according to *New York Times* columnist Bruce Weber, certain board members expressed disappointment that Akalaitis's "reputation for favoring a bleak-viewed and somewhat arcane strain of drama" failed to create the "kind of buzz" that draws audiences as well as corporate and private donor interest.[4]

Joan K. Davidson, also a member of the executive committee, explained that the board felt not enough work was being produced at the Festival, and that the work itself was not varied enough. Davidson argued that, despite the fact that she liked Akalaitis very much and respected her as an artist, there is a difference between being a talented director and a producer. She stated that the board wanted "the place to be hopping with all kinds of energy and activity, the way it was in Joe's glory days," and that there had been "a withering in the commitment and devotion" of some of the theater's longtime supporters whom the board expected "to come bouncing back enthusiastically now."[5]

The board cited various reasons for Akalaitis's dismissal including her lack of "personal forcefulness and charisma," her "aloof, occasionally abrasive manner," her "disdain for the fund-raising function of her position," her "predilection for grim, arcane projects that many felt alienated the audience built up by Mr. Papp," and her failure to generate "enough work to keep the five theaters at the Public busy."[6] In a gossipy follow-up piece in the *New York Times*, Weber wrote that there had been "only ten" subscription offerings at the Public this season, the only full-length, multi-character production originating at the Festival being Akalaitis's own production of *Woyzeck*. Weber then rumored that the theater's board was displeased that the expensive and limited run of Akalaitis's revival of *'Tis Pity She's a Whore* occurred while several of the Public's other stages remained dark.[7]

The most disturbed, and disturbing, response to Akalaitis's firing was a scathing *New York Times* piece written by Frank Rich, the paper's chief theater critic at the time. In Rich's view, the Public during Akalaitis's tenure "became an empty shell, a ragtag fairway for theatrical sideshows rather than the main event."[8] Regarding the decision to dismiss Akalaitis and replace her with George Wolfe, Rich asserted that the theater's board "should be applauded for ending the misery with relative promptness" and had the audacity to suggest that "somewhere, Papp may be smiling, or at least breathing a sigh of relief. Certainly anyone who cares about the future of the New York theater is."

Comparing Wolfe's "flair for talent scouting, show business and self-promotion" with that of Papp, Rich praised Wolfe's "artistic range whose broad sweep has more in common with Papp's inclusivity than Ms. Akalaitis's narrow, academic vision," adding that, "as for Ms. Akalaitis's record on Lafayette Street, it would be nice simply to forget about it, and get on with tomorrow."[9] While Rich had never been a fan of Akalaitis's work, the unabashedly mean-spirited tone of what his *New Republic* colleague Robert Brustein called "a characteristic kick-the corpse" piece, calls into question Rich's personal aesthetic agenda and his relationship with the Festival's board of directors.

Rich allowed that Akalaitis was in part a victim of bad luck, that she was a talented director who inherited an institution in economic turmoil. He nevertheless considered her failings to be numerous and inexcusable. The Public's stages, he argued, were all too often dark. And when they *were* occupied, the offerings were appearances by solo performance artists, readings, special events, or what Rich referred to as "plays by writers on Ms. Akalaitis's shortlist of Drama 101 Modernists" such as Beckett, Garcia Lorca, and Brecht. Clearly irritated by what he perceived to be Akalaitis's grim, academic, and hopelessly dated tastes, Rich stooped so low as to attack the Public's understated lobby café and bookstore for being "a sentimental homage to the bohemian heyday of San Francisco's City Light's Bookstore."

Personal and professional biases aside, Rich's article was full of inaccuracies and is an example of irresponsible journalism. Writing that Akalaitis's producing agenda consisted "mainly of theatrical snacks," whereas Papp served the New York theatergoers "a steady diet of original new plays and musicals, not to mention frequent mountings of Shakespeare," Rich failed to note that Akalaitis herself directed Shakespeare's *Cymbeline,* both parts of *Henry IV,* and the Jacobean tragedy *'Tis Pity She's a Whore.* Akalaitis also had been preparing to stage *Henry VIII* in Central Park, and to produce *All's*

Well That Ends Well and *Timon of Athens* as part of the Festival's upcoming season. Rich even lambasted Akalaitis for limiting her co-production ventures to a single company, Chicago's Goodman Theatre, which "frequently hired her as a director." None of these facts was true. Despite Rich's accusation that Akalaitis had no plans for expanding the Public's production season in the near future, Akalaitis had commissioned more than twenty new plays, and she was in the process of securing new works by Eric Overmyer and Elizabeth Egloff, Steve Carter's Carribean adaptation of *Medea,* and a new chamber opera by Philip Glass. She was putting together an in-house repertory company that was to present a series of new plays "one after another in a fluid way that avoided the punitive process of being locked into production budgets, previews, critics."[10] And she even wanted to direct *A Christmas Carol.*

As even her detractors pointed out, Akalaitis had inherited a financially troubled theater during an economic recession that had caused public and private support for the arts to decline drastically. Toward the end of Papp's reign, the Festival's budget was cut from $15 million to under $10 million and its staff was cut from 120 to sixty.[11] Even so, Akalaitis had been willing to undertake both the financial and artistic risk of developing new works and supporting individual artists. She managed to commission $80,000 worth of new plays and to alter the playwright's contract so that the artist would receive higher pay. Furthermore, Akalaitis was interested in both *Angels in America* and *Marisol* from the outset. The Public lost the chance to produce the former when the Mark Taper Forum decided to bring it directly to Broadway, and it lost out on the latter when Rivera chose to open his play at Hartford Stage rather than risk its future at the hands of potentially savage New York reviewers.[12] Finally, Akalaitis directed a single production at the Goodman Theatre, *'Tis Pity She's a Whore.*

Interviewed the day after she learned of the executive committee's recommendation, Akalaitis stated that the news of her dismissal came as a shock, that she was under the impression that her relations with the board were positive, and that she was leaving involuntarily:

I want to say that I'm not resigning. I have been fired, or some verb like that. I think that's the verb. . . . The box office on every show this year has exceeded projections. We've come in splendidly on production budgets. I was concerned about contributed income, individual and corporate, but I thought the theater was a lively, artistic, social, stimulating place. I was quite proud, am proud, of the work that was done.[13]

Several of Akalaitis's colleagues spoke out publicly on her behalf, and withdrew from upcoming Festival commitments in protest of her dismissal. Costume designer Gabriel Berry suggested that the board's treatment of Akalaitis had "poisoned the atmosphere and made artists feel they have to choose between JoAnne and George [Wolfe]." Berry, feeling that she could not "condone an institution that would behave like that," consequently withdrew from the Festival's upcoming production of *Marisol*. Lighting designer Jennifer Tipton likewise withdrew from a scheduled production of *All's Well That Ends Well* at the Festival in protest over Akalaitis's firing. Tipton observed that, "we're seeing the same trend in theaters as we're seeing in dance companies. Ballet companies used to be run by choreographers, then by dancers, and now by boards. In the theater, it's less clear since the structure is not as simple, but in both cases it means less work that is provocative and that makes the audience think." Director Anne Bogart observed that, during Akalaitis's leadership of the Festival, artists were more involved than they ever had been during Papp's reign:

JoAnne opened the doors wide and genuinely asked artists and staff, "What do you think?" It's very different from power being [located] in some dark corner that people are afraid of. . . . JoAnne's management style—which is not at all how Joe did it—is a style that scares boards. And that fear breeds brutality.[14]

And director Robert Woodruff, who had recently won a special grant to work with the Public on Egloff's adaptation of Dostoevsky's *The Devils,* suggested that the board's decision to disregard Akalaitis's seventeen-year relationship with the institution and cast her away with such rapidity did not "show much respect for a life in the theater. How can a theater do this and then say they're going to make great art? You can't divorce the politics of the arts institution from artistic creation in terms of values."[15]

Akalaitis's dismissal from the New York Shakespeare Festival, like her work itself, does not lend itself to easy analysis or even description. The theater's board got what it thought it wanted, and Akalaitis has continued to receive directing opportunities from major theaters around the country. That summer (1993), she was invited by Lincoln Center Theatre to stage a revival of Jane Bowles's *In the Summer House,* a surrealistic American drama originally produced on Broadway in the 1950s, and she since has gone on to direct at the Guthrie in Minneapolis, the Shakespeare Theatre and Arena Stage in Washington, D.C., the Court Theatre in Chicago, Actors' Theatre of Louisville, Theatre for a New Audience, New York Theatre Workshop, and New York City Opera. She has also served as co-chair of the M.F.A. Directing Program at the Juilliard School and is, at present, chair of the Theatre Department at Bard College.

Nevertheless, Akalaitis's dismissal left those who create, write about, and attend theater to speculate upon the tangled relationships between artists, non-profit cultural institutions, and the press, and to ponder difficult questions such as: What is the purpose of a board, and how much power should it wield? Should a board's jurisdiction extend beyond fiscal matters? How much influence should a board have, if any, in determining the artistic vision of an institution? To what degree should an institution's fiscal obligations and responsibilities be allowed to impinge upon its artistic ones, particularly in times of financial hardship? What is the relationship between artistic and financial risk? Are they inseparable? If so, is risk to be avoided at all "costs"? Is the financial survival of an institution the *raison d'être* of its existence, and, if so, is survival itself a worthy goal? Had Akalaitis's dismissal, as *Newsweek's* theater critic Jack Kroll suggested, reopened "the fault line that divides the commercial from the noncommercial theater, the 'uptown' from the 'downtown?'"[16] And finally, what does not only the event itself but also the manner in which it was executed and written about in the *New York Times* reveal about the concerns, values, and priorities of the American theater?

Wolfe's appointment to head the New York Shakespeare Festival was received with widespread enthusiasm. The theater community regarded him as an intelligent and talented director with a strong social agenda and, most importantly, the ability to fill Papp's shoes. On the very day that Akalaitis's dismissal was announced in the *New York Times*, the paper printed a "companion piece" portraying Wolfe as "a visually-oriented director with an intellectual bent who stages productions with confidence bordering on boldness. His administrative skills have yet to be tested. . . . Many people expect him to rely on professional managers."[17] That this description could just as easily apply to Akalaitis made it all the more apparent that her ousting boiled down to the age-old conflict between art and commerce. The Festival's inability to embrace Akalaitis's artistic vision or, at the very least, to allow it time to unfold, had something to do with the fact that neither her work nor her person was perceived by the theater's board as upbeat, accessible, and therefore marketable. Yet, as Robert Brustein pointed out, "these are ways of saying that Akalaitis is an artist rather than an administrator, and artists are notoriously single-minded and tunnel-visioned." A number of other adventurous theater artists such as Anne Bogart, Liviu Ciulei, and Adrian Hall had recently been fired from artistic directorships by their boards for failing to attract audiences or enough contributed income. Brustein suggested that we may better understand these artistic upheavals within the context of what he calls the "New Aesthetic Populism":

> The causes are social, political and economic, with pressures to compromise and conform coming from critics, audiences, foundations and the government alike. The result is that theaters these days are not being led so much as administered, the power of artistic directors having been transferred to managers and boards. "We have always been more comfortable with management structures . . . than with the troublesome intangibles of the creative imagination," I wrote some years back, and the crisis has only deepened.[18]

Akalaitis herself did not set about to disturb or provoke controversy, although she is aware her work may have done so. As she explained to a reporter who had attended the performance of *The Mormon Project* workshop, "You don't do art to change the world. You do art about the world."[19] And Akalaitis's work is, among other things, a very personal response to the current state of the world. Participating in her work can be difficult and demanding, in part, because Akalaitis looks out into the world and sees chaos, violence, darkness, and irrationality. As a director, she is able to engage this "insanity," endowing it with meaning, form, and shape onstage. Ideally, she would like her actors to do the same—to *be* insane, obsessed, disturbed, disrupted—yet also to be able to watch themselves going through this turmoil. A number of actors who have worked frequently with Akalaitis, those from Mabou Mines and others such as Joan McIntosh, Jesse Borrego, and Lauren Tom, are adept at negotiating this balance of involvement and detachment; other actors find it difficult or impossible. Furthermore, when Akalaitis puts this material on the stage, particularly within the volatile contexts of sex, politics, and religion, audience members who would prefer not to look and listen become disturbed. Yet as theater critic Michael Feingold writes:

> A nation that will not listen, that willfully destroys itself is tragic, and a theater artist first of all has to have a sense of that tragedy. Artists who hector their societies on the right way to live are forgotten. . . . Artists who confront their society with a vision of itself, however scandalous in the moment, live on.[20]

In an essay written in September of 1992, theater director and theorist Herbert Blau proposed that we must reassess the social function of theater in America. He argued that our nation's regional theater network is subject to boards and bottom lines without the intellectual matrix that exists in many other countries. In France, Blau pointed out, major writers, artists and intellectuals such as Camus, Sartre, Duras, and Boulez have traditionally been involved in the theater. It is also common practice in France for an "underground" artist to attack the Comédie Française and end up directing it ten years later. Blau suggested that, in our own country, provocative directors such as Lee Breuer and Richard Foreman should have their own theaters, and expressed hope that Akalaitis's stewardship of the Public would set a precedent for hiring intelligent, innovative people to run major cultural institutions.[21]

Whatever her shortcomings as an administrator, Akalaitis was deeply concerned, during her tenure at the Public, about the social function of theater and, in particular, about developing new artists and audiences. At the New York Public Library's "Theater and the World We Live In" forum, she expressed her belief that the mandate of all cultural institutions should be to cultivate not only younger, but also more diverse audiences. She pointed out that the primary reason these people do not attend the theater is, of course, that many of them simply cannot afford the price of theater tickets. But Akalaitis also wondered aloud what exactly the theater wants to, and can, say to youth and people of color, particularly those who live in the inner cities.[22]

Akalaitis went on to discuss what she saw as the increasing commercialism of the nonprofit theater. In her view, the major difficulty of working in the theater today, of surviving as an artist, is that "it's all about money, everything is about money. . . . every day, the marketplace aspect of nonprofit theater is getting more extreme." She was troubled by the fact that today it is so much more complicated to "get into theater." Akalaitis recalled that when she moved to New York City, she was "sort of a mindless bohemian" who moved into a cheap apartment in the East Village, formed a theater company, and from then on, she was in the theater. After a while, like many of her generation who did not attend theater school but simply started their own theaters, she began directing. She observed that today, on the other hand, there are many young directors who "are in their twenties or thirties, wear suits, have keys to the doors of the institution, and have their own parking space," yet have done nothing but assist other directors. She also referred to the young actors who, upon graduating from Juilliard, for example, have agents telling them, "You look okay. I can get you a job in television, and then you can pay off your

Juilliard debt." Akalaitis fears that these actors will never again work in the theater, that they will always be deferring to agents who tell them they must "do another movie."

Finally, Akalaitis spoke of her then recent appointment to lead the New York Shakespeare Festival. She confessed that being involved with a large institution had always been "two-sided" for her, and that she was "personally terrified of being subsumed into the institution." At the same time, she genuinely appreciated having a stage on which to direct and perform. She explained that she did not have the position of Artistic Director "all figured out," and that her response to being named Papp's successor was, "Now I have to open the door, go into this room, sit at this desk and figure out, in the process of doing it, what it means."

Akalaitis is an artist whose work and person have been problematic for certain members of New York's theater community. She is attracted to plays that are dark, disturbing, and "serious." She believes that the relationship between artists and cultural institutions must allow for questioning and dissent. She is perceived as an intellectual, yet cannot easily explain her creative process. As she explained to Chicago theater critic Richard Christiansen, "I never know where things come from. I just like the fact that you can put a lot of stuff on the stage. . . . So I'm not much of a theorist. But I do tend to direct things I don't understand [very] well."[23] And, of course, she is female. Yet however difficult or "uncharismatic" Akalaitis may be, she is an intelligent, authentic, mature artist who has devoted her life to the theater. She believes that making theater is a process of exploration and discovery, that plays and people need time to reveal themselves, that questions are more important than answers, and that one must occasionally be willing to let things "be awful for a long time." As with all of her work, Akalaitis approached her Artistic Directorship as an investigation. Unfortunately, the investigation was painful, thwarted and, as some no doubt saw it, a failure.

I conclude with some thoughts inspired by yet another rehearsal process directed by Akalaitis, one in which I did not participate but was granted permission to observe. The production was Shakespeare's *Henry IV, Parts One and Two,* produced by the New York Shakespeare Festival in February and March of 1991. In December of 1990, I observed the cast "stumble through" the following series of beats that together comprised an original prologue to *Henry IV, Part One:*

On an empty stage, the actress playing Doll Tearsheet dances with a young child, circling round and round the stage. Akalaitis suggests that perhaps they are eating a pizza together. There is nothing cute or sentimental in the relationship between the two characters. Doll and the child are interacting in a relaxed, playful, and informal manner; their relationship appears casual and contemporary. Eating a pizza is an activity that an adult and child might enjoy together in a contemporary daily life, and Akalaitis's suggestion makes odd but perfect sense. As it turns out, the pizza does not ultimately become part of the production, nor does a Vietnamese potbellied pig with which the company spends an entire day rehearsing.

The music changes and the entire acting company floods the stage, moving in a fashion that might best be described as "stopping-and-starting." The actors move rapidly and sharply, zigzagging across the stage, every now and then stopping abruptly to stare either at the audience or at an imaginary, invisible event that is occuring far upstage. There is something disturbing, even challenging, about the actors' collective gaze. As they move about the stage, they appear to be wondering, questioning, exploring, and discovering things about themselves, each other, the audience, and the stage itself. Neither as actors nor as characters do they appear to "have it all figured out."

The music changes again and the crowd surges in on itself, becoming a chaotic mob jostling, bumping, bouncing, and slam-dancing in all directions. One character in particular is being manhandled by the mob. It is Richard II—the outsider, the misfit, the evicted one. The crowd opens up a bit, yet continues to push Richard around. It is almost as if the ousted ruler is being hurtled through space against his will. Suddenly, without warning, the ensemble splits down the middle as if some deep rupture has occurred in the ground on which the crowd is standing. As each half of the crowd backs into the wings in slow motion, the actors/characters appear to be even more engrossed in discovering what is happening to them.

The stage is empty for a few seconds, and then two actors emerge from the stage-left wing carrying an empty throne. Although the actors are supposedly playing servants, their physical behavior does not seem terribly deferential. Both of them large men, they lumber around the stage, carrying the throne in a rough, irreverent fashion. Akalaitis tells the actors that they remind her of "Israeli furniture movers," and she decides to incorporate this image into the production. She suggests that the actors enter again, as modern-day furniture movers. They do so, and what had originally been haphazard and sloppy is now hilarious. The actors are focused; they have discovered their "objective." The "movers" exit, and the stage is once again empty save for the throne. Yet the emotional residue of what has occurred in the space remains.

The music shifts and George Tsypin's erector-set-like scenery rolls onstage. There is something eerie about the way the set travels into the empty space. It appears not to move mechanically but rather to "make an entrance," almost as if it were a character with a personality of its own. The activity of the actors has created a atmospheric, emotion-filled "architecture" into which the scenery now enters. The scenery, in a sense, "picks up the ball," adding further visual and emotional texture to a space into which the actors will soon return.

Later that day, Akalaitis comments offhandedly that the Prologue, which is not part of Shakespeare's text, "is about making theater." I am perplexed both by the remark and by the seemingly cavalier spirit in which it is voiced. I suspect, however, that Akalaitis is dead serious, that the Prologue is indeed a metaphor for her own process of making theater. Because this book has focused upon a subject that does not lend itself to tidy endings, I prefer not to analyze this metaphor but instead to offer a few closing thoughts.

As I participated, observed, and reflected upon the the creative processes that gave birth to *'Tis Pity She's a Whore* and *The Mormon Project* workshop, I became aware of a number of aesthetic priorities that characterized Akalaitis's approach to making theater: her emphasis on the physicality of performance, on acting and design as theatrical manifestations of image, on the actor's sensitivity to the here and now of theatrical space, and on the emotional power of scenic objects. She has a striking sense of theatrical composition and is a skilled choreographer of actors' bodies in theatrical space. At the same time, she has a genuine desire to share power with her actors in the collaborative investigation of text and character.

From her early days with Mabou Mines, Akalaitis has recognized the importance of working collaboratively. She considers actors to be intelligent individuals who are able to think creatively and independently rather than merely execute the vision of the director, and she endeavors to create a democratic rehearsal environment in which all participants have the freedom to invent and explore. She also believes it crucial for actors to develop a sense of ensemble, or *esprit de corps,* over the course of a rehearsal period, and thus expects each actor cast in her productions to participate in daily physical warm-ups and exercises. Whether the actors are exploring images, movements, and gestures in one of the exercises or working on a scene from the play itself, Akalaitis continually reminds them that they are "in it together."

Drawn to subjects and texts that address aspects of chaos in the individual and society, Akalaitis also embraces the chaos of the unknown as an inevitable aspect of the creative process. The physical exercises she has devised serve as formal structures that shape and contain this chaos, allowing the actors to investigate personal, textual, and scenic images in an emotionally "safe" environment. As the actors perform the exercises, they begin to see themselves not only as components but also as creators of the overall stage composition. They become active participants in the image-making aspect of theater, an area traditionally considered the province of the director and designer. As the membrane between acting and design becomes more permeable, the actors perform with, and within, the design instead of merely in front of it. The integration of acting and design, while not always achieved in production, is thus at the core of Akalaitis's directing process.

Physicality, emotionality, collaboration, chaos, seeing the space, seeing yourself in the space, actor and image, acting and design. . . . The image of JoAnne Akalaitis making theater about making theater illuminates but does not define. It is an image that I hope will provoke further questions and curiosity about her work.

[1] Alisa Solomon, "Public Executions," *Village Voice* 30 March 1993: 95.

[2] Bruce Weber, "Shakespeare Festival Dismisses Papp's Heir," *New York Times* 13 March 1992: 14.

[3] Solomon, 95.

[4] Bruce Weber, "New Theater Boss Plans Change," *New York Times* 22 March 1993, nat'l. ed.: B2.

[5] Weber, "Shakespeare Festival," 14.

[6] Weber, "Shakespeare Festival," 14.

[7] Weber, "New Theater Boss," B2.

[8] For all references attributed to Frank Rich, see "Opening a Window at a Theater Gone Stale," *New York Times* 21 March 1993, nat'l. ed., section 2: 1+.

[9] Robert Brustein, "Akalaitis Axed," *New Republic* 26 April 1993: 30.

[10] Solomon, 98.

[11] Weber, "Shakespeare Festival," 14.

[12] See Solomon 98; and Brustein, 30.

[13] Weber, "Shakespeare Festival," 1+.

[14] Solomon, 95.

[15] Solomon, 95.

[16] Jack Kroll, "Fireworks Behind the Scenes: Art and Commerce Clash at the Public Theater," *Newsweek* 29 March 1993: 63.

[17] Glen Collins, "Wolfe's Selection is Greeted with Praise," *New York Times* 13 March 1993: 13.

[18] Brustein, 29–30.

[19] Elizabeth Maupin, "*Mormon Project* Defies Theatrical Conventions," *Orlando Sentinel* 24 June 1990: F1.

[20] Michael Feingold, introduction, *Grove New American Theater,* ed. Feingold (New York: Evergreen-Grove, 1993) xvii.

21 Herbert Blau, "The Play of Thought," interview, *Perforing Arts Journal* 14.3 (1993): 22–23.

22 Akalaitis, "Theater and the World."

23 Richard Christiansen, "Setting 'Pity': JoAnne Akalaitis Lights the Fuse on a 1633 Drama," *Chicago Tribune* 11 March 1990, section 13: 10.

Part Two

Interview with JoAnne Akalaitis

August 17, 1990
New York City

On the day that Ryszard Cieslak's obituary appeared in the *New York Times*[1] you recalled that he taught you one of the most important things about acting—that it happens in the body. You've also spoken about your belief that the essence of theater is bodies moving in space onstage. Would you talk a bit about Grotowski and what his ideas have meant to you?

Yes, actually the weird thing is that there was a memorial in New York for Cieslak, and Grotowski was there. And he stood up and basically insulted all of us who do theater in America.

His work is very different now.

I never embraced Grotowski's aesthetic. And I never quite even embraced his methodology. But there was this amazing person, Richard, who was a transcendent actor who lived in his body. His performance lived in his body and he was able to communicate that. Grotowski's ideas actually are quite abhorrent to me because they're kind of elitist. It's not that I don't respect the work he did, because I saw those performances in the late sixties. I'm sort of shocked at his denouncing all of us at Richard's memorial.

What do you mean when you say that his ideas were elitist?

No, they *became* that. He developed all of this paratheater and got subsidies to do workshops and alot of people flocked to them. Actually, I should take that back. I don't abhor his ideas because I don't quite know what they are. But it really is an example of an amazing person rediscovering something personally, and then taking a whole bunch of people on that voyage whether those people should be on that voyage or not. And often that voyage involves spending a lot of money for tuition or to enroll in some workshop.

Did you work with Grotowski personally?

I did, yes.

How did you arrive at the physical exercises that we've done in rehearsal? Did you develop them gradually over time?

Oh, I don't know. I just get ideas from . . . I think they came from me.

And do they change when you work on each project?

They do.

During both 'Tis Pity She's a Whore and The Mormon Project workshop, we had similar tasks to explore. The idea of stopping and starting, for instance.

That actually came up a couple of years ago and it became very important to me. I think at the time I was working on *Green Card* at the Taper. I invented it. Or, I didn't invent it, I *saw* it. There are certain things that are indigenous to a production or to a company, and I discover them in working.

Stopping-and-starting is something that actors often have a hard time doing—especially during *The Mormon Project* when we had to combine it with the three different Mormon *mudras*.

It *is* hard to do.

It seems that much of the training actors receive somehow doesn't prepare them to work that way. Nari[2] has said that—this is taking off from the stopping-and-starting idea—there's a sense in which you ask the actor to "go from A to C." And, according to Nari, that can be difficult, and even frustrating, because the actor must supply the transition on his or her own.

Yes.

You've also referred to Genet's idea that each scene should be performed as if it were a play, in and of itself.

Yes. That was a very big influence on me. It's not that you deny transitions. Actors figure out—they negotiate a way from one thing to the other. And they have to do that.

That's a very foreign thing for some actors to do.

Yes, but I think a lot of things are foreign for actors, and it's because actors have not been trained in a physical way. They've not dealt with certain physical realities or body work. Or they think they have, and it's off-putting to them. They don't understand, and I think directors often don't understand either, that performance is profoundly physical.

Do you think directors should know how to move themselves? Or understand it?

Maybe they shouldn't have to. Maybe they shouldn't have to know how to move, or even understand how to put actors in some kind of movement ambience. But what they need to understand is that they *don't* understand it. Do you know what I mean?

You say during the slow-motion painting exercise, "If you don't know what painting you're in, just make sure you know *that*. That you don't know."

Yes. Robert Wilson brings in this Japanese woman, this choreographer who's very in touch with all the aspects of the production, very in touch with the performers. And actually I think Bob knows a lot about movement, but he also knows how to get an expert in there to help him. I think that there are many denials among American directors. One is the denial of design. Another is the denial of the actor as an empowered, collaborative partner in the production. And the third is movement—space—the body in space.

What do you mean by "the denial of design"? Many directors speak a great deal about design.

Well, I think it's not just directors. There's an anti-visual bias in the American theater that's been going on for a long time. And journalists try to put together this idea of the *auteur* director as a visually oriented director because *they*—the journalists—don't understand the visual. *They're* uneducated. They're not dealing with the amazing power of the development of design in the American theater. They think that if there's some kind of "look" onstage it denies the playwright. It's a very simplistic way of looking at theater. And I think a lot of directors come at it—not because of any criticism or scholarship, but because it's basically been the way of thinking about theater—from the point of view that the set is the background for the unfolding of events that the playwright has written. And, it's so screwed up.

It was very exciting to be around John Conklin and Pat Collins during 'Tis *Pity She's a Whore*.[3] They knew so much about the play. But it seemed that the actors were having trouble adjusting to playing in that big space.

Yes, but that's fine for the actors. Actors *should* have trouble. Actors basically are working in a very private, hermetic, deeply subjective way—which they should be doing. This hopefully will translate into a public, objective, physicalized way of working. The actor then has to put herself or himself into space, and that's a really hard thing to do. Actors say, "Oh, the set, it's so hard to work on." They all say that. They should say that. They need to say that. And then they need to get on to the next step, which is to understand that the set supports them and embraces them. And they have to figure out how to dominate. I often say that the actors have to possess the space. And they usually do.

You've spoken about the whole feel of Futurism in 'Tis *Pity*—that the actors needed to internalize *that*—the rhythm, the form, the speed. That also is something that actors trained in a conventional way never think about. They *are* used to thinking about their characters and their private . . .

Yes, except when you offer actors some kind of information—it could be dramaturgical information about character or some kind of historical exegesis—they love it. They really love it. I've noticed that. Some don't—some just want to work on their character. But, for the most part, they're not overwhelmed. They're grateful for information.

Why, when actors do a speed-through, is it usually so good?

I think all directors say that. It's always true. I don't know, there's something—you can't *do* it, you can't *perform* it as a speed-through, but you see everything. Everything is crystallized and condensed. And it's a joyous, exciting, competitive, collaborative experience. However, actors do learn from doing speed-throughs. Because you say, "O.K., well, do it that way." And they won't do it exactly that way, but they'll do it more that way. Whatever the beats are, you have to encounter them very quickly instead of wending your way to them. And actors like speed-throughs. Everyone likes them. You don't have to deal with the blocking, you don't have to deal with the scenery. You see the skeleton of the play but it's not just a skeleton. It's enlivened. It's filled out.

You've mentioned that Oliver Sacks's book *Awakenings* was very important for you. Could you speak more about that?

Well, I think I've explained it in a lot of other books and interviews. And I'll explain it again. It's this idea of being locked into—I'm trying to figure out what it really means because there's something about it that captures my imagination and, in some way, I have to deal with it in my aesthetics of theater. And I think part of it is that you sort of run toward something, and then you get stopped and locked and then paralyzed. And you keep trying and trying and trying to get out of it. So that's a sort of movement explanation of what it is. I started with it in *Endgame* for which it was specifically, thematically relevant. And it made a lot of sense for certain characters, especially in Beckett. The character of Clov, for instance. And then it made a lot of sense in [Büchner's] *Leon and Lena*. And I find it often makes a lot of sense. You're stopped, and then you're released, and then you're sort of hurtled—self-propelled into space. And then something else stops you. And then you're released again. Or then you're transfixed. All of these are images that are in Sacks's book. And it's not necessarily that—I think it has *a lot* to do with Beckett, but I don't think it has a lot to do with Shakespeare, thematically. But it does have a lot to do with an actor understanding something that could be very, very dangerous and on the edge and, movement-wise, chaotic.

How did you become interested in Genet?

Well, I think everyone's interested in Genet. I can't even remember how I discovered Genet. Genet is simply a great twentieth-century writer, and at some point around the sixties he was in my life. I think I saw *The Maids* at the Actors Workshop in San Francisco and I saw *The Blacks* in New York. And a lot of people I talk to, through the years, saw *The Blacks* and remember it as a very important theater event. I saw *Endgame*, I saw Genet—and those were really big.

Genet is not produced very much in the United States.

No.

You've referred to *Endgame* as one of the greatest, if not *the* greatest modern play ever written. Is he a writer that you're particularly attracted to? You and Mabou Mines have done a lot of his work. Were you drawn to Beckett's work personally or as a member of Mabou Mines?

I've never been involved with Beckett except personally. And there's nobody like Beckett. The interesting thing to me is the difference between Genet and Beckett. And I know Lee [Breuer] has said that he's more attracted to Genet. On the one hand, Beckett is very classical and ordered and intellectual, in the best sense of all of those words. And Genet is very Greek—classical in a different way. And sort of an adolescent, a naughty adolescent. You know, I think Genet has a lot to say to us now. He has so much to say to us. He's a great poet. And Beckett is a great poet. In some way I'm not interested in working on Beckett, but in another way I am. I would love to work on *Waiting for Godot* or *Happy Days*. With Beckett you just get back to . . . poetry.

Beckett and Genet are often anthologized together in terms of the history of the French avant-garde.

They're completely different.

Beckett is very difficult technically.

It is, yes. But Genet is technically difficult, too. And you don't really know it because there's this kind of exuberance. On one level, there's all this high poetry, this overly baroque poetry. And on the other level, there's this kind of natural, scatalogical, trashy talk. But what the actor has to do to negotiate between those two is amazing. I think that *Endgame* is the modern masterpiece. But I think *The Screens* is the play of the century. I'm not quite sure what I'm saying when I say that.

You've said that you dislike Brecht.

I shouldn't say that. I have profound reactions against Brecht. And it's complicated. What I think has not happened in American theater, or maybe English theater, is that no one has figured out who Brecht is in our theatrical lives. Nobody knows what to do with Brecht. Certainly I think Brecht is a great theater poet, and a great poet. I'm very attracted to the early plays like *Baal* and *In the Jungle of Cities.* Those are my favorite plays. And I went to the Berliner Ensemble and I saw the great Brecht masterpieces. I saw *Mother Courage,* I saw *Good Soldier Schweik,* I saw *Threepenny Opera,* I saw *Coriolanus.* That was really long ago and, at the time, I was willing to be wowed by it. And it was a time to be wowed. But, there's no way to ignore the fact that Brecht had a very clear political agenda that is to many of us, at this time, abhorrent. It's almost like a Stalinist thing. And in some plays—like *Arturo Ui* which is a delightful play—the level of the polemic is so naive I wouldn't even know how to direct those plays. And then there are other plays, like *Galileo* and *Mother Courage,* which are basically Broadway hits. They're very commercial plays written for some kind of star. And then there's his early poetry. But I think when you deal with the heart of Brecht it is a mistake to ignore his politics. Because he was a political man. That's what his plays are about. And for all of us to say, well, we can do these plays without dealing with his politics, in some way seems ignorant.

It seems naive of *us*.

And that whole idea about acting is not a new idea. I think that the alienation effect is basically a Greek idea. It's very, very classical. You see yourself doing something, and you sort of refine it while you're doing it, and you put it out into space and communicate something—which is another step, another level—toward the audience. For Brecht, that was political. And that seems to me extraordinarily naive on his part. It's a great acting idea but to use it politically is very, very naive. The more I talk about it, I'm sort of irritated with Brecht. And when you deal with Genet whose politics are so perverse and so chaotic and so insane, and whose poetry is also so perverse and so chaotic and so insane . . . . In the twentieth century, the kind of poetry that we may really have to deal with is Genet's poetry. Genet's poetry deals with the Third World. And he is the only major contemporary writer I can think of who has taken a stand in the Third World. In some way Beckett—which is not to put him down—and Brecht seem kind of rarefied. They're very much from the European tradition. Genet literally took the leap in that he *lived* among Palestinians in Jordan and places like that, underground for many, many years when he was not writing plays. And there's something very interesting about him not being a part of the literary world, even though he was a great poet, but being a part of the real world in his own fucked-up, wild and crazy way. It's interesting to see how that informs theater because what's happening in the world now is that there are a lot of people who are dying of AIDS. Like Ethyl Eichelberger—I don't know if you know about this, but he committed suicide. And there are a lot of homeless people. And these are the people that Genet embraced in his life—in his life*style*—and managed to put into his writing. And, in some way, he's so completely contemporary. I don't know how you get these people in. And that shouldn't be anyone's mandate, it really shouldn't. But I don't know how you can do theater now without dealing with . . . everything. With this epidemic, with all this violence, with all these people being shot on the streets of New York, with this global ecological nightmare that is descending on us minute by minute. It's not that you have to do plays about it. But it simply has to be there.

Sometimes it seems that, as actors and as everything else, our frame of reference is so small. It's easy to insulate oneself.

But I don't think that actors *are* insulated. I think that they're people like us. They listen to National Public Radio and they watch television. It's that they have been programmed to separate their work from that kind of consciousness. And you can't put it in every play and it doesn't belong in every play. It probably doesn't even belong in *any* play. But if you're not working with people for whom the bottom line is some kind of social reality, then you're not working. Then you're not doing it.

To get back to Beckett, he received the Nobel Prize because he wrote about human suffering. Although I suppose he didn't live it in the way that Genet lived it.

Yes, but Beckett did because he was part of the Resistance. He was a very brave person, he was wounded in the Resistance. I think Beckett *did* live it. And he lived it in an entirely different political world, which existed almost a generation before the world that Genet lived it in. Genet has truly lived it in the modern world. Right at this instant, we are at war in the Middle East. Genet would love that guy—the King of Iraq. There's something about Genet that would really get off on him. Because he's this macho idiot. And he's an Arab nationalist. You know, we're living in a dream world. We don't realize that there are Arabs all over the world, including in Detroit and Chicago, who are saying, "Right on! We don't care about Kuwait. We're Arab nationalists. Everyone has said we've been dogs for hundreds of years, and now suddenly we're on the front page of the *New York Times,* and we want that and we need it!" . . . the genius of Mabou Mines was that everyone was in power. And that *was* the genius of the company—that everyone had power. Some people less than others, but there is simply nothing like that. And I don't think there ever will be. This group of people came together, and certain people were very articulate and very domineering and others weren't, but I think the way it shook down is that, in some strange way, everybody got their say and everybody got to do what they needed to do. I was talking about that at the Public Theater. If Joe Papp likes something that I don't like, or if he hates something that I like, what do you do about it? And the thing that you do about it is that you allow it to happen. I think that's what Mabou Mines did. There were things that certain people were doing that other people thought were awful, but the unspoken contract was that you got to do whatever you wanted to do. And it's quite a good way of working.

And if somebody didn't like it, they didn't have to do it with you.

No. But that is not the way artistic organizations are run. Basically, there's an artistic vision and—this is a great way to do things—this artistic vision says, "You're on the wrong track with this, you have to get back on track" or "We've got to cancel this" or "You can't do this."

You mean, the power—

Yes, but it's a good kind of power, too. Because the reason people run these institutions is not because they're idiots or maniacs. It's because they have some kind of vision. It's because they believe in theater and they want to do something.

But not even a group like the Wooster Group is as democratic as Mabou Mines.

No, Liz LeCompte is the Artistic Director of The Wooster Group, she's the head of the Wooster Group. And the Wooster Group is, from what I can tell, very collaborative in their workings. But basically, in the public view and in their view, it's run by one person. That's fine. It's not to say that Mabou Mines—the director has always been the director. But, really, the internal workings of Mabou Mines was a consensus deal. There was a consensus mechanism. And whatever the outside world sees it as, that's how it worked.

When you speak about the actors in Mabou Mines being "empowered"—which is a word that's so bandied about today—are you referring to the fact that they were free to work on whatever they wanted to work on?

It's not just that. I think that the revolution Mabou Mines created for actors was that they were empowered to speak out about all the aspects of a production, including design. And, in one sense, that was a pain in the ass. It was very, very tiresome. But, on the other hand, there's nothing like it. I actually think that, design-wise, Mabou Mines is quite weak. I'm being sort of ruthlessly objective. I know that Mabou Mines is known for its visual sensibility and it does have that, but I think the design has been not quite as strong as the acting, not as strong as the sense of performance. And I think that's the thing— that there were no designers, and these were sort of artists, or whatever, and they didn't know anything about theater. All that was great, and that was its own kind of revolution. It was like a stepping-stone in history that designers now can use for their own work. But the greatest thing was not just that the actors in Mabou Mines went on to be directors and playwrights—it's how powerful the actors are [sic] in a piece.

I've seen that kind of unempowered behavior on the part of actors, that kind of deferring behavior among actors who are intelligent people and who have a lot going on. That's been in part what has made me want to do more than act. It's sad that so much of that kind of conditioning goes on.

It is. And that's the way that the system works. Actors go to Hollywood. And it's very interesting that now they all become directors. They're smart. They're realize where the power is. Because the power in theater is held by directors and producers. That's where it's at unless you're a major star. It happens all the time that stars dictate how a play's cast and who directs it. A lot of people object to that, but I'm not so sure whether it's objectionable. I don't know. Personally, it's objectionable to me because I insist on controlling the whole production.

At the same time, it has to be very collaborative. Those things are not mutually exclusive. It's an exciting, amazing kind of tension—people are helping me, and collaborating together, and giving me and the piece their own individual artistic history, and yet I am putting it all together. And basically directing it, in the simplest sense of what directing is.

You would sometimes refer to the physical exercises we did in rehearsal as "actor research." And you'd sometimes see an image from those exercises and actually use it in the piece. Or maybe try it out and then discard it. Is that part of what you're talking about? Because that's our own personal exploration.

Yes. . . . Do you think that violates an actor's—

No, not at all. Because even though you've asked us to work from the inside and see ourselves from the outside, *you* can see us from the outside in a different way.

Well, yes. I mean what I say with most of those exercises—that it's for the actors. Sometimes I get very bored and zone out. And other times I do the exercise myself, in my imagination. And then other times I do that *and* really look. And there are always great things, it's always great. It's amazing what actors do. Nobody could do better than actors in their work, in being inventive.

I appreciated those exercises very much. It was wonderful to be able to do them before a rehearsal.

Yes, we had this casting discussion about Falstaff in the *Henry* plays. It could be that a big star will play Falstaff. And I said to the casting department, "You have to tell these people—and I'm very happy to have a big star or a minor star—that there are no exceptions. I work the way I do. Everyone has to lie down on the floor and everyone has to stand up. Everyone has to do these exercises. No matter who that person is, she or he has to do these exercises, and there *are* no exceptions, and that's the way I work."

When we were doing the attraction and repulsion exercise, you'd often say, "Now, remember, this is physical. This is not psychological." And I would hear this and think, "Okay, I'll just keep it physical," but something inside of me couldn't help being activated simply by doing that physical action of going toward or away from someone.

Yes, I think the physical *is* the psychological. That's what Bob Wilson said many years ago—that the mechanical is the emotional, or something like like. And, for me, it was not about creating plays or improvisational situations or some kind of improvisational scenes. It was really understanding how the physical . . . . Certainly [doing the exercises] *is* psychological, it's absolutely psychological, but to deal with [the physical] is such a primary, basic and, for many actors, novel experience that it's important to stay glommed on to it. Otherwise, the exercise becomes narrative. And I think that it's very important in acting to be pre-narrative—in all these plays, the Shakespeare plays, the Chekhov plays—to be open to some kind of physicalized state that does not define what the physicality of the character is too early. To be in a kind of primeval, subconscious, unconscious state that is open to the whole world, or *worlds,* of the play. So that's the background, sort of the base of it. And then when you go on to do the really articulated work, you always have that to fall back on. And it's very secure because it's completely primitive physicality. And out of that you make it really detailed for the performance. And you *have* to make it detailed for the performance.

Something that's been meaningful to me, as a performer—and that's been reinforced by working with you—is the importance of not pretending. It's a double-edged thing because, in a way, you are always pretending in the theater. Many people have talked about this paradox, but if I feel that I have to pretend a lot, it's very difficult for me to perform. I really enjoy working on Beckett, for instance, because I don't feel that I have to do any pretending. It was also very easy for me not to pretend while doing the physical exercises, or even while doing *The Mormon Project* itself that, at least on the most obvious level, deals with something very far removed from my own experience. When you concentrate during the exercises on actually being in the room, being aware of your own body and the other bodies around you—you *are* operating in a pre-narrative realm because you're dealing with *your* knee and *this other person's* body and *this* wall. And then when you start letting your character seep in, you're still responding to *this* floor and *this* arm. And I think that's another thing that's not often focused upon, at least in my theatrical experience— dealing with what's really happening in front of you at each moment.

Oh, I know exactly what you're talking about. I am stunned by what theaters are doing. I don't understand what directors are doing. I don't understand how directors are talking to actors. I don't know what's going on. There are simply no ideas about how to put it together. Basically people are either doing plays or making these grand career moves like, "I'm doing this piece and I need to have this actress be in it."

I've also found that doing physical tasks often allows what's inside to free up and come out.

It's a very simple thing. It's the inside and outside coming together. There really is nothing like it. And, oddly enough, very few actors can do it. I never thought of that—it's so weird, isn't it—that very few actors actually do it, put the two together. I thought that Denzel Washington was doing it. I went to the opening [of *Richard III*] the other night, and the critics were so mean to him. I thought, "Why should this really, really talented guy ever want to do a play again?" He was actually doing something onstage, he was actually working. And his physical work was so interesting. Did you read the *New York Times* review?

No.

Mel Gussow said, "He contorted his body so much that he kept talking over his shoulder." Which he did. It was so great. I was really impressed by the way he used his body. He's an important American actor, and then he tries to do something very important. . . . Why should he ever do another play? He's going to get better and better. He was doing something onstage. He was talking and he was making sense. He walked onstage and I thought, "Hey, here's a guy who's working." And they just shot him down.

---

1 Ryszard Cieslak was a member of Grotowski's Polish Laboratory Theatre until it ceased touring in 1980 and is best remembered for his performance in *The Constant Prince* and *Apocalypse cum Figuris*. Cieslak's obituary appeared in the *New York Times* on June 16, 1990.

2 Actor Erik (Nari) Avari appeared in *The Screens, 'Tis Pity She's a Whore* and *The Mormon Project* workshop.

3 Conklin designed the sets and Collins designed the lights for the Goodman Theatre production of *'Tis Pity She's a Whore*.

Interview with
David Leong

June 10, 1992
New York City

I'm particularly interested in the way that JoAnne works with her collaborators. In the *Voice* article[1] you mentioned that when you work on a production your title varies, depending on your relationship with the director and the temperament you bring to the assignment, from fight director to fight coach with many subtle gradations in between. How would you describe your role when you work with JoAnne?[2] It's appeared to me that you have a great deal of collaborative power.

I would say input. In terms of power, I would say that she trusts me a lot. She trusts my judgment and my ideas for those sections of the play that need to be physicalized. She asks for my artistic input. And because of the level of trust that I have in her, she's very open to my ideas. We know each other pretty well. It's now at the point where we don't really have to discuss each idea to the nth degree because she knows—actually, she may not even know. In other words, even if I'm able to articulate something verbally she may not really be able to see it. She'll say, "I can't see it. I hear it, but I have to see it in front of me and then I'll know." And most of the time the material that I come up with is something that pleases her.

You've been fortunate to have worked with some of the best directors in the country. Is there anything that's particularly inspiring—or challenging—about working with Joanne?

First of all, to be quite basic, I know it's going to be different. Her artistic appetite is further to the left politically. And there's an element of not knowing what's going to come next in the process. It is a challenge but I love that sense of not knowing. I think that working with JoAnne forces me—or actually, I put some pressure on myself—to do things that I've never done before. It stretches me. I may actually not know what I'm going to do a week ahead of time, but I do know that something will be there and it will be unlike anything I've done before.

But isn't that the way you usually work with directors?

Well, with a few. With directors like Michael Kahn, Liviu Ciulei, Garland Wright, and JoAnne, I put the pressure on myself to do things in ways I have never done before. And, at the same time, to make the artistic statement that is needed at that particular point in the play—to keep what I do in harmony with the play. With other directors I could literally describe to you what I was going to do six months from now, and I guarantee it would turn out like that. That kind of work I do for bread and butter. To make a living. It doesn't satisfy the artist in me at all.

What about JoAnne's political sensibility? Does it impinge upon your work with her? Dramaturgically, or in any other way?

No. No, it doesn't. Because along with the fact that JoAnne is a feminist, she really knows the time period in which she has set the play. She studies the sociopolitical environment in a very thorough manner. And when I work with JoAnne, I'm often—but not always—doing something that has do with fighting, which was based on the sociopolitical norms of the day. In other words, no matter what the play, there are accepted conventions of dealing with violence. There are rules set down by society: "Yes, you can use these particular guns, these weapons are legal, these are not legal, these kinds of things are allowed, these aren't, this is how you treat men and women. . . ." So much of what I do in studying the martial arts of a specific time period, is in fact studying the sociopolitical system because that's where the particular type of fighting originated. Someone in power, someone in charge of that government says, "These are the types of weapons and this is the attitude," and, by some sort of decree, says, "This is the way we feel about violence." So, really, JoAnne's research is confirming things that I've researched on my own. Because if she sets 'Tis Pity She's a Whore in Fascist Italy, my study of that period is going to involve reading about that particular society's attitude toward violence and the use of weapons—that's the research I'm doing. If she's doing a play in 1575 or 1625 England, my research about the Elizabethan style is going to tell me what was going on politically and socially at the time. You know, this is the first time I've ever been asked this question and have been able to make sense of it. So, there's nothing that's ever in conflict. The choices I make in terms of movement and fighting techniques all support her choices.

What do you think is unique about JoAnne's way of working?

What's unique is her process of making decisions, arranging and rearranging the space, and giving a vision to a play. I think she operates at an almost subliminal level, an unconscious level, and sometimes you can't bring to the surface in concrete words exactly what it is she's doing. She couldn't even explain it herself. It either moves you for some reason and you feel it on a visceral level, or you don't. I'm not saying it's something positive or negative. It's just an observation about the way she works. Other directors I work with make conscious choices and can articulate why. That's not always good. JoAnne often can't. I feel that if, in conversation with her, you said, "JoAnne, why are you going to do this?" she probably wouldn't be able to tell you. She'd probably say, "I don't know. I just am."

I don't think she enjoys being pinned down. So even if she perhaps had a glimmer of why she was going to do it, she might still say, "I don't know."

One valuable resource to me when I'm working on a show with JoAnne is sitting around with the other collaborators. I look at the set design and the costume design and the lights, and I get a feeling of the shapes and the forms that are used, the lines, the weights. If I were to have a first meeting with JoAnne alone and she said, "This is what I want to do," and there was nothing in front of me, I don't know if I'd be able to make my presentation. I need to see a model or sketches. And I think we all are that way when we talk to JoAnne. We sit and we talk, and each one brings in ideas. It's about refining things.

You've referred to yourself as a designer, as part of the design team. Do you see JoAnne more as a designer's director than an actor's director?

Oh, no doubt about that. I think you knew the answer to that question.

You work closely with actors and are often in a position where they confide in you. From your point of view, what kinds of things may account for frustration on an actor's part?

I think there's so much in an actor's world that is not tangible. There are so many choices that have to be made. Their moment-to-moment existence up there on the stage is not like learning a tap dance or juggling or sword fighting.

It can be terrifying.

Yes, because it changes all the time. And that's one of the beauties of acting—that is, if you are able to live in a world where things are so constantly in flux. And I'm talking about offstage as well. Onstage, if you're really doing your job as an actor, everything changes moment-to-moment depending on the audience and the way you're feeling and the way your fellow actor is feeling. Working on a fight or a movement sequence is a more concrete, tangible thing even if it's developed in a very process-oriented way, which happens with all of JoAnne's plays. Even if we don't know where we're going with it, to move in space, to lay your hand down on this table, to grab someone by the throat and choke them are very tangible things. And the actors need that in their life. They have to have something that they can grab on to. When they leave a fight rehearsal they can say, "This is what I did. And I'll do it the same way tomorrow." And it's something that's solid. It's like learning to tap-dance.

Or play the piano.

Yes. Actors need that. And even though they live in that intangible world, I think they're always wanting tangibles. An actor would love to know that the choice he or she is making at the moment is right, and will work every time. But that's not the way it works.

JoAnne brings a certain amount of "not knowing" to the rehearsal process.

Exactly. So when an actor says to her, "Can you help me out here?" she often can't because she operates at another level. She can't verbalize it, she can't coach them in the way that they want coaching. So it may be frustrating for them. It's not my job, but if on the first day of rehearsal I could spend an hour alone with the newer actors explaining to them the way JoAnne works and how they best could use her input, they might find it easier to give something back to her. Because JoAnne's a director who doesn't really explain her process. As a matter of fact, I was a a faculty meeting at the Juilliard School last week. And one of the things we talked about was offering a master class for actors that was all about learning how to work with directors. That's never been done before. Directors often study how to coach different types of actors. But how in the world, over a short rehearsal period, does an actor learn how a particular director thinks and works? Because many directors don't articulate it. I would say ninety percent of the directors that I've worked with can't articulate what their "concept" of the production is when I have my first meeting with them. You know, that word "concept" is really an academic one. It's something you study in graduate school. Many directors would say, "I don't know what 'concept' means." So it would be great if actors learned that if they listened and watched carefully enough, they might find out a lot about how a director works. For example, they might watch the way that JoAnne operates outside of rehearsal, the way she comes into a rehearsal, the way she listens, the way she communicates with designers.

That's an extraordinary request to make of an actor. It's a radical notion.

But it's not something that shouldn't be accomplished. It would only help them. Isn't it funny that when a director decides to do a play, there's a number of things they do to prepare. They do historical research. And if they're going to do a play by, let's say, Brecht, they don't read just that particular play. They read as many Brecht plays as they can because they're trying to get inside the author's head. Well, why don't actors read a director's reviews or watch videotapes of a director's other productions? They'd then come to the first rehearsal already knowing something about their role as actors. But some actors don't even read the play itself. They should research the director before they accept a role, but they're so hungry and grateful to simply work.

What about the physical exercises that JoAnne does in rehearsal? Do you see them as critical somehow? On some subliminal, unconscious level, as you put it?

If you're willing, as an actor, to open yourself up to it. I think that being in a play of JoAnne's is a life choice you make for that specific period of time. It's the ideal way to approach doing theater, and unfortunately I myself don't even live up to it. But, as an actor, I think it's really important. For the time period that you work on that play, it's important that it encompasses you. It's part of your life. And that's what JoAnne expects of her actors. It's as far away from commercial-ism as you can get in the theater, from the attitude that this is just a job—you come in well-prepared, you do it, and you leave. JoAnne expects her actors to live and breathe it.

Could you speak about some specific projects that were your personal favorites? Maybe you could describe the way you developed the fights for *Cymbeline*.

Out of all the experiences I've had working with JoAnne, I think that *Cymbeline* was probably the most challenging and the most creative. And I wish I had more of those experiences. With *Cymbeline,* JoAnne kept mentioning the word "surreal." You know, she doesn't give you a lot. Actually, it's funny, because by not giving you a lot she gives you an awful lot. Excuse my redundancy. When JoAnne says "surreal," she is throwing the ball back into my court. Then it's my job. So I went and researched the visual artists of the time. I also talked to art teachers. And I remember extracting three or four qualities that seemed to dominate the whole surrealist movement. One of those qualities was transformation, melting. Dali's clocks, for instance, are melting and becoming something else. When JoAnne told me the number of actors we would cast as soldiers in the production, I said "O.K., well, we can't do a whole battle scene." To this day, people still think I had about fifty people onstage. In fact there were only about twenty-five. My choice based on that smaller number of soldiers was to have each actor play more than one soldier. They could actually transform from one soldier to another, though not necessarily to a different army. And I also had the idea, based on the transformative process I'd been studying, that instead of seeing one battle scene from beginning to end, the group of soldiers would be in about fifteen different little vignettes on the battlefield. So I said to JoAnne, "I'd like to approach this battle as if we're watching a TV with a remote control. As if we're watching Channel 4 and we see a war. Maybe it's a big panoramic view. And then we press the remote control, and we go to Channel 5 and see another view. We might go to a close-up of a soldier wailing over the death of his best friend. And then we press the remote button again and we transform to another view." I said that I didn't have to do one clean story from beginning to end, I could do these flash vignettes. At the end of each sequence, the actors would freeze and, through changes in lighting and music, we'd go on to another scene. And sometimes I'd keep certain actors frozen into the next scene, so that those soldiers would then become actual pieces of scenery. JoAnne liked that idea. I had to work carefully with the set and lighting designers, and with Philip Glass, the composer. They all loved the idea. And JoAnne was eager to give me as much rehearsal time as it took to pull it off.

The fights in *Cymbeline* seemed to be a microcosm of the piece as a whole.

Yes, I was also able to use the scenic elements in a transformational way. At one time a stick would become a bow, at other times it would become a sword, a rifle, a spike or whatever. And then there was this big, sort of unidentifiable "machine" that hadn't been used in the play at all but was stuck on stage left. And I said to JoAnne, "Let me try to move this thing around and allow it to become on the battlefield whatever the audience wants it to be. As long as it's a force that is acted upon." And that fit in with her ideas, because everything I was doing was at once concrete and not concrete. I didn't have to tell the story exactly. I created a mood, a feeling. We knew who won and who lost, but it was less specific than some of the other works that I've done. And I actually liked it a lot more.

What was it like working on two different productions of '*Tis Pity She's a Whore*?

You know we won an Obie for it in New York. Conceptually, it was a tighter design than the Goodman production.

Did John Conklin change the design?

No, but some of it was refined. I don't think the acting was as good as it was at the Goodman, though. The New York production was tighter, all around. It was in some ways easier to put up and in other ways more difficult. I had never recreated the same show with a different cast. I would have preferred to reconceive my ideas totally, rather than try to keep the same ideas.

Because you create a fight for the specific people who will be doing it.

You have to.

What about the critical reception JoAnne has received since she took over at The Public? Do you think it's been unfair?

I think it's gotten a lot better lately.

What do you think JoAnne's contribution is and will be to the American theater?

JoAnne's a very important director, no doubt about it. She has a socio-political-feminist approach to the classics that, if you allow it, can strike you in a deep way. She achieves this through a constant integration of all the theatrical elements: music, light, sound, etc. Her images are strong, she's a very sculptural director. And she is able to touch upon the issues that lie at the base of the play and stir them up. She doesn't try to provide answers but she gets those issues rumbling within you.

She disturbs.

Yes, you go away with all that kind of jumbled up inside and it's yours to do with what you will. I think the way that JoAnne approaches her work is definitely unique.

The idea of theater artists and audiences allowing themselves to be jumbled up by a play is an exciting one. It can also be difficult. But then JoAnne herself is not an easy person to talk and write about.

Oh, yes, because when I was walking here I was thinking, "God, what am I going to say? I've never been asked to talk about JoAnne and her work." But I came up with a little bit more than I actually thought I'd be able to.

---

[1] Robinson, Marc, "'They Fight': The Thrusts and Parries of David Leong," *Village Voice* 28 April 1992: 104.

[2] David Leong has worked on several productions with Akalaitis including *Cymbeline* (New York Shakespeare Festival, 1989), *'Tis Pity She's a Whore* (Goodman Theatre, 1990 and New York Shakespeare Festival, 1992), and *Henry IV, Parts 1 and 2* (New York Shakespeare Festival, 1991).

Interview with Joan Elizabeth

October 21, 1992
Chicago

When did you first encounter JoAnne's work?[1]

I went to see *Dead End Kids,* and it completely destroyed any conceptions I had about musical theater. When I was growing up, I went to see musicals or very ordinary productions of things. But, later, I was making films at NYU and became very interested in layering sound tracks, and in ideas about the ways we take in information and how much we can accept at once. And then I went and saw this play, and it changed my ideas completely about what happens in the theater. It was the first experimental thing I ever saw. Although I did see one thing earlier. I saw *Dark Ride.*[2] It fascinated but completely confused me because it wasn't about a subject I really could grasp.

What was it like seeing JoAnne perform?

I didn't realize it was her. The only thing I remember from the show was somebody saying, "What a coincidence!" which I thought was hilarious because I love coincidences. And JoAnne later told me that those were her lines.

And when did you first meet JoAnne in person?

I starting meeting her just casually, socially, because I started working with Anne Bogart. And David Warren, who used to assist her, introduced me to her. After *Dead End Kids,* I always went to see her plays. And she came to see some of Anne's stuff. She came to see *Cinderella.*

What was it like auditioning for JoAnne? Was it a different kind of an audition?

Well, since she knew me from before, I think, and she knew that I was from a broad background that included [experimental] work, she was great to me in the audition.

What did you have to do?

The first time through I just read for the character of Philotis. It was very simple. JoAnne didn't really give me any direction. She had me read through the scene once or twice. She liked what I was doing so she didn't change a lot about it. But what was more interesting was the movement audition. She wanted to see how everybody moved, so she brought us in, in groups of about seven or eight. And she put on that kind of Carribbean salsa music she always plays in rehearsal, and just had us move. The first time she just wanted to see us move around, to "feel the space." And she would demonstrate it. And I fell in love with the look of her, this woman who was such an intellectual. So she was demonstrating "feeling the space, sensing the space." We had to do that. Some of the actors were very resistant. They were threatened by it, they didn't understand what it was or why it was important. But I was loving it because I so much missed working with Anne, and JoAnne was doing all that stuff. And she had us do slam-dancing without touching. And she was demonstrating that as well. And we also had to do starting-and-stopping.

Do you think that JoAnne is interested in using, or is attracted to, a certain type of actor?

She seems to be attracted to actors who are easily very physical.

Actors who appear comfortable in their bodies?

Yes, and who like to use themselves. And who are connected physically. It's not just that they can move, but that they move to express emotion. So, not necessarily an actor who is great at musical theater. Someone who could tap-dance, for instance. Or even someone who could really shake it out. Some people can move but it's not connected. Actors like Jesse Borrego and Jared Harris really use their whole bodies. They're interested in pushing physical and psychological limits. It seems to me that the actors I've seen JoAnne work with have that ability.

JoAnne has said that the physical and the psychological are the same thing, and that she instructs actors doing the exercises to "keep it physical" because it's not what they're used to focusing on.

That's interesting, because I always wondered why in rehearsal she'd keep hammering, "Relax your face, don't try to do it with your face." She was trying to create the sensation that the emotion was coming out of the body as a whole rather than just through the face or the eyes.

Something that really stood out for me during the Chicago rehearsals for 'Tis Pity was the time she spent working with the ensemble to create a kind of collective facial mask during the wedding scene. There was one rehearsal, before you all had the actual prop masks you'd be using in performance, when she asked everyone onstage to, "Remember a time that you were really ashamed of something and make a mask of that."

Yes, she really asks you to expose yourself, even for a group scene like that. And to expose things that she can't even really talk about.

Do you think that JoAnne's directing process is unusual?

Among the more run-of-the-mill directors I've worked with she's unusual because she's so physically oriented. You almost never have the opportunity to work physically with other cast members, which I think is imperative. When I've seen actors do their best work, and when I've seen them give their most exciting performances, there's a sense of ensemble that you can't create unless you're used to working with each other's bodies in an uncensored way. And JoAnne, from the first day of rehearsal—

—from the audition—

—from the audition, gets you used to "looking where you're not supposed to look," as Anne Bogart always says. Looking at somebody's body where it's usually not appropriate. Looking at them for a longer period of time. It's a whole exploration of breaking down physical barriers.

Both JoAnne and Anne speak about "getting too close," of breaking that theatrical taboo of being too close together or too far apart. Of avoiding that common middle-distance that you use when you talk to somebody in a scene.

Right. And I've always thought that that's the great thing about the physical exercises. Because in any other rehearsal process, you're going to spend the first few weeks always at that middle-distance. It's about being polite. It's about the space that's comfortable and polite to be interacting in with somebody with whom you're not in love or angry or whatever. It's neutral space. So you have to go through getting to know each other, and being polite and asking if you can violate that space, and then getting comfortable—it's takes ten times as long. And you can be in previews and still be saying, "Do you mind if I touch you here?" Which drives me crazy because it seems to really get in the way of the work that can come out of being in a dangerous physical position. You put yourself in a physical position that's dangerous and you're going to have emotions that you don't expect. And that's where interesting acting might come from.

What was it like performing the physical exercises?

JoAnne has led exercises where she'll ask you to do things like "Let your body fill with evil." Something like that, if you're a Catholic girl like me, is interesting because you really get to see where your own resistance lies. And whether you can get through it or not, in an exercise, is not really the point. What's important is that you become aware of what you don't want to do. Or, conversely, of what really excites you. So then when you go to work on a scene from the play, you can begin from that place of awareness you discovered during the exercises. You don't even have to think about it.

JoAnne refers to the exercises as "research" for the actors. Did you find yourself remembering things you discovered in the exercises—or even physically remembering things—and then using them when you were actually doing scene work?

I would notice when I was "going away" during an exercise. Even a simple thing such as noticing it happen with somebody I don't like in the cast. Or with somebody I'm really attracted to. Either one of those people can be difficult to look at. If you don't like someone, it can become very hard to act with them because you never want to commit to any *emotional* time. Even if you "commit," in the way that actors know how to do, you've really not done so on a deep level. And if there's somebody you're really attracted to, you may also create more distance and then you can't spontaneously respond to each other. So you've already begun leaving yourself out of the process.

And do the exercises make it easier to deal with these two kinds of people?

They make you aware that you *have* to deal with these two kinds of people. In a nonthreatening way, they allow you to be very physical. And to explore all different kinds of things, because the exercises take you through many different emotions. The slow-motion exercise, for instance, teaches you about trust. And whether you like the other actors or not doesn't really matter. You have to be able to trust each other as an ensemble onstage. And, right away, you have a physical understanding of everyone in the cast. So you feel like you can go up and talk to them, give them a hug or a soft touch. That's another thing JoAnne does, she always makes sure she touches her actors.

You were speaking about the way the exercises allow you to connect to the other cast members. Was there more of a trusting, ensemble-feel in the two productions that you've worked on with JoAnne, or were there still the inevitable tensions between people?

Well, there are two things. The exercises allow you to trust each other and communicate without a lot of lag-time about asking and being polite. So you are freer, physically and emotionally, in rehearsal. And that leads to . . . stuff. That's one given, but then there's also the layer of what the play asks of you emotionally. *'Tis Pity* is such a dark play, and JoAnne had such a strong view of what it was about.

I've often thought that maybe the play itself—on a sort of deep, unconscious level—brought up "stuff," as you put it.

Yes, and it also seemed to me that there was something fundamental JoAnne was grappling with in this play—the victimization of the female by men.

What did you think about the Futurism/Fascism concept?

I felt that the root of the production, for JoAnne, was the dynamic between men and women. Women were victimized and brutalized by this male-dominated society. And the Futurist Manifesto incorporated those ideas. So Futurism and Fascism were intellectual and visual ways of speaking to what she really felt the play was about.

I'm thinking specifically of the exercise where you are creating a group composition in slow motion of, for example, "The Dangerous Place." Did you feel that this exercise encouraged you as an actor to take on more responsibility for the shape of the production as a whole?

Yes. And it also teaches you how to compose with each other. To compose a state of mind or an emotional state. If you're doing exercises with each other about composing the painting of "Evil" or "The Devil," you may discover yourself in a physical position that expresses that. If you can then recreate that physical position in a scene, the emotional state is also recreated. You don't have to be doing backbends—it's just that if you physically position yourself on a different level and at a certain spatial distance from someone onstage, it may also set up the emotional scenario you want the audience to be perceiving. So you can just be there and then act.

Did the exercises help you connect to the physical space? And when you've seen a production JoAnne has directed, do the actors seem to you *in production* to possess a strong connection to the space and to each other?

Yes. No doubt about it. Because most of the time, as actors, we don't even deal with our connection to the space.

What about the set?

There's the scenery and then there's you. And it's completely separate. And half the time, as an audience member, you look at actors on the set and you don't even know why the set has to be there, or what it is, or you don't quite know how to deal with it. And it doesn't really seem to be designed for actors to be on anyway.

What was it like performing on the *'Tis Pity* set?

Oh, I loved that set. I like sets like that because they place you in an alternate reality. Anything that's going to be working to release my preconceptions about how to behave in a space is going to be more interesting. It's always more fun to deal with a landscape that's surreal, that's unusual, that's not literally where you are, than it is to act in a little room with a bunch of magazines and props and espresso cups.

Are you referring to something like a Victorian interior that recreates the *actual place* where the action of the play occurs?

I'd rather see a design that expresses the psychological state of the play. Because, as an actor, that's what you have to deal with. You don't have to waste time pretending to look out a window that isn't there.

Faking.

Yes. Or doing something with your demitasse cup. I know that's a style of acting, but I think that movies can do that better. Plays should be about something else.

When I would watch the Goodman production of 'Tis *Pity,* I felt at times that the set itself, or even some of the large group scenes on the set, had more emotional power than many of the more intimate scenes. Seeing a single person in the arcade, or the image of people in that red bedroom, was a tremendously emotional experience. And I think that's one of JoAnne's strengths as a director, and perhaps also something that tends to frustrate certain actors.

Yes, I agree with that. That's a really good point. Because the other side of the coin is that a physical space like that can be overwhelming.

Do you think the actors felt at times that they were competing with the set?

I'm sure. We're lost on the set. You go out there and you have in your mind, "O.K., I'm in my Dad's study." Because there is the level of entering into what you have to create as real, as the physical space your character exists in. And you go out onstage, and there are half-naked statues covered with twine. It's like, "What drug was I on when I ordered these art pieces?" It ends up being more work for you as an actor because you've got to rationalize what's around you. You've got to deal with it as something recognizable or the audience will never buy it, the play won't be rooted in any kind of . . .

Do you think JoAnne might have an easier time, say, with actors who are used to working with directors like Ariane Mnouchkine or Peter Brook?

I don't know. I think there's a style of performing, a style of theater, that's just more demanding. At the same time, the actor can also end up . . .

A pawn. Serving the director's vision.

Which always struck me as a huge irony. Because this style of theater demands so much more of you as an actor. So much more of your imagination, your intelligence, your physical and emotional commitment. You can't slack off or you'll look really bad. Because you're serving a very specific master. You're really trying to carry out someone's idea. And so, consequently, if you do it very well, you can end up looking like a lackey to their master. When in reality you're working ten times harder than you have doing any kind of conventional play. What I've always thought is that you can't use mediocre actors in work like JoAnne's, because it will just fall apart. It will be insufferably bad.

Do you think that the free play of the actors' personalities—their ability to really use themselves and feel like themselves and let themselves go onstage—can easily get stifled in this type of work?

It depends on whether you believe that setting up parameters allows you to be free. There's a German philosopher who said that what makes you free are the conditions—the rules—by which you live your life.

The structure.

Yes, the structure makes you free. And I think that, in a way, is true. Your brain knows how far it can go before you lose your mind. It has those built-in checks and balances. If you're taking drugs, or if you actually go crazy, then those parameters are released so you go too far and you can't go back. But knowing there's a wall ahead of you that will tell you how far is too far, you can run full-force beyond what you ever thought was possible. Even if you hit the wall and get hurt, at least you know you won't go past it and lose youself.

I think JoAnne's exercises give the actor a set of structures, or "walls." And then when the work on the actual text begins, those parameters cease to exist and the actor may feel somewhat imperiled.

Or perhaps JoAnne doesn't know how to articulate the parameters as clearly when she is working on the text itself. It's very interesting to contrast working with Anne Bogart and with JoAnne. Anne sets up such physical boundaries. Everything is so choreographed that it creates, or even imposes, another "text" in the scene. You're dancing one dance and speaking another dance. And that sets up an emotional tension in the scene. But JoAnne doesn't give you as many physical boundaries, she doesn't make the scene into a ballet. Which really appeals to me because you are still working formally but you're not so constrained.

---

1 Joan Elizabeth is an actress who appeared in both the Chicago and New York productions of *'Tis Pity She's a Whore.*
2 Len Jenkin's *Dark Ride* was presented by the Soho Repertory Theatre in New York City, in November of 1981. JoAnne Akalaitis played the role of Mrs. Lammle.

Interview with Anne Dudek and Genevieve VenJohnson

Conducted by Ron Russell, Education Director, Theatre for a New Audience

February 8, 1999
The New School, New York City

We have with us two actors from *The Iphgenia Cycle,* who have been with the production since it was first done in Chicago.[1] Genvieve VenJohnson is a member of the Chorus and Anne Dudek plays Iphigenia.[2] JoAnne Akalaitis sends her regrets that she was unable to attend tonight. She left for Washington, D.C., earlier this afternoon to work on her next project, but she did give me some thoughts to address. What I'd like to do, first of all, is recap what these two plays are about. *The Iphigenia Cycle* is a pairing of two plays by Euripides, *Iphigenia at Aulis* and *Iphigenia in Tauris.* The two plays were actually written in the reverse order of the way they're presented. *Tauris* was written around 412 B.C. and *Aulis* was written around 407 B.C.

The first play is about Agamemnon's decision to kill his eldest daughter Iphigenia in a sacrificial rite to Artemis. The Greek armies gathered at Aulis have been told that they will not be able to sail to Troy unless Artemis, who has stopped the winds, is appeased. So, eventually, over the course of the play, Iphigenia makes the decision to sacrifice herself for the good of Greece. She is brought to the altar, Agamemnon brings the knife down to kill her, and suddenly, in Iphigenia's place, there is a dying deer bleeding all over the altar. This is taken as a sign that Artemis is accepting the sacrifice, the winds come up, and the Greeks sail to Troy. We pick up after intermission, about eighteen years later, well after the Trojan War. Again, just to recap the story, when Agamemnon returns from the Trojan War with his paramour Cassandra, he finds that his wife Clytemnestra has herself taken a paramour, Aegisthus, who is essentially running Agamemnon's kingdom back in Mycenae. Aegisthus and Clytemnestra murder Agamemnon in his bath, and murder Cassandra along the way. This results in the youngest member of the household, Orestes, the brother of Iphigenia, being told by Apollo's oracle at Delphi that he must kill his mother Clytemnestra in order to exact vengeance. He does, and he is promptly pursued by a group of nasty old goddesses called the Furies who run around with snakes in their hands. The Furies carry the dead body of Clytemnestra and sort of shove it in Orestes' face, but of course no one else can see it but him. Apollo tells Orestes that, in order to rid himself of the Furies, he must go to the barbarian land of Tauris across the Black Sea, rescue a statue of Artemis, and bring it back to Greece. It turns out that Iphigenia is the very priestess of said temple of Artemis in this land of the barbarian Taurians. And, of course, what happens is that the family is reunited through the sister and the brother who make their way back to Athens by the end of the play. There's a kind of a happy ending, a little Euripidean *deus ex machina* with Athena coming down and saying, "Thoas, king of the barbarians, don't kill these people. Let them go back to Athens." Another important thing that I want to bring up is the role of the Chorus in these two plays. In *Aulis*, the Chorus is a group of women from the nearby town of Chalkis who have come to view the armies on display. There are a lot of men without shirts running up and down the beach and these women are coming to see them. In the second play, however, the Chorus is a group of six slave women held captive—do we find out in the play, or do we assume, that Thoas the barbarian has captured them?

GV: We're not told, exactly. We have a little ode where we refer to our city having fallen and being taken away in ships by barbarians.

These women, of course, want to get back to Greece but they're being held captive by King Thoas. So they are two very different Choruses, which helps define the distinct world of each play. I think that one of the most salient aspects of this production is the way that the Chorus is handled. It's difficult to describe, but the Chorus has a new kind of vitality that breaks out of the traditional, formalized modality in which a Chorus is expected to operate. The Chorus is very exciting in that it has an actual character-driven presence onstage that enhances the argument in the first play, and the emotional desperation in the second play. Let's start talking about the arc of these two plays performed in sequence. What does this arc demand of you as actors? What does it do for you? What challenges does it pose?

AD: The first major challenge is that Iphigenia is about sixteen to eighteen years old in the first play and about thirty-six years old in the second play. It's difficult as an actor to portray someone who's thirty-six and who has lived through what Iphigenia has lived through. There's also a reversal of her role in the play. In the first play, she's the willing victim of a sacrifice—willing and unwilling, in a way. And in the second play, she is a priestess who must sacrifice Greeks to Artemis, the same goddess who saved her from death in the first play. So, in terms of that arc, you can ask, "What happens when the victim becomes the victimizer? What is the pyschology of that? How does a person who has been abused turn around and abuse others?" Iphigenia, in the first play, sees herself as someone who'll be famous for willingly giving up her life for Greece. She very willingly goes to her death thinking she'll be a hero whereas in the second play, which was actually written first, Iphigenia is feeling very angry that her father killed her—that they took her by force. In retrospect, she sees that a wrong has been done to her, that someone has victimized her. It is that anger that drives her through the second play as an older woman who is now a priestess consecrating victims to be sacrificed. Iphigenia's psychological state in the second play is that of a person who must make her heart steel, who must not have any feelings for the people she sacrifices. She talks a lot about how, when she first came to this barbaric island, she wept for the Greeks she had to kill. But she can't do that anymore. I think of prisoners of war and how, throughout history, the great massacres have happened when people turn their hearts to steel. They refuse to feel anything about what they're doing because it would be just too awful. Likewise, Iphigenia wouldn't be able to survive eighteen years, or however long she's been there, feeling for the people she's killing. And through that hardened heart, her brother Orestes enters and they run off together back to Greece. Iphigenia's one hope that someone will save her from all this is fulfilled and she becomes a feeling, loving person again. So the arc, I think, begins with Iphigenia as a very loving, feeling daughter who loves her father and country dearly. And she goes on a tremendous journey of wanting to be famous, feeling a victim, being a barbaric woman and hard-hearted killer, experiencing the triumph of hope, and finally feeling happy and having a loving life once again.

GV: I suppose I should talk first about the function of the Chorus. We have feelings about and responses to the events of the story, and, in that way, serve as a conduit for the audience. We also serve as the conscience of Euripides who was provoking certain issues of his time. It was almost heresy to question the gods in ancient Greece, so Euripides puts doubts into the mouths of his characters. For example, Clytemnestra asks, "If there are no gods, why should we suffer so?" which, for its time, was a very inflammatory question. In the first play, JoAnne Akalaitis envisioned the Chorus as a group of "suburban housewives." Many of our husbands are at the Bay of Aulis, waiting to sail across the sea to serve their nation of Greece. Our husbands want to be heroes and they're with the rest of the Greek heroes, with the great general Achilles and with King Agamemnon. And we're there, as enthusiastic and patriotic as any of them. There has been a wrong committed, the men are going to set things right, and we're all for it. As we witness these arguments between King Agamemnon and his brother Menelaos, however, we begin to question the validity of their mission. Is it really honorable to sacrifice your daughter in order to bring Helen, a woman we all think is a harlot, back to Greece? So we are a kind of witness to Iphigenia's emotional journey and are able to express both the horror and the adoration. In that sense, we experience nearly that same arc as she does. And then, in the second play, we find ourselves in these horrific circumstances where we are attendant on a priestess who is sacrificing Greeks. So all the horror and mutilation is a terrible part of our journey. And this arc, too, is nearly the same for us as it is for Iphigenia.

So is there a kind of essential link between Iphigenia and the Chorus?

GV: The Chorus feels that Iphigenia is a heroine. Yet we are also six individuals with our own stories. You'd have to speak to the other five women to hear how they link up with Iphigenia. My character is very traditionally Greek. I devoutly believe in the gods, it's my religion. A young woman willing to sacrifice herself because the gods have ordained it is an amazing thing to me. We have parallels in our own society today of people who are willing to "go to the wall" for their religion or belief system.

And in the second play, have the Chorus hardened their hearts to the task at hand?

GV: Iphigenia goes back and forth—she tries to keep going but she's angry. I'm extremely connected to that, and I suffer a great deal. I take my cues from Iphigenia. She has been able to commit to her beliefs in a way that I never have. The work we're doing is emotionally grueling but we have to do it to survive.

AD: When I was a kid, my mother told me that if someone's mean to you at school it probably means that they're having a hard time themselves.

I think that's also the story of *Iphigenia in Tauris*. Iphigenia's being a jerk. She's really mean, she's hardened. And she behaves that way as a means of survival because she herself is so angry. But she's very sad about things and is struggling not to be sad. It doesn't mean that she doesn't have feelings, longings, desires, or hopes. But it's true that people who hurt the most are those who are most nasty to other people. That's what the play is about for us. We suffer a lot, and, because of that, we are difficult women to be around.

Can you speak a little about the process of working with a director like JoAnne Akalaitis? Both of you have observed that working with JoAnne is very different than working with most directors. JoAnne has long been perceived as someone who is a bit of a rule-breaker, a director who takes classical or great modern texts and updates or twists them in some way. I think this is a misperception and that JoAnne is actually quite conscious of the traditional readings of classical plays. But she's very adept at giving that traditional reading a contemporary heart, and at creating a work that speaks to us today. I think she's uncompromising in her refusal to use an old modality if it doesn't make sense. Because JoAnne also has an incredible visual sense, what sometimes happens is that people walk into a production of hers and feel as if there's a set of downtown, experimental trappings masking the play. Anne, you were interviewed by someone last night who defined *Iphigenia* as "performance art," which seems to me radically misguided. It's interesting, though, that JoAnne's work gets labelled in that way. What I'd like to explore is how you work with a director who has a strong visual sense, who has that sense of how the thing is going to look and how it's going to be portrayed. Does JoAnne give you some intellectual, esoteric definition of how you should behave onstage and then say, "Now you figure it out?" More specifically, how do JoAnne's ideas about both the visual design and the actors' physicality—and I'll let you talk about the *mudras*— how are those "exterior" ideas communicated to you and how are you expected to work within her framework? Why don't we start with the Chorus. Can you tell us a little bit about the *mudras* and how those were incorporated?

GV: The Chorus uses a specific movement vocabulary that was created in part during a two-week workshop prior to beginning rehearsals in Chicago. JoAnne used the workshop to explore the world of the play, to familiarize us with her approach to exercises, and to experiment a bit. And out of that workshop came some gestures and movements that were inspired by Indian *mudras,* or archetypal gestures. JoAnne wanted to use *mudras* that would be emotionally evocative.

For the viewer?

GV: For the viewer and also for the actor. That's the idea. JoAnne believes that the mechanical becomes emotional. So that when you do something technically or mechanically, the repetition of that will catapult you into an emotional response. That for me was a very different approach. And I think several of us found it particularly challenging at first. We were given so many gestures and weren't really sure what they meant. For JoAnne, it all came from an instinctive place. But for us, on an emotional level, we had to sort of connect the internal dots to support our movements and gestures.

You began with the raw material of the Chorus's texts and ended up with a certain movement vocabulary. What kind of exercises did you use along the way? I'm referring, for example, to the sculptural exercises and things like that.

AD: Well, in terms of creating the *mudras,* JoAnne asked us, "What gestures do we have in our culture? What gestures mean something?" And we'd try out certain gestures, and she'd remember those that she liked. That's how some of the *mudras* were born, and others were born out of actual Greek gestures. For example, we use a Greek gesture of supplication. And there are some gestures that Joanne just made up instinctively and liked the way they looked. When "dream" is mentioned, for example, we do this movement [places her hand next to her forehead and does a kind of waving, rippling gesture]. And there's also a kind of "migraine" one [demonstrates a gesture that suggests she is suffering from a painful headache]. There wasn't any further explanation to us about why our character is performing this gesture at this particular moment, and what it means. The process wasn't about that. It was about trusting that JoAnne wanted to mark that moment with this particular gesture, that it was important to the visual picture and would create an emotional response for the audience. And, as an actor, you trust that and at the same time ask yourself, "What is this gesture doing to me emotionally? O.K., I'll use that in what I'm doing right now. How do I come out of this gesture and then go on with the scene?" And that's what working with those gestures is like.

GV: And then we did exercises where we would try to become more comfortable in space, and with the bodies of the other actors. The six women of the Chorus almost always work as a unit. We are six individuals that at times must move and speak as one. But the entire company did these kind of sculptural exercises where JoAnne would give us a word like *violence* or *love* or *victory,* and we would explore as a group what that image means to us, what it makes our body do and how we can connect it to our personal energy. We also explored what happens if we allow our bodies to become a sculpture that reflects "victory"? And then, how would we create a sculpture that expresses "victory" with three bodies? And sometimes we would simply put an image or idea "inside" and let it work on us.

What about that stopping-and-starting exercise?

AD: Oh, yes. JoAnne did that with us as a sort of preliminary exercise. I think it reflects her taste in acting and what it means to play a scene that is very agressively attacking what you're saying, then letting the moment drop and attacking something else. A thought comes into your head, you attack it with all of your mental, spiritual, and emotional capability, then you let it drop and there's a new one, and then a new one. I think that's the way JoAnne builds action onstage and her theater in general. And the stopping-and-starting exercise is a physical representation of that aesthetic. She'll say, "Feel what it's like to walk across the room with as much purpose as possible and then stop. Really stop." And then she'll say, "It's really hard to do. It's difficult to walk with purpose and really stop. And then make a decision to move. And go. And then stop." We would do this for about ten minutes around the rehearsal room and it was interesting. You're just walking around the room but you have a specific goal in mind about your movement. Then, after executing the physical representation of stopping-and-starting in the exercise, you take that attitude into a scene or use it as a way to break up a monologue. You think, "O.K., I attack this part of the speech which is about this. And then I attack this part which is about something else." It gives strength to whatever is called for in the text. If it's quiet, you attack the quiet. If it's loudness, you attack the loudness. If it's sadness, you attack the sadness. And then you move on and leave it behind. JoAnne read us something by Jean Genet which indicates this idea on a larger scale; according to Genet, each scene should be played as an entire play complete within itself. Again, it's the idea of completely attacking a specific moment of a play and then moving on to the next thing. There's no blurring between moments. Each moment stands as itself.

Can you give us a little more definition of how that illustrates JoAnne's taste or aesthetic in terms of acting? Is it just the attack?

GV: I really think JoAnne appreciates boldness and emotionally challenging theater. She believes in emotion, which is odd because she gets labelled a cerebral or visually oriented director. I'm not sure why that is. But she certainly comes from a very raw, bold, emotionally committed place. And that seemed to be the way to approach the work when I figured out what she wanted. Because she doesn't speak traditional actor-director language. She doesn't talk about motivation or transitions.

AD: For example, I have a line where I say, "I have decided that I must die." And I think a more traditional director might say, "Now, you know, you really have to understand what it means to die. Take that in. What kind of thoughts have been going through your mind to bring you to that decision?" JoAnne, on the other hand, says to me, "I want you to say the line the way you'd say you've decided to quit smoking, or you've decided to go to the pizza store and get a slice of pizza, or you've decided to wear black today." And that's her way of directing me to say the line. So, I'm sort of confused and I think, "What does she mean by that?" But then I take that bizarre analogy she's given me, which was very incongruous at first, and I think, "O.K, I'll try it like that." And then something wonderful happens. Or, she'll break down one of my long speeches and say, "This part is sad, and this part is really mad, and this part is sad again. Now do that." And so you do it, and something happens to you emotionally, and it works. It's very different from a director who might ask you, "What were you doing offstage before you came on? Is your head itching here?" It's not at all like with JoAnne.

It seems that, because JoAnne herself responds to the text in an instinctual manner, she offers her actors the opportunity to fill it instinctively as well. And that's exactly what we see onstage in *The Iphigenia Cycle* and in many of JoAnne's productions—a very instinctual reading of the text that doesn't bog itself down in outmoded notions of how a classical play should be done. I love the example of JoAnne directing you to say your line in the same way that you'd say, "I've decided to go to the pizza store," or "I've decided to quit smoking," because it's an extremely contemporary rendering of that line. It makes the line fresh rather than wrought with the emotional circumstances that clearly exist in the play. Can you tell us a little more, Genevieve, about the way the choral odes were first approached? We have six actors; we have these large pieces of text, some of which are narrating the circumstances of the play, and others are responding to the events happening onstage; we have a musical director because many of these odes are sung; and we have a choreographer. And, of course, we have JoAnne Akalaitis.

GV: If it was a speaking ode, JoAnne divided up the text based upon the quality of our voices and who we were as individuals. She'd take all of that into consideration, along with the meaning of the line, and say, "You're going to say this line, you say this line, the two of you do that line together, you do this passage up to here and then stop, now you pick it up." And often it was sort of blended, vocally. If someone had a higher speaking pitch and JoAnne wanted more of a chord, she would add two other people on the line. If it was a particularly dark or serious passage, she'd put someone with a lower voice on it. When it came to the singing odes, the composer assigned lines based on the quality of our singing voices.

Did he come in with the music already composed and then put you into it, or did things change during the course of the rehearsals?

GV: Some things changed. I think he also approached the material instinctively. He actually composed a few pieces before we met, then came in and listened to our voices, then wrote new pieces and altered some of the music he had already written. I wasn't in the two-week workshop prior to the Chicago production, but when I joined rehearsals and he heard my lower register, he composed the dirge for me. He asked me what my lowest note was and had me start there. So he worked with who we were. With Ginger Farley, the choreographer, it was the same thing. She'd say to us, "What can your body do? What would you do here? Do something. Let's see. Oh, I like that, let's keep that." Ginger also worked with JoAnne in terms of texture. JoAnne often wanted a sharper texture on some of our long passages, so she'd ask Ginger to come up with movements that were very sharp or angular. Or smooth, in another place. And, for Ginger, it became a process of trying things and deciding, "No, no, no, yes." The whole thing was very organic.

We were talking about how you were expected to respond, as an actor, to "exterior" or scenographic elements. A specific example I'm thinking of is that, in _Iphigenia in Tauris,_ JoAnne decided to have Iphigenia and Orestes use microphones. So you're in a Greek play and you're given a microphone. What is the internal process of using that microphone?

AD: JoAnne told me what to do. She said, "Here's a microphone. You come onstage and you say the speech really fast. And that's it." So that's how I started. I just came onstage and said the speech really fast. And I remember JoAnne saying, "People think microphones are really sexy. They're factual, too. They're about speaking the facts." So you take these little "gifts" she's given you and ask yourself, "O.K., *why* am I coming onstage and saying this speech into a microphone really fast? What is the speech about?" That's how I began to fill in what is going on internally. JoAnne will give you a framework—you're speaking really fast into a microphone—and you have to figure out for yourself not necessarily why *she* has made that choice but why *you, as the charcter,* have done so. She gives you a box and then you have to color it in, as opposed to creating your own shape and the director sort of shaping it with you. So I decided, "O.K., this speech is a statement of fact. According to the text, I woke up from a dream that my mother's dead. So I speak very quickly because, I have to relate some background information and I want to get to the part about the dream." JoAnne may say, "O.K., we have this pool here . . . because I like the water." And you have to figure out, "When am I going to use this pool? When does it make sense to walk over to the pool?" She's not too quick to explain in great detail *why* she's done something because, I think, that's not terribly important to her. Her choices are instinctive; they seem emotionally and psychologically right to her. But, as an actor, you *must* know why you're doing something. So you invent a justification that makes sense.

It's fascinating to hear about JoAnne's work from the perspective of the actors. Because a lot of people consider JoAnne's work somewhat didactic and a bit like a lecture in theatricality. As if, perhaps, she sat at home with a lot of books for about a week and decided, "This is exactly what the production is going to look like and this is exactly what I'm trying to say." I'm not necessarily trying to defend JoAnne Akalaitis against her critics But the fact of the matter is that she is an artist. She may in fact decide to have a microphone onstage because it's sexy, and what we should take away from that is not some didactic

truth about the use of microphones in Greek drama, but rather "How does that microphone affect this particular character?"

AD: And how do *you*, as an audience member, feel about sitting in a chair and listening to microphones? When we began rehearsing, JoAnne had no idea what certain lines meant and would ask, "Could somebody explain this to me?" That's how she started to work on the play: "What does this mean?" And then she'd have an idea about it. It wasn't as if she was figuring out that a microphone is going to do this and this and this. It was more that she felt like having it onstage, and it seemed right to her.

It seems that JoAnne is giving the audience a question rather than an answer. She's asking, "Why might there be a microphone onstage?"

AD: She's doing right by the play, in her own instinctive way. She's really trying to tell the story of the play the best way that she can. I don't think she's trying to put anything on top of the story. She's using these elements to express the story as she sees it.

What, for each of you, are the themes of these play? I'm not asking, "What was Euripides trying to communicate?" because we can never really know. We can only guess. But what excites you about doing these plays? Was the relationship between the ancient gods and our contemporary "gods," for example, ever discussed in rehearsal?

AD: I don't really remember having talked about the gods with JoAnne. I think we just assumed their fundamental importance to the plays. The psychologist Dr. Robert Michaels spoke to us about how the Greeks gods weren't all-knowing. A god had to hear or be told something to figure something out. And each god represented a certain attitude or aspect of life. So when these cults, such as the cult that the Chorus has created for themselves, would worship a certain god or goddess it was also an attitude they were worshipping. There were cults to Aphrodite or Artemis, which were cults to particular aspects of life. If a woman was murderous or sacrificial, for instance, it was said that she was overcome by a particular goddess. The psychological equivalent would be, "I'm overcome by this idea." Or, "I'm overcome by this emotion." The Greeks viewed their gods very personally. In the second play, Iphigenia tells the story of Tantalus who served the gods a meal of his own children. She says she doesn't believe the gods are evil, even the gods who ate Tantalus's children, but rather that mortals themselves are killers and lay their guilt about that on the gods. They blame the gods for making them do things for which they themselves are responsible. This is a very interesting theme in terms of Iphigenia's emotional journey, which begins with doing something for a god. She says, "My father is listening to this goddess and I have to die. This is a great cause. Artemis wants the fleet to sail." And eventually she realizes that all the horrible things that have happened, all the things that people said the gods have commanded them to do, were in fact their own doing. And she says, "No, that's not right. I kill people myself. I take responsibility for doing that. The gods aren't evil. The gods are wonderful. No god would make anyone do this. I do it myself." It's interesting that Euripides, who came from a culture that didn't value women, has written a play about a *woman* who goes on this amazing journey and has this revelatory experience. Iphigenia herself says, "A man's life is worth more than ten thousand women." The wonderful thing about the Greek myths is that each story contains a million stories within it. *Iphigenia* is a story that everyone knew. But is it the story of a stupid teenager or a loving daughter? Is it the story of how great or how absurd war is? Is it the story of how terrible or how wonderful the gods are? I've lived with these plays for almost two years, and they have told me about twenty different stories based upon what I'm going through in my life. You go to the theater and, depending on who you are and where you are in life, you think, "This story is just like what happened last week with that man on the subway." And you discover as much about yourself as you do about the play.

So the play really does encourage you to examine your own personal and political point of view about these issues. Genevieve, in what ways do you connect to the play?

GV: Well, I have to agree with Anne. My personal connection to the play lies in the consideration and discussion of the human, mortal relationship to the gods. I think of the big questions we ask ourselves today: What are the values that we hold most dear? What is honor? What is duty? Who is responsible for the choices we make? What motivates those choices? It's interesting that Euripides is the only classical Greek playwright who specifically called for a Chorus of women. And I think he did that because he wanted the Chorus to evoke a sympathetic response. Euripides took this well-known myth about Iphigenia, honor, and all the supposedly wonderful things that happened in order for the army to sail to Troy, and considered what it really might have been about. What was really going on? What was the emotion associated with these events? Was it really the gods' command? Who made this choice? A Chorus of Greek women raising these questions is very different from a Chorus of Greek men. I'm not just speaking about Euripides from a feminist point of view. He was a rebel, an innovator, an outspoken critic of his time.

It would be interesting to hear from the actors about the critical response in Chicago, where the production was voted one of the top ten plays of the year by the *Chicago Tribune*. In New York, the critical response has been mixed and several of the flagship critics have really attacked the show.[3]

AD: There are a lot of non-Equity, lower budget, young, start-up theater companies in Chicago. It's a huge, crazy theater scene, with new companies springing up every week. And I think that the young JoAnne Akalaitises of the world gravitate to a place like Chicago rather than New York because the Chicago press is much more of an advocate for theater. The Chicago theater community and audiences are very supportive of innovative, unconventional theater; I think that's one of the reasons why the critics embraced it. There is a lot of theater going on like this, and in the case of *Iphigenia,* it's produced with a budget and directed by JoAnne Akalaitis. That's a treat. In New York, it seems there's a lot of "back story" with JoAnne that might color a critic's view of her work.[4] Perhaps they come in expecting not to like it. It's difficult, as an actor, to open the newspaper and read that you're ugly and completely unskilled and involved in a worthless project. But, in other ways, it doesn't affect you. I still believe very strongly in this play. I know how it originated, and I know the thoughts and feelings that went into its creation. Even so, it's hard to understand why the same production would be perceived so differently by two groups of people.

GV: This is not an area I can easily comment upon. Why did they like it? Why didn't they like it? I'm a native New Yorker, and I think the difference between the Chicago and New York theater scenes exists because there's so much not-for-profit, noncommercial theater in Chicago. It's a healthier environment for artists in that they are given more room to try, and possibly fail. It's always been a lot riskier here in New York, budgets being what they are and the environment being more competitive. Perhaps the New York and Chicago theater critics think they're writing for different audiences. The Chicago critics will review a piece and see themselves more as advocates of the theater community at large. It's not that there aren't things they dislike, but they see their mission somewhat differently.

I think we have to cultivate our own critical response and our own way of thinking about productions. Hopefully, the critics will come along once that audience culture develops.

Question from the Audience: Do you experience a difference between New York and Chicago audiences?

GV: As we've said, there's so much theater in Chicago that it has engendered a very healthy community. But I won't say the audience, as a whole, is a more educated one. Audiences here in New York are exposed to, and knowledgeable about, so many different forms of culture. But here in New York you have the top-end, the huge commercial productions. That next layer—which Theatre for a New Audience is involed in—is much thinner. In Chicago, there are more what I call "artistic houses," and the depth of that layer has created a different sense of audience.

Question from the Audience: Given that everything about these plays is so grand—the characters, the setting, the action—is there a danger in trying to make them contemporary? Might they become too ordinary?

AD: I think ordinary people do amazing things all the time. I don't think that people in our contemporary society are any different in their basic human nature than the characters in *Iphigenia.*

GV: Sophocles said, "I write men as they should be, and Euripides writes men as they are."

AD: So I don't think that the classic nature of these plays necessarily makes the characters better or more heroic than people who are alive today.

Question from the Audience: I wonder if some audience members or critics expect to see mythical grandeur. So it's not so much a question of what the production does, but what it doesn't do.

AD: I read one review that said, "Agamemnon is a great king. Why don't we see this great king?" But Euripides writes a man who thinks one thing one second and another thing the next, who doesn't know what to do or how to handle himself. It's really kind of touching. That's the play Euripides wrote.

GV: What I wonder is, "Why do we have classics? What makes a classic?" If we can't relate to the characters in a classic work, it probably doesn't deserve to be here and won't last. The reason that we're doing these plays now is because there is something about the characters that touch us. We always think that people are so different from ourselves.

I think it's a mistake to approach Euripides' Iphigenia in the same way that you might approach Aeschylus's Oresteia. In a traditional Aeschylan or Sophoclean piece, the hero enters—and remember we're talking about the greatest heroes ever, the Trojan War heroes—and the Chorus has a very grand, poetic prologue about him. In Iphigenia, our first image of Agamemnon is that of a man who is very indecisive. He's being instructed on how to be a king, in fact he's being yelled at, by an old slave—the lowest person in Greek society. And in JoAnne Akalaitis's production, Agamemnon is literally on the floor, tearing up pieces of paper while the old slave stands above him and says, "Be more like a king." That's Euripides sending us a very clear message. Before the play begins, we think, "Oh, Agamemnon is the great hero of the Trojan War. He's going to enter wearing robes of gold." But JoAnne has him come onstage wearing a bathrobe at four o'clock in the morning. He's visibly upset because he doesn't want to kill his daughter, and he has to be instructed on his behavior by an old slave. I think that humanistic perspective is integral to Euripides. It's what separates him from the other Greek dramatists and brings him closer to us.

Question from the Audience: We haven't said anything about setting, or lighting or costumes. And I'm interested in the way JoAnne Akalaitis dealt with those aspects of the production. Was she as specific and demanding as she was with the actors? Did she have her own ideas about the design?

AD: My costumes are not as fun as the Chorus's. I wear a white dress as the young Iphigenia. In the second play, I wear a kind of black hip-hop outfit and swimming cap. And finally I wear a beautiful red silk evening dress at the end.

GV: The costumes were created by Doey Lüthi, the costume designer, in collaboration with JoAnne. In the first play, the Chorus women wear black vintage cocktail dresses of different design. And in the second play, we wear these very strange red and orange "retro" bathing suits with different surgical pieces added to the design. I think

JoAnne and Doey were dealing with the fact that Tauris is an island surrounded by water, and they wanted to create costumes that would somehow reflect this watery environmment.

How does JoAnne treat Clytemnestra in the production? Is she a passionate, histrionic heroine?

AD: She's a strong, dignified, passionate woman. She's very feminine. She's a queen.

Clytemnestra's position is probably, for most audience members, the most convincing in the play. Because she very simply dismantles Agamemnon's argument that "We must protect our society's core moral value, which is the family. If we allow the barbarian Trojans to steal our women, we're no better than they are. We must protect our families." And Clytemnestra says to him in no uncertain terms, "So the way that you're going to protect your family is to kill you daughter?" Agamemnon has no answer. He has to resort to political platitudes about the good of Greece. Ora Jones, the actress who plays Clytemnestra, is incredibly direct. Her Clytemnestra is a great and powerful queen. But if you're asking whether she comes off as a woman who's later going to kill her husband with histrionic vengeance, no, I don't think so at all. JoAnne Akalaitis's production of *Iphigenia at Aulis* ends with the image of Clytemnestra carrying her young child Orestes downstage and off, as Iphigenia appears, sacrificed, behind a scrim. At that moment, I completely understand why this woman will eventually kill Agamemnon.

1 *The Iphigenia Cycle,* directed by JoAnne Akalaitis, opened at Chicago's Court Theatre in April of 1997. The rehearsal period was preceded by a two-week exploratory workshop, also held at the Court Theatre. The New York production opened at the American Place Theater in January of 1999, presented by Theatre for a New Audience in association with Court Theatre.

2 Anne Dudek is an actress who appeared as Iphigenia in both the Chicago and New York productions of *The Iphigenia Cycle.* For her role in the New York production, she was awarded the Joe A. Callaway Award that encourages participation in the classics and nonprofit theater. Genevieve VenJohnson appeared as a member of the Chorus in both the Chicago and New York productions of *The Iphigenia Cycle.*

3 *New York Times* reviewer Peter Marks, for example, accused Akalaitis of "dumbing down Euripides with tacky modernist conceits that offer little insight into the characters' agonized struggles." Marks went on to attack "the signifiying gestures [see discussion of *mudras* above] and blatant modernizations [e.g., the delivery of monologues into microphones] that are Ms. Akalaitis's signature" as smart-aleckly, amateurish and "potent only for their shock-value." See "So, Iphigenia, How's the Family," *New York Times,* 26 Jan 1999: E5.

4 Dudek may be referring here to Akalaitis's brief tenure and subsequent dismissal as Artistic Director of the New York Shakespeare Festival, previously discussed in Chapter Six.

Interview with JoAnne Akalaitis

January 8, 2000
New York City

In our earlier interview, you spoke about certain denials that you felt existed in the American theater at that time. One of these was the denial of design, which manifested itself in the phenomenon of a set being nothing more than a backdrop for the unfolding of the events in a play. Something that is very much at the core of my interest in your work is that the scenic environment you and your designers create is never simply background. On the contrary, it is fundamental to the emotional life of the play. I'm wondering if your thinking about any of this has changed, or if it's something that remains important to you.

I think designers are certainly more important now. I went to see *Wrong Mountain*, the new David Herskovits play on Broadway last night. And it has a very bold, perhaps not great, design. But it is designed. Apparently it's the only serious play on Broadway this year, whatever we think of it. But it is definitely designed. So I think *that's* great. Julie Taymor did *The Lion King* . . . she's a great designer. That's designed. Design is more important than it was ten years ago. And it should be.

Do you think that certain theater writers and critics tend to assume that if a show is "designed" then the acting is somehow neglected?

I think they're the most ignorant people. I went to the Public Theater, for the first time since I got fired, to see Andrei Serban's *Hamlet* with Liev Schreiber. It was a fantastic production, with some very faulted directorial gestures. But this was the *Hamlet* of *Hamlets*. I had read the review in the *New York Times* and thought, "Oh, this must be good," because the review was so dismissive. When I was in Washington, D.C., working on *The Trojan Women* with [set designer] Paul Steinberg, we came out of our hotel, bought the *New York Times*, and read this review of *Macbeth* at Theater for a New Audience. Jeff Horowitz, one of the great producers in New York, was doing classical theater. The review dismissed the production. Paul and I both asked ourselves the same thing, "Why is Ben Brantley being so dismissive?" We have so little classical theater and he's knocking it off instead of dealing with it. And Paul said, "Maybe it's good, maybe it's bad. We don't know. We can't tell from the review because Brantley is not saying, 'I disagree with this production for these reasons.' He's just knocking it off." So no one gets a chance to do anything. And, you know, it was so strange that *The Iphigenia Cycle* was completely dismissed. What it means is that people are more afraid to do things.

You mentioned that you no longer block plays. How did that evolve?

I don't know how that evolved, but I realized I stopped blocking plays. And it's because the actors do it better than I can. Eventually, of course, it's all very choreographed, very seriously blocked. But I just stopped blocking. And it's a lot of fun to let that go. The actors are amazing. So I let them sort of wander around the stage, and they figure it out. And sometimes what they figure out is very complicated. With *Life Is a Dream* in Chicago, there were two actors who had to walk down a set of stairs—jump down the stairs—to music by the Balenescu Quartet and David Byrne. And I couldn't believe what they were doing. They were actually dancing.

And they just invented that?

Yes. So not blocking the play is very interesting to me.

When you used to block plays, was it something that you enjoyed? I'm kind of terrified of it, myself.

Everyone is. My recent boss, Michael Kahn, said the worst thing in the world is the first blocking rehearsal. And it is. So now I don't have that. I just have the actors walk around the stage. And I think it may be difficult for them. Or perhaps not. I may be saying that I don't block anymore because it's my version of reality, but I really think it's true. There's a lot of improvisation that actors do in rehearsal that ends up being fantastic.

And do elements from these improvisations become set eventually?

They do become set eventually, over weeks and weeks of rehearsal. So it's very, very messy for a long time.

Does that make the actors anxious?

I think some actors don't like it because they want to be told what to do. And some actors are empowered by it. I have to say, I kind of love it. Actors have an incredible instinct for space. They really know what to do.

Are you referring to actors with a certain level of experience?

I don't think student actors do, but I think grown-up actors really do.

You've said that it's very exciting for you when an actor is able to "see their way to the liberation of being a body in space." But I wonder if, for some actors, the idea of being "a body in space" is frightening.

I think it's a lot of fun for actors. Once actors experience it, they love it, whatever age they are. There are very few actors I've worked with who didn't want to do it. Two or three older men didn't want to do it.

They didn't want to do the exercises?

They just didn't want to move around. But most actors just love it. It's not terrifying, actually. Once they realize how safe it is and how much fun it is, they're completely into it.

Do you still do the physical exercises in rehearsal?

I do less of the exercises than I did before. I have a warm-up. I do stopping-and-starting. I do composition in slow motion. I do less. But what I always do is warm-up.

And do you do this physical work throughout the rehearsal process or just during the early weeks?

I do it pretty much every day. Because, in a funny way, *I* need to do it. It's hard for me to walk into rehearsal and just start. When we were doing *The Trojan Women* last year, we danced to Marvin Gaye. That was our thing. We'd put on Marvin Gaye, we'd all dance, and then we'd cry all day over *The Trojan Women* because it was such a difficult play. And, for some years, I've very much liked having a vocal coach there to do a group warm-up. The group experience is very important to me. So I really like doing a warm-up, or even hanging out with the actors or inviting them for dinner. I remember when we were working on *Iphigenia* last year and we rehearsed on New Year's day. It was very, very cold. And it seemed like the coziest, most wonderful thing in the world for us to be rehearsing a Greek play on Tenth Avenue and 16th Street when the whole world was sleeping. It was really fantastic. So, part of this kind of moving around in the exercises involves making a little *family* that moves around.

I recall you saying once that theater was spiritually ennobling because it created community. I see this very much where I teach, at Rutgers University in Newark. It's a commuter school so the students don't live on campus. There are several very active student organizations such as the Islamic students' group, the African-American women's

group, the Latino group . . . but they're all very separate from one another. And theater seems to be one of the few places on campus where a diverse group of students work together in an energized, passionate way. Some of my students have said, "You know, when we walk around on campus we usually never say 'hi' to anyone. But when we see people from our theater classes, we *always* say 'hi' to each other."

Wow. This whole "separate" thing really upsets me. You know, when I went to see John Leguizamo's show *Freak,* there were so many Latino people there who might not go to theater normally. And at Bard, some students did a Langston Hughes show, *Soul Gone Home,* which I thought was fantastic. I looked around and I saw so many Black and Latino people there, including faculty, that I had never seen in the theater before. That's always a disappointment.

We spoke a lot about audiences in our earlier interview. At that time, you felt that a great deal of work needed to be done to bring theater to younger, more diverse, and more economically disadvantaged audiences. Do you think we've made any progress in this area over the past ten years?

Actually, I'm sort of depressed about it. When I went to see *Wrong Mountain* on Broadway with my daughter, I realized that she, who is thirty-one years old, had never been to a Broadway show. At intermission, she said something amazing. She said, "Broadway is basically like watching a movie or television, right? Is that what Broadway is supposed to be?" She's very smart. I said, "Well, this is the most advanced kind of Broadway. But, yes, I guess it is." I looked around at the audience and nothing had changed. And that was a very cool audience because there were a lot of actors there, a lot of young people there.

When you say, "Nothing had changed," are you referring to the demographics of the *Wrong Mountain* audience?

Yes, it's pretty much the same, even though this was a Broadway audience with a lot of younger actors because they were papering the house. I thought the same thing when I went to the Public Theatre to see *Hamlet* with Liev Schreiber. Yet I respect that audience because they're people who are there for culture in New York. But nothing has changed over the past ten years. It's not as if large numbers of diverse people want to go see *Hamlet*. That's not what's happening. The show has to be very culturally specific, like *Freak*.

I don't know if that's a phenomenon unique to New York or if it happens across the nation as a whole.

I think it's happening everywhere. I think it's even worse in other places. I love the audiences because they are so curious and passionate but I wish they had another face. Jennifer Tipton told me a story the other day about getting into a taxi cab in Minneapolis to go to the Guthrie Theatre. The taxi driver was a woman. And she said, "I love theater. My favorite playwright is Beckett." And Jennifer said, "Oh, you're an actress?" And she said, "No, I'm a taxi driver." Minneapolis is a city where you get into a taxi cab and say, "Take me to the stage door of the Guthrie Theatre," and they know where it is. It's a cultured city.

Most of my students have never seen a play. Several of them have never read a play.

I ask my students at Bard, "Name three directors." They can't. "Name three designers." They can't. "Name three playwrights." They can't. Now they're seeing a lot of plays because we're bringing them to New York. They're very smart. But I just don't understand why *Wrong Mountain* is the only serious play on Broadway when forty years ago there were twenty, thirty plays a season on Broadway. Last night, I thought, "Here I am on Broadway. How lucky I am that I have complimentary tickets. How nice it is to see all these people. And to be at the Eugene O'Neill theater, which is beautiful." There was something about the culture of Broadway at a serious play, whatever you think about the play, that was a lot of fun. I thought, "Here's the old Broadway. This is what it's supposed to be."

You're not directing at the moment, but what are you interested in now? What writers are you reading or thinking about? During our last interview, we spoke a lot about Beckett and Genet.

I taught Beckett and Genet, actually, this semester and it was very exciting. It was amazing how the students responded. They responded more to Beckett. They really loved Beckett.

Why do you think that is?

Because I think Beckett is more humane. Genet is so naughty. We didn't have enough time for Genet, I have to say. But the students just loved Beckett and their work was great. It was very moving to me, to see young people really connecting with Samuel Beckett. I'm interested in the Greeks—Euripides, actually. I had a great time doing some Strindberg projects. I'm interested in opera.

You directed an operatic version of Durrenmatt's _The Visit,_ didn't you?

Yes, at City Opera.

How did you enjoy that?

I loved it. I love working with singers. I love working on opera.

What is it like working with singers?

Well, they're actors. Except they sing.

Are they temperamentally different than actors?

No, they're great. They like to be downstage, of course. And they remember the blocking because it all goes with the music. Singers are great. I'm mad for them. It's very easy to work with them. The other thing I like about opera is that the rehearsal period is very short. You can't rehearse for a lot of hours each day because the singers can't sing all day. So it's a lot of fun. It's so interesting.

Do you deal with the emotional aspects of performance with them?

Yes, oh yes. I would love to do more opera. It's not so much that I like opera but that I like working with *them*. Singers are fantastic. They walk into the room with their coffee, and then they open their mouths, and you can't even believe what comes out.

You've been very involved over the past few years with the plays of Euripides, who you've described as the most rebellious and contemporary of the Greek playwrights. And I've been thinking a lot about your observation, during our last interview, that Genet—who is nothing if not rebellious and contemporary—is very Greek.

I'm trying to think about why the Greek theater was the greatest theater before Shakespeare. And I think Euripides was the greatest playwright before Shakespeare. Shakespeare is a lot like Mozart in that he's very open. But with Euripides and the Greeks—there's also Sophocles's *Antigone* and *Philoctetes* and some other plays—there's a sort of doomed, chaotic version of life. It's a very, very crazy version of life. It's also a very big version of life. And I think that's what Genet is like. Genet is so dangerous. I think that's why he's not produced and that's why the Greeks are not produced. They're very upsetting.

Have you worked with your students on the Greeks?

I just taught Euripides, actually, at Bard. And I had a very interesting group of students. There were six of them and the work that they did was incredible. I asked them to write a tragedy. And I also taught Euripides at NYU last year. One student at NYU wrote a tragedy about mistaken identity. She was great, an art history student. I loved what they did. They worked very, very hard. They had to write a paper about the way a person in the Athenian democracy could learn from tragedy. I couldn't get over the papers they wrote. We studied *The Bacchae, Iphigenia at Aulis, Iphigenia in Tauris, Helen* and *Hecuba* this past semester. We had a ball.

And did they also perform from the plays?

They got up and, of course, we read. And one of my favorite students directed. We talked a lot about the Choruses and they tried to figure out what the Chorus would be like onstage. It was a fantastic class.

In your production of *Iphigenia,* the Chorus was very powerful.

There's nothing like a Greek Chorus. When I did *The Trojan Women* in Washington, D.C., it was again an unbelievable experience working with a group of people who have to be in the same world. It's amazing.

The *Iphigenia* Chorus was six individual women who, at the same time, seemed to possess a kind of collective mind.

In both the Chicago and New York productions, each member of the Chorus had to write her own history. They invented names for themselves, and then they exchanged their own stories about who they were—for example, whether they were married or not married. They didn't tell me any of those stories, it was *their* story. For *Iphigenia,* they invented their own cult and wore necklaces with these little balls. And for *The Trojan Women,* it was the same thing. The Chorus created their own stories, and then they gave their stories to each other. So they were private, separate from the rest of us.

You wrote in the *Iphigenia* program that we don't identify with the characters in Greek tragedy but, rather, we react to them on some deep level. And we can never completely understand them because the things they do are so enormous and terrifying.

Yes, I talked a lot about that with my students this past semester. We were trying to think, "Is there a story that we know that's a tragedy?" Like the killing of Matthew Shepard. Or the girl whose baby died because she didn't nurse it enough. Or the girl who left her baby in the closet. Those are tragic events, but are they tragedies? The thing about the Greek tragedies is that they're out of control. And the stories in the Metro section of the *New York Times* are out of control, too. But the Greeks are beyond that. It's been said, "the Greeks are us" . . . but the Greeks are *not* us. The Greeks are beyond us. And that's the great thing about these plays. What we do is learn from the Greeks. I'm not sure how but I'm very interested in the possibility. There's a great book called *The Greeks* by Piere Grimal. It's a very important book and the introduction is amazing. Grimal says, "the Greeks are not us. We are not the Greeks." They're different in every way. Their religion is not like Christianity or any other religion that we know. It's catastrophically different. The thing about Greek tragedy is that it's a very odd form. Someone comes onstage and talks for a long time, then the Chorus comes out and dances and sings, and then someone else comes onstage and talks for a long time. And somehow this form, in an almost Jungian way, knocks us out. The Greeks figured it out. They knew what to do.

At the SSDC talk about five years ago,[1] you mentioned that you wanted the actors to talk to the audience more. And they do that in Greek tragedies, don't they? They talk out.

That's interesting, they do talk out. They do in Shakespeare, too. But what I mean by "talking out" is being more generous, internally. I don't mean formally talking out. I mean being inside and talking out.

So that even when you're addressing another character onstage you're also talking out.

Yes. I talk to actors all the time about that—to be more generous, to play the house, to open up to the house.

Is that related to your interest in Grotowski's idea of the "partner in security"?

Well, the "partner in security" can help that. Yes, it could be related. Some shows I do I never talk about the "partner in security" because it just doesn't come up. And I have to say, the more shows I do the less comes up. My rehearsals are shorter now. I think you can do everything in a five- or six-hour block. Except maybe a big Shakespeare play with a lot of scenes. That's where I've changed a lot. I used to feel I had to rehearse all the time. Now I feel I can walk into the room and say, "We're going to be here from noon to five," and we can do a good day's work.

For how many weeks do you normally rehearse?

Whatever the theater has available. And often it's not a lot. It might be three-and-a-half weeks, but you can do a lot in three-and-a-half weeks. The thing is, you have to have the security that you can do it. Because in those days, when we would come back from a lunch hour and then have three more hours of rehearsal . . . it was horrible, just horrible. I also think that we don't need the "ten out of twelve" rehearsals.[2] Let's have less tech, let's have less rehearsal, less everything. And do it right. Because we *can* do it right. What happens is that the actors go away and do their work at home. So if we have a five-hour rehearsal, they come back feeling better.

Do you still enjoy working out of town?

No.

You did, previously.

I did a lot. I like being home now. That's why I like working at Bard.

You work on classics a lot. Are there any contemporary plays you'd like to direct?

Well, actually, I'm going to do a play at Bard that I did at Louisville, by Jack Kerouac.[3] There are good contemporary playwrights. Irene Fornes I love. I was asked to direct her new play at Signature,[4] but I couldn't because I was teaching at Bard. I'm interested in younger playwrights. And also some older playwrights like Marlene Meyer who has a new comedy that's being read at the Women's Project. I'm interested in the student playwrights—they're very young. When they give me their plays I say, "I'm not a good person to critique it," because I don't know quite how to critique a play. But I'm thrilled that so many people want to be playwrights. At Bard, forty students signed up for Playwriting I.

Do you think they really want to be screenwriters?

I don't think. Young people are interested in writing. There are a lot of young people writing poetry. There's a class called Exploding Text at Bard with a zillion people in it. The professor, Bob Holman, does those poetry slams. He's a great colleague and friend. Young people want to be writers. I don't know what that means, I don't have a clue. But they're writing like crazy. I think it's interesting that so many nine-teen- and twenty-year-olds are writing.

How do your students feel about writing critical papers?

My students had to do a lot of very serious writing. They had to write about the way that Ionesco, Beckett, and Genet emerged from the 1930s, 40s and 50s, and their research materials were picture books that I left in the library. I thought they did pretty well. And I think my Euripides group did amazingly well because the question of how someone in a democracy learns from tragedy is a very difficult thing to figure out. I gave them a lot of hints, but . . . And there were a couple of students who were way ahead of me, much smarter than I am.

Do you think that our audiences today are open to learning from Greek tragedy?

Yes, from seeing the audiences. Isn't *Iphigenia* a great play? Isn't it a zany play? What an experience it is to work on a Greek tragedy. I was so lucky to be able to do *The Trojan Women* in Washington, D.C. . . . oh, my god, what a play . . . we cried all the time. And during *Iphigenia* we cried all the time. It's so deep and expansive and serious. It's bottom-line drama. And I felt so lucky to be able to do that.

Are you preparing to direct anything? Is there anything that you're going to work on soon that you're excited about?

Yes, I'm very excited about *In the Penal Colony,* which is a Philip Glass "opera." He calls everything he does an "opera." We had a meeting about it yesterday. It's going to be performed at ACT in Seattle, then in Chicago, and then probably in Cambridge. It's going to travel around. I have no idea how we're going to do it, because it's like a machine and . . .there's a string quintet, with two singers and three actors. Philip played some of the music yesterday and it sounds great. So I'm now involved in Kafka-land, which is a great place to be. Kafka is amazing. Kafka is very disturbing.

Didn't Kafka have a very sad, troubled life?

Yes, very sad. John Conklin and Jennifer Tipton and I are working, trying to figure out how we're going to do it. We don't have a clue. But the music sounds great. And we're going to do *The Screens* again at New York Theatre Workshop, which is very exciting. But I want to direct less. Because right now I'm more interested in reading.

What are you reading right now?

I'm reading Philip Roth's *I Married A Communist.* I think he's a great writer. I'm not sure that this is a great book . . .

Are your students interested in going into theater professionally? At certain colleges and universities there are large numbers of students who want to make a career of theater. And at times it seems to me

almost unethical to be preparing so many young people to be going into this profession.

That's a very good point.

Now, if somebody has a passion they should follow it—

—sure—

—but I wonder if we are reinforcing the delusion that there's a career out there waiting for them. How do we guide them, or talk to them about following their passion while, at the same time, dealing with the realities of making a life? I remember you once saying that theater isn't a career, it's a hobby.

It's funny, I've come around 180 degrees on this. At Bard, after two years, the students have to do something called "moderate" from the Lower College into the Upper College. In other words, they're accepted into a department as a major. In math, or physics, or Latin, you know whether someone has talent. But you don't know in theater. And maybe you don't even know in math. I say that I've come around 180 degrees on this because there were a couple of students about whom I thought, "They can't moderate, they have no talent." But Bard is a liberal arts college. And so, by virtue of their enthusiasm, they are now moderated as theater majors. I was talking to the head of the anthropology department who was saying, "A student has a right, if that student is very serious, to moderate in my department." And I understand that. I'm going to be teaching an advanced directing seminar. The students who wanted to be in the seminar presented scenes, and I was supposed to choose three out of six. I said, "I'm taking them all." I do have students who will be directors and actors, but it takes so much drive. In a lot of these meetings, I say, "Your senior project was great. What do you want to do next year?" And they say, "I want to be an actor." And I don't say anything because there are very few people who are going to be actors. But do you think that we're sort of misleading them?

I don't think so. We would be if we were to keep telling them, "You're going to be great, you're going to make it." But I don't think we are. And the arrogance of certain acting teachers who say, "You'll never make it. . . ."

I'm sort of new at this. It was different at Juilliard, which is the most professional, competitive place in the world. That's something else. Now I'm looking for a play to do at Bard because we haven't done any real plays.

What do you mean when you say "real plays"?

Well, I think we should do an actual play. Because what they've been doing are deconstructions.

In class?

In production. And I inherited that.

Who has been directing, the students or the faculty?

The students. And I have to say, we've done great work. But I just said, "O.K., I want to do some plays."

---

1 On November 27, 1995, Anne Cattaneo and David Diamond interviewed Akalaitis at ArtsConnection, New York, N.Y. for the Society of Stage Directors and Choreographers.

2 A union-approved technical rehearsal that runs for ten hours within a twelve-hour period.

3 Akalaitis adapted and directed *Ti Jean Blues,* based upon the writings of Beat poet Jack Kerouac, at the Actors Theatre of Louisville's 1998 Humana Festival of New Plays. She staged a revised version of the production at Bard College in the spring of 2000.

4 New York's Signature Theatre Company devoted their 1999–2000 season to the work of playwright Maria Irene Fornes.

Interview with Anne Dudek

February 15, 2000
New York City

When did you first meet JoAnne?

It was at the first audition for the *Iphigenia* workshop. Being cast in the workshop meant that you would also be in the production. I was still in college so I was pretty young, and I thought it was kind of amazing that I was having this audition. I worked very hard on it because I was nervous about meeting JoAnne. I didn't think I would get cast; I just didn't want to embarrass myself. I walked into the theater and JoAnne was sitting there, reading the *New York Times*. There was a set for another play onstage, *The Philadephia Story*. So I began looking around the set, thinking, "I didn't expect there to be a set here. This is going to change what I'm doing because there's a wall here and there are some stairs I can use." And then it was time to start.

Did you audition with a monologue from the play?

Yes, I chose one of Iphigenia's monologues. I had choreographed the entire speech and felt very at one with my little piece. At one point, I did a kind of slow kneeling movement which, was a physical way I had found to express what was going on in the monologue. And something about what I did interested JoAnne. She had me sit in a chair and said, "Now, don't do anything that you were doing before. Just say the words to your Dad." I did the monologue again and felt an incredible emotional connection to what I was saying. It was, in a way, a microcosm of what was to happen in rehearsal. I left, and then I was called back for another audition. There was a Chorus involved in *Iphigenia*, so JoAnne had us do movement exercises in groups of about five. In one of these exercises, we had to walk incredibly slowly but exactly the way we walk in our daily life. JoAnne singled me out and said, "Annie, that's not the way you walk." And I thought, "O.K., my goal is not to be embarrassed and I'm embarrassed." But then my goal became to find out, "O.K. How *do* I walk?" Then JoAnne had us make up these little gestures. I wasn't quite sure what we were doing, but it was fun and I became very interested in the little gestures I was inventing. Then I did another monologue, from the second play, *Iphigenia in Tauris*, where Iphigenia is an embittered woman. I began saying my lines, and JoAnne stopped me and said, "No. This woman is tortured, she's been through everything." Once again I felt embarrassed . . . I was twenty-one at the time . . . but I responded by doing something physically and it turned out to be very interesting. It was very much the reverse of what had happened in the first audition. I remember thinking, "I'd really love to work with this person because she has a simple way of asking me to do something and I can respond to it." It was not an intellectual kind of suggestion that JoAnne had given me; it was something that activated my own creativity and made me feel that I was having a good audition. And that was my experience of JoAnne. It was a sort of embarrassing audition process. I had been so nervous that my palms were sweating and I didn't even know if I was going to say the words correctly. But, in the end, that really didn't matter and I left thinking that some good work happened.

And what had been your training in acting, beforehand?

Most of my training has been based in the Sanford Meisner technique, which, in the simplest way, is about responding to and evoking a response in the other people onstage. You don't get lost in some strange, mushy land of emotions. It's very much about discovering and acting on those impulses within you that you don't normally express in your everyday life.

And when these impulses occur onstage they are completely authentic.

Exactly. You pay such close attention to the other person that it evokes a response in you. You allow that response to happen, whatever it may be, and express it. You play a scene in order to get something—to make the other person in the scene fall in love with you, for example, or to stop them from killing you. You try plan A, plan B, and plan C, all of which are designated for you by the playwright. But, as an actor, you have to figure out how your character executes these strategies—these are your impulses. Perhaps your character bites the other person. But it's very much based upon what that other person is doing. He or she may evoke something in you that would make you want to bite them. What's so exciting about being onstage is that you can never think up beforehand the way the scene will go. It, and you, would never be as interesting as what happens when you don't premeditate and simply pay attention to what the other person is giving you.

So the actor needs to be able to live onstage in such a way that those impulses can occur.

Yes. The most important thing that you have onstage is your partner. One of my acting teachers compared it to having a crush on someone at a party. You're interested in that one special person and everything you do at the party is for them—the way that you pick up your coffee cup, for instance—even if you're talking to someone else.

You're hypersensitive to them.

Right. And that's how you have to be not only toward everyone onstage but also toward the architecture of the stage or room. What particular qualities in the space might cause you to move? How do you respond to the walls? The stove? All of these things—the architecture of the space, the movement vocabularies the other actors are offering you—are there to inform what you do onstage.

I've always felt that the set is a living presence in JoAnne's work. In her best productions, the actors are affecting and being affected by the space she and her designers have created. Everything is working together to tell the story of the play.

The space is alive, even if you're alone onstage with some particle-board. It's part of the whole package that makes up the scene.

And the space itself is emotional.

Yes, and you respond to that as an actor. I think JoAnne wants that to happen. One of the exercises we did before rehearsal was looking around the space—really seeing it and each object in it. It's interesting because we're not used to being aware of our space and the way it affects us.

How did you, personally, respond to the *Iphigenia* set?

The set was a huge, open space with a Day-Glo yellow-green tile floor, a white staircase, and a big expanse of sky that seemed to go on for-ever. There was nothing about it that made me feel, "This doesn't belong here in my imagination." I never asked myself, "Here I am in Greece, why is the floor bright green?" The set was never shocking to me; it was just there. In fact, I really loved it. The set made you want to run across it because you knew that your movement would be very articulated. The stage was very brightly lit which made you feel as if everything was under scrutiny. The set and the lights encouraged you to be clear as an actor. You couldn't be mushy, physically or emo-tionally, because the space itself was so clear. You couldn't get away with "making it up" because the audience would see it. There was a terrifyingly steep set of stairs at the back of the stage. The Chorus was especially concerned about having those stairs because we had to do some crazy things on them and we were scared for our lives. It was great for me, though, because the play itself is about being scared and all the horrible things that might happen. I felt as if I could fall off those stairs at any moment and that might be the horrible thing that would happen. There was such a sense of danger. You had to enter at the top of stairs, say your lines and then go down this very steep slope. The physical environment really supported the emotional life of the play.

You certainly have to be present as an actor when you're dealing with all of that. The set forces you to be, as they say, "in the moment."

Of course. Something like a scary set of stairs or a bizarre prop onstage really makes you deal with the concrete reality of those objects in a very honest way. The set makes you want to be clear and the lighting makes you want to show something to the audience. And what's the point of showing them something that's isn't truthful?

JoAnne used a lot of flourescent light in *Iphigenia*. How did that make you feel?

I'm not really sure what flourescent light evokes. You have to deal with it, though.

For me, they create a feeling of coolness. Everything onstage is exposed, just as you were saying before about the bright lights. But there's nothing warm about the space.

I think that relates to something interesting about acting. Actors often want their character to be redeemable in some way—"I may do horrible things but I'm really a good person inside." You're afraid to play a character who isn't necessarily a good person, to allow yourself to be ugly onstage. I have this instinct, too, and I try to resist it. Now it's a very bold statement to make about the entire world of a play, but perhaps the flourescents are saying, "We're going to show you these people, and it might not be very pretty."

Wasn't there a scene in *Iphigenia in Tauris* where the Chorus enters with photographs on stakes? I remember it being beautiful and horrible at the same time.

Yes, the photographs were of the Greeks that Iphigenia sacrifices. The image was based on an actual practice that goes on in some country—I forget where. The graveyards are fields of poles topped with photographs of killed soldiers. JoAnnne does such thorough research. She gives you these great little dramaturgical gifts, and one of them was a book of the actual photographs of these men. And there was one photograph that was so disturbing—this man wore a number to mark him that was pinned right into his flesh. At the same time, we were laughing because the models for our photographs were University of Chicago students and some of them were on the stage crew. So, on the one hand, I'm looking at "crew guy number five" up on the pole and, on the other hand, I'm thinking, "man with pins through his chest." If you're open to it, there is always something for you to be moved by in the physical space that JoAnne creates. The space will evoke something in you, especially if you understand the research behind it.

You also had to deal with the fact that you're in this Greek world— maybe it's long ago but maybe it's also right now—and you're speaking into a microphone.

I liked using the microphone because, in a certain way, it reminded me of Beckett's plays. Beckett gives the actor a very particular set of textual and physical requirements; he sets up a very contained system. But beneath that rigid structure, and Beckett's particularity and peculiarity, is a vast world churning with life and mystery When I learned I'd be using a microphone, my first instinct was to ask myself, "Is this like Beckett? Is what's important the fact there's this story playing over and over in Iphigenia's head?" Throughout *Iphigenia in Tauris,* she tells the same story to the Chorus women over and over again like a broken record. It's so human, so psychologically accurate and funny. And that's the way the first play opens—with Iphigenia telling her story into the microphone. JoAnne wanted the speech rattled off very fast, which also reminded me of Beckett. You can't move around the space; you're subject to the position designated for you by the microphone. JoAnne also spoke about microphones being sexy and the way that people respond to them.

When you hear a miked voice, it sounds as if it's coming from inside of you. Perhaps this has something to do with their sexiness.

It's interesting to speculate on the audience's response to the microphone but that can be dangerous for an actor. The work I did was very technical. When I spoke quickly, I would lose some of the clarity so I had to work hard to make my words understandable. It was also terrifying because I had to be onstage naked in a pool of water right before I used the microphone. I had to run offstage, and change into my clothes and swim cap in the dark. It was like a clown act backstage. Then I came onstage and had to deliver a two-page speech very fast. There was something comforting, though, about just standing there with the microphone in front of me. Using a microphone in that context didn't seemed absurd to me at all. The play is not a kitchen sink drama, by any stretch of the imagination. The audience needs to know the information conveyed in Iphigenia's speech, Iphigenia herself feels that people need to know the information, she needs to tell it, she gets something out of telling it, and she feels a certain way about it. So the microphone made complete sense and prepared me for the rest of the play. Having to deal with the microphone as a kind of container made me aware of that underlying emotional layer that I could tap into as the play went on. And I think that JoAnne's physical exercises did the same thing for me; they were also elements of containment. The slow-motion composition exercise—where you fill your body with hate or terror, for example, and then move to create a group painting of that emotion—really loosened me up. It's a collaborative effort and everyone is responding to the exercise and to each other in their own way. Your mind is sort of simultaneously watching and not watching what you're doing. After the exercise was over, it wasn't so much a physical shape or action I'd remember but a sense of strength. The exercises make you feel very powerful; they also make you feel uninhibited because everyone's doing them together. You're given a set of requirements: You're moving in slow motion, you're working on a particular emotion, you're creating a composition or "painting" with the other actors, you're using your relationships with these people and you're using the space. So there's a very specific structure involved and, as in Beckett, there are strong currents operating below the surface. You have a physical container and within that something inexplicably emotional happens. I felt like jelly, as if something inside me had been awakened that I could use later in rehearsal.

Do you think a certain type of actor responds particularly well to these exercises, or are they are so powerful that they affect everybody in some way? Also, what do you think happens between the actors as they're doing the exercises?

It's funny. We did an exercise where you walk around the room, stop in front of another person and [she claps twice] the two of you have a few beats to settle into a picture. Everyone's responding differently to the exercise and you begin choosing your favorite people to do these little scenes with. It's interesting how that happens. There may be a kind of chemistry between you and a certain person, and it will be enjoyable to do the exercise together. It might be a little more awkward with someone else. And certainly there are actors who aren't very physically oriented or who don't like the exercises . . . but maybe even they get something out of it. It's interesting that, during the break, everyone talks backstage but no one ever mentions the exercises—you know, that weird thing we were doing for an hour before rehearsal. You might leave a scene and say to the other actor, "Wow, the way that happened was really interesting. Should we do it again?" but no one really talks about what happened when we filled our bodies with terror and made a slow-motion painting. The exercises may be somewhat embarrassing to talk about because they can create inexplicable emotional responses in you that may have nothing to do with the play.

I think there are a couple of reasons why the exercises are so powerful. First, there's something about having to adhere to the structural requirements of the exercises—creating a group painting of an emotion, within a particular architecture, in slow motion—that forces you to behave in an absolutely authentic manner. There's no faking or pretending. And second, most people are not terribly comfortable with their bodies. JoAnne talks about color flooding through your body, being aware of the spaces between your organs, the blood, the fluids, the semen, the urine. . . . The exercises throw you into a very intimate relationship with your own body and the bodies of the other actors.

We want to look pretty, we want to walk in an elegant fashion, we want to be good at sports. Our physicality reveals things about us and that's why it's so important onstage. JoAnne is very interested in *mudras*, which are stylized gestures from classical Indian theater. She wanted to develop, especially for the Chorus, a language of gestures that the audience would understand. One of these—the hand moving outward from the temple of the forehead in a rippling, wave-like movement—denoted psychic ability and the dream world. It actually looked like a brain wave or light wave emanating from your head. Now, it's a bit weird to be in a scene with someone and suddenly make a waving motion from your forehead. But it's also part of the world of your character and a way of conveying another bit of information to the audience. Because as much as your primary goal as an actor is to be attentive and responsive to the other people onstage, you are telling the story of the play to, and for, the audience.

Watching, and trying to decipher, the *mudras* seems to drive some people—critics, that is—crazy.

It's interesting that people react that way. There's a monologue in the play where Iphigenia is pleading with her father for her life, and she says, "I touch your beard." Why would she touch his beard? That's such a bizarre thing to do. But the classical gesture of supplication was in fact to hold someone around the knees, reach up, and touch their beard. So there's a physical gesture inherent in the line. From the actor's perspective, there are actually two things going on: You're addressing another actor onstage and you're communicating with the audience. In modern plays, your lines are usually directed to the other person onstage so your gestures are also directed to that person. But classical plays often call for you to turn out and deliver a monologue to the audience so why not do the same with your gestures? People think of theater as language. You study plays in English class, not in dance class. If it's appropriate to address the audience with verbal language, why can't you do the same with physical language?

Gesturing to the audience is fundamental to the Kathakali dance-drama of India and the Kabuki theater of Japan. But in our theatrical culture, it seems strange. It might be accepted in "performance art" or stand-up comedy but not in mainstream theater.

No, at 46th Street and Sixth Avenue, here in New York City, it's not accepted.

JoAnne mentioned that she doesn't block plays anymore. She lets the actors decide where to move.

I feel fortunate that JoAnne was one of the first directors I worked with since leaving school because I was so naive about what was expected of me. I've since learned that you have to be very efficient at rehearsal because you're on a tight schedule in the American regional theater. You only have three weeks to rehearse a play. JoAnne said to us, "O.K., let's just do the play. You block it out however you want." I remember being frustrated and thinking, "Why isn't JoAnne telling me what to do? Just tell me what to do and I'll do it." But I wanted to give myself over to the process so I thought, "O.K., I'll just have to decide this for myself." So I would make these huge physical gestures, without thinking about what was supposed to happen because I thought JoAnne was doing that. And so many wonderful things did happen spontaneously, probably because we had all been going through the exercises together. For example, we were working on the scene in the second play where Iphigenia is reunited with Orestes. There was a little pool taped out onstage, and I thought, "Maybe we just fall into the pool together. Let's use the water." And that's what ended up happening in the production. JoAnne will often designate very specific gestures and blocking, but there are also moments where you've come up with an idea and feel a sense of authorship. Even if your idea has been adjusted a bit, you feel that your impulsive life is being expressed in the play, which is very rewarding. JoAnne really trusts her actors.

Do you think most actors really prefer to be told where to go and what to do in terms of movement and blocking?

As I said before, it's not easy to know where you should move and what you should do onstage. The best you can do is pay close attention to the other actors and to the architecture of the space, and allow those elements to inform your movement. At the same time, there's something great about being allowed the freedom to move however you will or to invent gestures. And JoAnne creates a rehearsal environment where that type of collaboration can happen. In *Iphigenia in Tauris,* the name "Helen" is repeated over and over again as the woman responsible for all the trouble. One day in rehearsal, I said "Helen" and spit. And that became a gesture that we used in the production. A critic might see a gesture like that and think, "Why are they spitting? That's so stupid. That's so JoAnne Akalaitis." But, in fact, that particular gesture arose from a genuine place of, "I've done all I can as an actor. I've prepared for this scene. I'm really paying attention to what's going on around me."

And audiences, not having any ideas of the way JoAnne works with actors, will see these Greek women spitting in unison and think, "Oh, that's one of JoAnne's quirky, weird touches. She directed the actors to do that."

JoAnne is a powerful person who inspires power in her actors. She really does see things the actors are doing and says, "Let's use that." She may also suggest a physical idea that you don't understand at all. You wonder, "Why am I doing this?" but you trust her. You think, "O.K., I'll do this over and over again, and eventually it will make sense to me in some way." And it always does. Whenever she's asked me to do something, I will do it one hundred percent because I know it will eventually make sense. I have no doubt. And there *are* directors you doubt. They haven't shown you that they trust you as an actor, or that they've really researched and are interested in the play. So you, in turn, aren't as willing to give yourself over to a directorial idea that you might not understand right away.

JoAnne is also willing to say "I don't know" in rehearsal. Something she said that has really stayed with me is, "Sometimes you just have to let it be messy for a long time. Sometimes there are problems you just can't solve right away." That says a lot about process and the way great art is made.

She gives you the time to feel, "I don't know what is happening." Inevitably you *will* know what is happening. There's certainly a structured rehearsal schedule. But the performance is created in a very honest way because JoAnne allows you to find things for yourself.

Did you do table work on *Iphigenia*?

Yes, we did. JoAnne gives you a lot of great dramaturgical information during the table work sessions and throughout the rehearsal process. She brings in newspaper articles that speak to the play's subject, books, movies and all sorts of things to inspire you. She's the first one to say, "I don't understand this line." And there will be someone at the table who can explain it. It's not as if she's sitting back and thinking, "This is for the actors. Now they'll catch up with me." We're all really working through the play together. Or she'll say, "Wait, who is this person mentioned here? How do you pronounce their name? Is there another way of pronouncing it, because we're checking all possible pronunciations." She's always curious, and this inspires the actors to be interested in the dramaturgical aspects of the play. It's a group effort of curiosity.

Actors are so often treated like children by directors, producers, agents, and others who wield power in the business. JoAnne doesn't do that at all; she treats actors as intelligent and creative beings. Perhaps that came from the life she led with Mabou Mines where all the actors shared artistic and administrative power.

Yes, she trusts that you can do your job as an actor. It's very empowering. And her not having to know the answer all the time makes it okay for you not to know as well. It also makes it okay for you to come up with ideas. I remember there was a point in the play where we were stuck—something wasn't working in the scene where Iphigenia questions Orestes about his home. We had these photographs, and I had the idea that maybe Iphigenia takes Orestes' picture. And JoAnne said, "Okay. Do we have a camera? Someone get a camera." It turned out to be a horrible idea. She finally said, "No, no, that's not going to work out." But she was open to it and to not having to solve the problem right away. And I didn't feel bad about having made the suggestion.

JoAnne wrote in the *Iphigenia* program that people say "the Greeks are us," but they're not us. She believes that we react to, rather than empathize with, the Greeks. While I understand that, from the perspective of a reader and viewer, I wonder if it makes any sense to an actor who *must* empathize with her character.

The Greeks aren't me. I'm not Greek. I need to go home and read about the Greeks. And as much as some acting teachers say that you must use the pronoun *I* when speaking about your character, you're never onstage thinking with one hundred percent certainty that you're Iphigenia in 500 B.C. Greece. You do have empathy for the character, not necessarily as a Greek but as a human being involved in a particular set of circumstances. I think it's the director's job to point you toward "being Greek." As JoAnne said, the Greeks are not us. But these plays evoke strong, psychological reactions because they're primal stories that deal with our greatest fears. My mother, of all people, wrote me a beautiful note before the show which said something like, "Your job is to act out for people their worst fears, as a way of helping them." Maybe that was the original function of these myths.

Yes, the purpose of catharsis in the ancient Greek theater was to help the society. JoAnne has described the Greek world as chaotic and out of control. And she's exposing this very disturbing world on a big stage, under harsh, unflattering flourescent light. I think there are some people today who would prefer not to acknowledge that these disturbing worlds, events, and relationships exist, let alone see them portrayed in the theater. So perhaps it's important if even a few audience members open themselves up to this play.

Iphigenia is a tragedy about completely screwed-up familial relationships. It's so horrible. In a way, the experience of watching a play like this is very much like dreaming. When you dream, your mind is working out your fears or telling you what you really think about something. And when you watch a play, you work things out through the characters. And JoAnne's right; it's not so much about empathizing with the characters but about allowing them to evoke something important in you. It's similar to having a mysterious dream. If you really think about it, you'll come up with an interpretation of that dream that is helpful to you.

Do you think JoAnne is making a mark on the American theater? Is it even possible, given that the critical community is not terribly receptive to her work?

I think JoAnne is well-respected now and her work is appreciated by many people in the theater community. But she has also been the target of rude and insensitive criticism. Perhaps what happens is that you learn about an art form in a particular way and get so much enjoyment out of it that you begin to think, "This is what theater is. This is what theater should be." When an artist like JoAnne comes along and does something that's not in line with your definition of the art form, it's startling. You can react like, "What the hell is this person doing? That's not theater." Or you can say to yourself, "This is something new. This artist has a unique way of describing the world and perhaps I can understand this play in a different way." I think art is about opening yourself up to all sorts of experiences and asking, "What's going on here?" The critic's job is to educate the audience. But there's not a mainstream critic out there with expertise about JoAnne Akalaitis and the kind of work she's trying to do. If the critic is not informed about, or even open to, the work in front of them, how can they give the audience a sense of what they're going to see? It's rare to find a director who is so clear about the kind of material and projects that interest her, who can look at a text and say, "This is what this piece needs to do," and who can express that onstage in a unique and honest way. I hope that other theater artists will learn from JoAnne and her way of working. That doesn't mean they should try to emulate her aesthetic because JoAnne's theater is so much a part of who she is as a person. It's not *about* an aesthetic outside of herself.

Interview with
Doey Lüthi

February 21, 2000
New York/Berlin

How would you describe the process of collaborating with JoAnne?[1]

Collaborating with JoAnne is a process of total immersion. By this I mean reading (both the text and a lot of background information on the Greeks, the gods, religion, history, etc.), listening to music, doing historical and contemporary pictorial research, eating Greek food, talking about the characters, looking at more pictures, looking at the actors, drawing, redrawing, bargaining about fabrics, looking at more pictures, eating more food, reacting to rehearsals, reacting to the actors, adapting to changes.

What, for you, is unique about JoAnne's way of working?

This search is what makes it unique, as well as JoAnne's willingness to throw everything overboard at any given moment (right through previews) in order to achieve something stronger, different, perhaps better, or truer to her vision. What is also unique is the *Gesamtkunstwerk*, the team of collaborators all striving to reach a common goal, sometimes together, sometimes individually, and the loyalty that JoAnne inspires in her collaborators. It is a process, which makes it both challenging and inspiring. The challenge is to try to support JoAnne's vision, whatever that turns out to be, and to remain flexible enough to be able to reach that goal.

In rehearsal, JoAnne is very willing to say "I don't know the answer to that question" or "I don't know how to solve that problem." Has this sense of "not knowing" been a part of your director-designer interactions?

"Not knowing" is definitely an aspect of working with JoAnne. This can be disconcerting, although only from an organizational, financial, time-constraint point of view—NEVER from an artistic one. Some advice I got from a 'veteran' before working with JoAnne for the first time was that you cannot control or rush the decision-making process, so enjoy it and allow it to happen. Often, however, JoAnne knows exactly what she wants, e.g., the Trojan Women are prisoners; their heads have been shaven; they have been robbed of their individuality, their lives, and their families; they have been kept in a holding place for ages, sleeping on concrete floors, terrorized by the Army. And they MUST be wearing mascara. There is never a moment of unadulterated realism.

Have you observed the physical exercises that JoAnne does in rehearsal?

Yes. It was great to watch the physicality and movement of the actors. That always informs my work with their bodies.

Do you have any personal favorites among the costumes you've designed for JoAnne?

One of my favorite costumes was that of Orestes in *The Iphigenia Cycle*. JoAnne wanted stylized rags, which I was moderately excited by at first. We slashed a suit horizontally into one-inch strips, leaving enough of the garment intact so that it still read as a suit but also looked as if something dreadful had happened. It looked like ribs. The body of the actor seemed to disintegrate; it seemed vulnerable, as if it had been ravaged. Of course a great deal of the effectiveness of the costume was thanks to Taylor Price, the actor playing the part, and to JoAnne's direction. The character stuttered and exhibited symptoms of Tourette's Syndrome to convey his torments. JoAnne and Taylor researched and worked on this very carefully and thoroughly. Orestes, hounded by the furies, became one of the most moving characters of the play for me.

As you know, the critical response to JoAnne's work has at times been quite harsh. What are your thoughts about this?

Yes, the critical response has been unbelievably harsh at times. It is often unjust and exceptionally cruel, the attacks frequently seeming to be personal assaults. JoAnne has not deserved that.

---

[1] Doey Lü thi designed the costumes for Akalaitis's productions of *The Iphigenia Cycle* (Court Theatre, Chicago, 1998; Theatre for a New Audience, New York, 1999) and *The Trojan Women* (The Shakespeare Theatre, Washington, D.C., 1998). This interview was conducted via electronic mail.

Select Bibliography

Akalaitis, JoAnne. *Dead End Kids: A History of Nuclear Power. Theater* 13.3 (1982): 4-34.

—————. Interview with David Sterritt. *Christian Science Monitor* 6 Jan. 1981: N. pag.

—————. Interview with Jonathan Kalb. *Theater* 15.2 (1984): 6–13.

—————. *Dressed Like An Egg. Wordplays 4: An Anthology of New American Drama.* New York: PAJ, 1984. 191-220.

—————. *Green Card.* New York: Broadway Play, 1991.

—————. Jacket notes. Philip Glass and Foday Musa Suso. *Music from* The Screens. Cond. Martin Goldray. Point, 432-966-2, 1991.

—————. "Theater and the World We Live In." Lecture. Performing Arts Forum Series. New York Public Library for the Performing Arts, 28 Feb. 1991.

Anderson, Porter. "Teasers and Tormentors: Jettisoning JoAnne." *Village Voice* 23 March 1993: 94.

Arnone, John. Interview. *American Set Design 2.* Ed., Ronn Smith. New York: TCG,1991: 17–31.

Aronson, Arnold. "John Conklin." *American Set Design.* New York: TCG, 1985. 14–27.

—————. "Shakespeare's Past is Present." *New York Times* 24 Feb. 1991, nat'l. ed., sec. 2: 5.

—————. "A Nineties Spin for Büchner's *Woyzeck.*" *New York Times* 7 Dec. 1992, nat'l. ed., sec. 2: 7.

Baker, Robb. "Mabou Mines: Animating Art." *Soho Weekly News* 12 Dec. 1974: N. pag.

Banu, Georges. "A Midway View." *Theater Three* 5 (1988): 35–40.

Barba, Eugenio. "Montage." *A Dictionary of Theatre Anthropology: The Secret Art of the Performer.* Ed., Richard Gough. Trans., Richard Fowler. New York: Routledge, 1991. 158–64.

Barber, Bob. "Experimental Theater Program Presented by Mabou Mines." Rev. of *Play* and *The Red Horse Animation.* Dir. Lee Breuer. Santa Barbara News-Press 13 Jan 1972: N. pag.

Barthes, Roland. "Diderot, Brecht, Eisenstein." *Image-Music-Text.* Ed. and trans., Stephen Heath. New York: Hill-Farrar, 1977. 69–78.

Bartow, Arthur. "JoAnne Akalaitis." *The Director's Voice: Twenty-One Interviews*. New York: TCG, 1988. 1–19.

Beckett, Samuel. *Collected Shorter Plays*. New York: Grove, 1984.

Berc, Shelley. "Lee Breuer's *Lulu*." *Theater* 12.3 (1981): 69–77.

Berson, Misha. "Keeping Company: Against Economic Odds, Ensembles Keep Trouping Along." *American Theatre* April 1990: 16+.

Bigsby, C.W.E. "Lee Breuer." *A Critical Introduction to Twentieth-Century Drama*. Vol. 3: Beyond Broadway. Cambridge: Cambridge University Press, 1985. 204–18.

Birringer, Johannes. *Theater, Theory, Postmodernism*. Drama and Performance Series. Gen. ed., Timothy Wiles. Bloomington: Indiana University Press, 1981.

Blau, Herbert. "The Bloody Show and The Eye of Prey: Beckett and Deconstruction." *Theatre Journal* 39.1 (1987): 5–19.

————. Interview with Jonathan Kalb. *Theater* 15.2 (1984): 6–13.

"The Play of Thought." Interview. *Performing Arts Journal* 14.3 (1992): 1–32.

Blumenthal, Eileen. "West Meets East Meets West." *American Theatre* Jan. 1987: 11–16.

Bly, Mark. "JoAnne Akalaitis's *Leon and Lena (and lenz)*: A Log from the Dramaturg." Theater 21. 1 & 2 (1989–90): 81–95.

————.Personal interview. 6 April 1992.

Bogart, Anne. Lecture, "Seminars for Working Directors." Drama League of New York. 13 Nov. 1991.

Breuer, Lee. *Animations: A Trilogy for Mabou Mines*. New York: PAJ, 1979.

————."How We Work: Mabou Mines." *Performing Arts Journal* 1.1 (1976): 29–32.

————."The Avant-Garde is Alive and Well and Living in Women." *Soho Weekly News* 2 Feb 1982: N. pag.

————."On The Gospel at Colonus." Interview by Gerald Rabkin. *Performing Arts Journal* 8.2 (1984): 48–51.

————."The Theatre and Its Trouble." *American Theatre* Nov. 1986: 38+.

————."How Tall Was Coriolanus." *American Theatre* May 1988: 22.

————."Lee Breuer on Interculturalism." Interview by Gabrielle Cody. *Performing Arts Journal* 11.3/12.1 (1989): 59–66.

Bronder, Keith. "Mabou Who?: Experimental Theatre at the Walker." Review of *Play, Come and Go* and *The Red Horse Animation*. Dir. Lee Breuer. *Minneapolis Daily* 5 Nov. 1971: 12.

Brook, Peter. "Any Event Stems from Combustion: Actors, Audiences and Theatrical Energy." *New Theatre Quarterly* 8 (1992): 107–12.

Bruckner, D. J. R. "Revival of Kroetz's *Leaves*." Review of *Through the Leaves*. Dir. JoAnne Akalaitis. *New York Times* 18 Sept. 1990, nat'l. ed.: B2.

Brustein, Robert. "Akalaitis Axed." *New Republic* 26 April 1993: 29–31.

——————. Review of *Dead End Kids*. Dir. JoAnne Akalaitis. *New Republic* 27 Dec. 1980: N. pag.

——————. "The Premature Death of Modernism." Review of *Through the Leaves*. Dir. JoAnne Akalaitis. *Who Needs Theatre: Dramatic Opinions*. New York: Atlantic, 1987. 119–23.

——————. "Fairy Tailspin." Review of *Cymbeline*. Dir. JoAnne Akalaitis. *Reimagining American Theatre*. New York: Hill, 1991. 178–81.

——————. "Shakespeare in Extremis." Review of *The Tempest*. Dir. Lee Breuer. *Who Needs Theatre: Dramatic Opinions*. New York: Atlantic, 1987. 111–15.

Bryant-Bertail, Sarah. "Oedipus and The Gospel at Colonus." Review of *The Gospel at Colonus*. Dir. Lee Breuer. *Theatre Studies* 34 (1989): 85–102.

Carney, Saraleigh. Review of *Through the Leaves*. Dir. JoAnne Akalaitis. *Stages* Dec. 1984: N. pag.

Christiansen, Richard. "Jean Genet's *The Screens* a Triumph in Guthrie Theatre's 4 $^1/_2$-Hour Offering." *Chicago Tribune* 4 Nov. 1989, sec. 1: 14.

——————. "Setting *Pity*: JoAnne Akalaitis Lights the Fuse on a 1633 Drama." *Chicago Tribune* 11 March 1990, sec. 13: 8+.

——————. "'Tis Pity Is Cleverly Imagined But Not Dramatic." Review of *'Tis Pity She's a Whore*. Dir. JoAnne Akalaitis. *Chicago Tribune* 13 March 1990, sec. 1: 20.

Cieslak, Ryszard. "Running to Touch the Horizon." Interview by Marzena Torzecka. *New Theatre Quarterly* 8 (1992): 261.

Clubb, Dare. "Dead End Kidding." *Theater* 12.3 (1981): 46–50.

Coates, Joseph. "Modern Arthur: Donald Barthelme Relocates the Round Table." Rev. of *The King*, by Donald Barthelme. *Chicago Tribune* 10 June 1990, sect. 14: 5.

Coe, Robert, Don Shewey and Bethany Haye. "Mabou Mines: Seven Actors with a Vision, Community with a Vengeance." *Soho Weekly News* 29 April–5 May 1981: N. pag.

Cohen, Debra. "The Mabou Mines: *The Lost Ones*." *The Drama Review* 20.2 (1976): 83–87.

Cole, Susan Letzler. "JoAnne Akalaitis Directs *The Voyage of the Beagle*: 'Quiet, boys, I'll direct this.'" *Directors in Rehearsal*. New York: Chapman-Routledge, 1992. 75–88.

Collins, Glen. "Wolfe's Selection is Greeted With Praise." *New York Times* 13 March 1993: 14.

Copeland, Roger. "Art Against Art." *American Theatre July/Aug.* 1989: 12+.

————. "Where Theatrical and Conceptual Art Blend." *New York Times* 1 May 1977: N. pag.

————. Review of *Dressed Like An Egg*. Dir. JoAnne Akalaitis. *New York Times* 17 May 1977: N. pag.

————. "The Presence of Mediation." *TDR* 34.4 (Winter 1990): 28–44.

————. "A Post-Mortem for the Post-Modern." *Theater* 22.3 (1991): 67–77.

Dace, Tish. "Mabou Mines Collaborative Creation." *Soho Weekly News* 18 May 1978: N. pag.

Daniels, Barry V. Review of *Through the Leaves*. Dir. JoAnne Akalaitis. *Theatre Journal* 36.4 (1984): N. pag.

Daniels, Rebecca. *Women Stage Directors Speak: Exploring the Influence of Gender on Their Work*. Jefferson, N.C.: McFarland, 1996.

Davis, David Brion. "Secrets of the Mormons." *New York Review of Books* 15 Aug. 1985: N. pag.

Davis, R.G. "The Politics, Packaging, and Potential of Performance Art." *New Theatre Quarterly* 4.13 (1988): 17–31.

Diamond, Elin. Review of *Lear*. Dir. Lee Breuer. *Theatre Journal* 42.4 (1990): 481–84.

Dollimore, John. *Radical Tragedy: Religion, Ideology and Power in the Drama of Shakespeare and His Contemporaries*. Chicago: University of Chicago Press, 1984.

Downey, Roger. "Hunkering Down with Mabou Mines." *American Theatre* Dec. 1992: 44–45.

————. "In Search of the Real Lulu." *American Theatre* July/Aug. 1985: 34–36.

Eichelbaum, Stanley. "Fine Troupe of Earnest Experimentalists." Review of *Play* and *The Red Horse Animation*. Dir. Lee Breuer. *San Francisco Examiner* 17 Jan. 1972: 30.

————. "The Floor is Part of Their Act." *San Francisco Examiner* 12 Jan. 1972: N. pag.

Epstein, Martin. Review of *Play* and *The Red Horse Animation*. Dir. Lee Breuer. *San Francisco Fault* 11 Jan. 1972: N. pag.

Fassbinder, Rainer Werner. *The Anarchy of the Imagination: Interviews, Essays, Notes*. Ed., Michael Töteberg and Leo A. Lensing. Trans. Krishna Winston. Baltimore: Johns Hopkins University Press, 1992.

Feingold, Michael. "Camp Followers." Review of *Cymbeline*. Dir. JoAnne Akalaitis. *Village Voice* 13 June 1989: 97.

————. "Lovers' Meatings." Review of *Through the Leaves*. Dir. JoAnne Akalaitis. *Village Voice* 3 April 1984: N. pag.

————. "Going for Bolingbroke." Review of *Henry IV, Parts I and II*. Dir. JoAnne Akalaitis. *Village Voice* 12 March 1991: 85+.

——————. "Sin and Form." Review of *'Tis Pity She's a Whore*. Dir. JoAnne Akalaitis. *Village Voice* 14 April 1992: 108+.

——————. Introduction. *Grove New American Theater*. Ed., Feingold. New York: Evergreen-Grove, 1993. xiii–xxii.

——————. "Life By Drowning." Review of *Woyzeck*. Dir. JoAnne Akalaitis. *Village Voice* 15 Dec. 1992: 95.

Flam, Jack. "Invader." Review of *A Life of Picasso Vol. I: 1881–1906*, by John Richardson. *New York Review of Books* 28 March 1989: 3–6.

Ford, John. *'Tis Pity She's a Whore*. Rehearsal script. Chicago: Goodman Theatre, 1990.

Ford, John. *'Tis Pity She's a Whore*. In *John Ford: Three Plays*. Ed., Keith Sturgess. 1970. Harmondsworth, Eng.: Penguin, 1985. 21–124.

Fox, Terry Curtis. "The Quite Explosions of JoAnne Akalaitis." *Village Voice* n.d. [May 1977]: N. pag.

Fuchs, Elinor. "*Cymbeline* and Its Critics: A Case Study/Misunderstanding Postmodernism." *American Theatre* Dec. 1989: 24+.

——————. "Is There Life After Irony?" Review of *The Gospel at Colonus*. Dir. Lee Breuer. *Village Voice* 3 Jan. 1984: 77-78.

——————. "Too Late for Kidding." Rev. of *Dead End Kids*. Dir. JoAnne Akalaitis. *Soho News* 19 Nov. 1980: N. pag.

Fusco, Coco. Rev. of *Dead End Kids, the Film*. Dir. JoAnne Akalaitis. *Facets Features*. Chicago: Facets Film Center, May 1987: 6.

Gainor, J. Ellen. Rev. of *Lear*. Dir. Lee Breuer. *Theatre Journal* 40.4 (1988): 552-53.

Genet, Jean. *Letters to Roger Blin: Reflections On the Theate*. Trans., Richard Seaver. New York: Grove, 1969.

Gevisser, Mark. "Leave It to Beaver." Review of *The B. Beaver Animation*. Dir. Lee Breuer. *Village Voice* 5 June 1990: 91.

Gilman, Richard. "The Preemptive Image." *American Theatre* Oct. 1987: 28–29.

Ginsberg, Merle. "'Dead End Kids': Nukes Were Never So Much Fun." Review of *Dead End Kids*. Dir. JoAnne Akalaitis. *Villager* 20 Nov. 1980: N. pag.

Glass, Philip. *Music By Philip Glass*. Ed., Robert T. Jones. New York: Harper, 1987.

Greene, Alexis. "Mabou Mines Turns Twenty." *Theater Week* 29 Jan.–5 Feb. 1990: 10-14.

Grotowski, Jerzy. *Towards a Poor Theatre*. New York: Touchstone-Simon, 1968.

Gussow, Mel. "Adapting Beckett's Prose for the Stage." *New York Times* 21 Sept. 1986, natl. ed., sec. 2: 7+.

—————. Review of *The B. Beaver Animation.* Dir. Lee Breuer. *New York Times* 25 March 1977: N. pag.

—————. Review of *Southern Exposure.* Dir. JoAnne Akalaitis. *New York Times* 28 February 1979: N. pag.

—————. "Other Ways at the Shakespeare Festival." *New York Times* 17 June 1990, sec. 2: 5.

—————. "Woyzeck, Antihero, Cannot Outrun His Destiny." Review of *Woyzeck.* Dir. JoAnne Akalaitis. *New York Times* 7 Dec. 1992: C14.

Gussow, Zakariasen, Stasio, Sterritt, Kroll. Reviews of *Cold Harbor,* Dir. Bill Raymond. *New York Theatre Critics' Reviews.* 44.19 (1983): 299–301.

Hackett, Regina. "'Kids' Written on Your Nerve Endings." Review of *Dead End Kids.* Dir. JoAnne Akalaitis. *Seattle Post-Intelligencer* 18 March 1982: N. pag.

Haff, Stephen. "Woyzeck's Erratic Pulse." *American Theatre* Feb. 1993: 12–13.

Hoban, Phoebe. "Going Public: Jo Anne Akalaitis Takes Over for Papp." *New York Magazine* 28 Oct. 1991: 42–47.

Holland, Peter. "The Director and the Playwright: Control Over the Means of Production." *New Theatre Quarterly* 3.11 (1987): 207–17.

Holmberg, Arthur. "[Kroetz's] Plays Seek 'The Reality of the Mind.'" *New York Times* 7 Oct. 1984: N. pag.

—————. Review of *The Balcony.* Dir. JoAnne Akalaitis. *Performing Arts Journal* 10.1 (1986): 43–46.

—————. "The Liberation of Lear." *American Theatre* July/Aug. 1988: 12–19.

—————. "Objects Speak Volumes in Two Design Exhibits." *American Theatre* April 1991: 55.

Howell, John. "The State of Mines." *Elle* May 1990: 122.

Hulser, Kathleen. "Ruth Maleczech: Pushing the Limits." *American Theatre* Sept. 1986: 46–48.

Hunter, Mead. "Interculturalism and American Music." *Performing Arts Journal* 11.3/12.1 (1989): 186–202.

"Is It Still *Endgame*?" Editorial. *American Theatre* Feb 1985: 26-27.

Jaffe, Susan. "Faust in War, Faust in Peace." Review of *Dead End Kids.* Dir. JoAnne Akalaitis. *Village Voice* 19–25 Nov. 1980: N. pag.

Johnson, Diane. "The Lost World of the Mormons." *New York Review of Books* 15 March 1990: 28–31.

Johnson, Wayne. "'Dead End Kids' Offers Message in Clever, Entertaining Package." Review of *Dead End Kids.* Dir. JoAnne Akalaitis. *Seattle Times* 18 March 1992: N. pag.

Jones, Robert T. "Chilling 'Dead End Kids' Gets Point Across." Review of *Dead End Kids.* Dir. JoAnne Akalaitis. *News & Courier* [Charleston, S.C.] 23 May 1983: N. pag.

Kalb, Jonathan. "Acting Beckett." *American Theatre* Dec. 1987: 20–27.

——————. "Whose Text is It Anyway?: *The Balcony* at A.R.T." *Theater* 17.3 (1986): 97–100.

——————. "The Question of Beckett's Context." *Performing Arts Journal* 11.2 (1988): 25–44.

——————. *Beckett in Performance*. Cambridge: Cambridge University Press, 1989.

——————. "A Life in the Gallery: Curating Twenty Years of Mabou Mines." *Village Voice* 1 Jan. 1991: 84.

——————. "Kroetz in America." *American Theatre* Feb. 1991: 22+.

Kaufman, Edward. "Mabou Mines at UCLA: Out of La Mama by Le Living." Review of *Play* and *The Red Horse Animation*. Dir. Lee Breuer. *The Staff* [U.C.L.A.] 11 Feb. 1972: 18.

Knickerbocker, Paine. "La Mama Offshoot: Mabou Mines Troupe Between Art, Theater." *San Francisco Chronicle* 12 Jan. 1972: N. pag.

Kramer, Mimi. Rev. of *Henry IV, Parts I and II*. Dir. JoAnne Akalaitis. New Yorker 11 March 1991: 76–77.

——————. "Victims." Review of *'Tis Pity She's a Whore*. Dir. JoAnne Akalaitis. *New Yorker* 20 April 1992: 78–79.

Kraus, Karl. "On Pandora's Box." Review of *Lulu*. Dir. Lee Breuer. *Theater Three* 2 (Spring 1987): 60–70.

Kroll, Jack. "Fireworks Behind the Scenes: Art and Commerce Clash at the Public Theater." *Newsweek* 29 March 1993: 63.

——————. "Making a Revolution Onstage." Review of *Woyzeck*. Dir. JoAnne Akalaitis. *Newsweek* 21 Dec. 1992: 67.

——————. "Major Doings in Minneapolis: The Genius of Genet." Review of *The Screens*. Dir. JoAnne Akalaitis. *Newsweek* n.d.: N. pag.

Lamont, Rosette C. "Interpreting a Russian Poet's Comic Language." *New York Times* 22 Nov. 1987, natl. ed., sect. 2: 6+.

Lassiter, Laurie. "David Warrilow: Creating Symbol and Cypher." *The Drama Review* 29.4 (1985): 3–12.

——————. Review of *Beckett Trilogy*. Dir. Lee Breuer. *The Drama Review* 29.3 (1985): 138-43.

——————. Review of *Help Wanted*. Dir. JoAnne Akalaitis. *Women and Performance*. 3.2. (1987/88): 162–64.

Laughlin, Karen. "Beckett's Three Dimension: Narration, Dialogue and the Role of the Reader in *Play*." *Modern Drama* 28.3 (1985): 329–40.

Leaming, Greg. "Not a Well Woman." Review of *Through the Leaves*. Dir. JoAnne Akalaitis. *New York Native* 21 May–3 June 1984: N. pag.

Lee, Ming Cho. "The Akalaitis Affair." Letter. *American Theatre* May/June 1993: 4.

Leiter, Samuel. *Ten Seasons: New York Theatre in the Seventies.* Contributions in Drama and Theatre Studies, #21. Westport, C.T.: Greenwood, 1986.

Leslie, Guy. Review of *Henry IV, Parts I and II.* Dir. JoAnne Akalaitis. *Theater Week* 11–17 March 1991: 33–34.

Leverett, James. "Adding to Beckett." *American Theatre* June 1984: 26–27.

——————. "*Cymbeline* and Its Critics: A Case Study/Why Did Reviewers Turn So Savage?" *American Theatre* Dec. 1989: 25+.

Levy, Ellen. "Individuals and Autonomists: 1970's Group Theater, 1980s Performance Art." *Dissent* (1987): 585–91.

——————. "Inspiration in Its Roots: The Place of Poetry in the Theater of Lee Breuer." *Theater* 18.2 (1987): 66–68.

London, Todd. "On Change and Mourning in the American Theatre." *American Theatre* July/Aug 1992: 21+.

López-Pedraza, Rafael. "Reflections on the Duende." *Cultural Anxiety.* Trans., Michael Heron. Ensiedeln, Switz.: Daimon, 1990. 55–78.

Lovelace, Carey. "Nuclear Energy for the Millions: The Filming of *Dead End Kids.*" *Art Com* [San Francisco] Spring 1983: 35+.

Mabou Mines: The First Twenty Years. Video Catalogue. Dir. Martin Lucas. Prod. Grey Art Gallery & Study Center, New York University, 1990.

MacDonald, Sandy. "Theater of the Concerned." *New Age* March 1981: N. pag.

Maleczech, Ruth. "Acting/Non-Acting." Interview by John Howell. *Performance Art* 2 (1976): 11.

Maleczech, Ruth and Elizabeth LeCompte. "Two Women Creating Their Own Worlds." Interview by Wanda Phipps. *High Peformance* 13.1 (1990): 34.

Marinetti, Emilio Fillippo Tomaso. "The Foundation Manifesto of Futurism." *Le Figaro* 20 Feb. 1909. Trans., R.W. Flint. N. pag.

Marks, Peter. "Jesse Borrego Feasts on Avant-Garde Parts." *Los Angeles Times.* 25 Dec. 1992: F22.

Marranca, Bonnie, et. al. "The Controversial 1985-86 Theatre Season: A Politics of Reception." *Performing Arts Journal* 10.1 (1986): 7-33.

——————. "*The Red Horse Animation:* Lee Breuer." *The Theatre of Images.* New York: PAJ, 1977. 113–22+.

——————. "Performance World, Performance Culture." *Performing Arts Journal* 10.3 (1987): 21–29.

——————. "The Self as Text: Lee Breuer's *Animations.*" *Theatrewritings.* New York: PAJ, 1984. 42–59.

——————. "The Theatre of Images: An Introduction." *Theatrewritings.* New York: PAJ, 1984. 77–82.

Massa, Robert. "The Kroetz Sonata." *Village Voice* 9 Oct. 1990: 105–106.

Maupin, Elizabeth. "Mormon Project Defies Theatrical Conventions." *Orlando Sentinel* 24 June 1990: F1+.

McDonnell, Evelyn. "Two Part Variations." *Village Voice* 5 March 1991: 83.

McNamara, Robert. "Franz Xaver Kroetz: A New Voice from Europe." Review of *Through the Leaves.* Dir. JoAnne Akalaitis. *Washington Review* Aug./Sept. 1984: N. pag.

Mehta, Xerxes. "Notes from the Avant-Garde." Review of *Dressed Like an Egg.* Dir. JoAnne Akalaitis. *Theatre Journal* 31.1 (1979): 5–24.

Mickery Pictorial—1965–1987: A Photographic History. Introd., Janny Donker. Amsterdam: Stichting Mickery Workshop, 1988.

"Mining New Media: Mabou Mines's Video and Performance Theater." *American Film* 8.4 (1983): 17–19.

Morra, Louis. "Mabou Mines: On and Off Stage." *New York Talk* 8 May 1984: 16–17.

Munk, Erika. "The Inventive Mabou Mines: Their Latest Triumph is JoAnne Akalaitis's *Dead End Kids.*" *Showbill* Dec. 1980: N. pag.

————. "'Dead End Kids': Signaling Through the Flames." *Village Voice* 12–18 Nov. 1980: 43+.

————. "Men's Business." Review of *Through the Leaves.* Dir. JoAnne Akalaitis. *Village Voice* 16 Oct. 1984: N. pag.

————. "Ky Exchange." Review of *Green Card.* Dir. JoAnne Akalaitis. *Village Voice* 23 June 1988: 121–22.

Musolf, Peter M. "The Illusion of Criticism: A Review of JoAnne Akalaitis's *Leon and Lena (and lenz).*" *Theater Three* 5 (Fall 1988): 105–10.

Naifeh, Steven and Gregory White Smith. *The Mormon Murders: A True Story of Greed, Forgery, Deceit and Death.* New York: New American Library, 1990.

Neely, Ken. "Lee Breuer's Theatrical Technique: From *The Animations* to *Gospel at Colonus.*" *Journal of Dramatic Theory and Criticism* 3.2. (1989): 181–88.

Nelson, Don. "'Dead End Kids': Have a Good Time While You Can." Review of *Dead End Kids.* Dir. JoAnne Akalaitis. *Daily News* [New York] 2 Dec. 1980: N. pag.

Novick, Jules. Review of *Dead End Kids.* Dir. JoAnne Akalaitis. *The Nation* 20 Dec. 1980: N. pag.

Nouryeh, Andrea J. "JoAnne Akalaitis: Post-Modern Director or Socio-Sexual Critic." *Theatre Topics* 1.2 (1991): 177–91.

Nyeboe, Ingrid. "The Shaggy Dog Animation." *The Drama Review* 22.3 (1978): 46–54.

Oestreich, James R. "Music Fit for an English King, Courtesy of a Minimalist: How Philip Glass Provided the Rhythm for *Henry IV.*" *New York Times* 24 March 1991, nat'l. ed., sec. 2: 5.

Oliver, Edith. "*Cymbeline* Undone." Review of *Cymbeline*. Dir. JoAnne Akalaitis. *New Yorker* 12 June 1989: 89.

Opera For the Eighties and Beyond: Mabou Mines. Issue 10. Washington, D.C.: Opera America, 1985.

O'Quinn, Jim. "Change of Will." Editorial. *American Theatre* May/June 1993: 43.

Osborn, Elizabeth M. "Directors at Work." *American Theatre* Sept. 1985: 30.

—————. "Worlds Onstage: John Conklin On the Set Designer's Art." *Village Voice* 21 April 1992: 97–98.

Overmyer, Eric. *About the Mormon Project.* New Smyrna Beach, Fla.: Atlantic Center for the Arts, 1990.

P. J. V. "Breuer's Mabou Mines in Brilliant Creativity." Review of *Play* and *The Red Horse Animation*. Dir. Lee Breuer. *Berkeley Daily Gazette* 18 Jan 1972: N. pag.

Parham, Sidney F. Review of *The Screens*. Dir. JoAnne Akalaitis. *Theatre Journal* 42.2 (1990): 249–51.

"Performing *Dead End Kids*: Statements by Mabou Mines Actors." *Theater* 13.3 (1982): 35–37.

Popkin, Henry. "Dire Laughter: An Interview with German Playwright Franz Xaver Kroetz." *Theater Week* 1–7 Oct. 1990: 24–26.

Quinn, Michael. "'Reading' and Directing the Play." *New Theatre Quarterly* 3.11 (1987): 218–23.

Rabkin, Gerald. Review of *Haj*. Dir. Lee Breur. *Performing Arts Journal* 7.2 (1983): 55–58.

—————. Review of *Cascando*. Dir. JoAnne Akalaitis. *New York Times* 5 Nov. 1976: N. pag.

—————. Review of *Cascando*. Dir. JoAnne Akalaitis. *Soho Weekly News* 19 May 1977: N. pag.

—————. "Mirror of a Master's Eye." Review of the *Shaggy Dog Animation*. Dir. Lee Breuer. *Soho Weekly News* 9 Feb. 1978: 27.

—————. "Is There a Text On This Stage?: Theatre/Authorship/Interpretation. *Performing Arts Journal* 9.2–3 (1985): 142–59.

—————. "Making Waves Together." Review of *The Photographer*. Dir. JoAnne Akalaitis, and *Gospel at Colonus*, Dir. Lee Breuer. 1983 BAM Next Wave Festival. *Performing Arts Journal* 8.1 (1984): 35–47.

Rawson, Judy. "Italian Futurism." *The Avant-Garde Tradition in Literature.* Ed. Richard Kostelanetz. Buffalo: Prometheus, 1982. 142–54.

Raymond, Bill. Interview. *Fresh Air.* By Lee Ann Hansen. National Public Radio. WHYY, Philadelphia. 12 Aug. 1987.

Reynolds, Eve. "Two Absurdist Theater Pieces Offered at Pacific Lutheran University." Review of *Play* and *The Red Horse Animation*. Dir. Lee Breuer. *Tacoma News Tribune* 12 Nov. 1971: N. pag.

Rich, Frank. "A Fantasy 'Cymbeline' in Victorian England." Review of *Cymbeline*. Dir. JoAnne Akalaitis. *New York Times* 1 June 1989: 17.

—. "Mabou Mines's 'Dead End Kids.'" Review of *Dead End Kids*. Dir. JoAnne Akalaitis. *New York Times* 19 Nov. 1980: N. pag.

—. "Off Broadway's Best Plays: *Dead End Kids*." *New York Times* 28 Nov. 1980: N. pag.

—. "'Through the Leaves': Kroetz Play in His Third this Season." Review of *Through the Leaves*. Dir. JoAnne Akalaitis. *New York Times* 6 April 1984: N. pag.

—. "'Henry IV,' Both Parts, As Directed by Akalaitis." Review of *Henry IV, Parts I and II*. Dir. JoAnne Akalaitis. *New York Times* 28 Feb. 1991, nat'l. ed.: B3.

—. "Jacobean Tale of Lust and Revenge, Updated." Review of *'Tis Pity She's a Whore*. Dir. JoAnne Akalaitis. *New York Times* 4 April 1992, nat'l. ed.: B1+.

—. "Opening a Window at a Theater Gone Stale." *New York Times* 21 March 1993, nat'l. ed., sect. 2: 1+.

Richards, David. "At the Public, This Bud's for You, Bard." Sunday View. *New York Times* 10 March 1991, nat'l. ed., sec. 2: 5-6.

—. "'Woyzeck' Ricochets Through a Mad World: JoAnne Akalaitis Stages a Searing Vision of Despair at the Public." Sunday View. *New York Times* 13 Dec. 1992, nat'l. ed., sec. 2: 5.

Robinson, Marc. "The Conversion of Saint Genet: A Revisited *Screens* and a Final Memoir Recast the French Nihilist as Political Partisan." *American Theatre* March 1990: 15+.

Robinson, Marc. "'They Fight': The Thrusts and Parries of David Leong." *Village Voice* 28 April 1992: 104.

Rockwell, John. "Mabou Mines Does Beckett, Own Play." Review of *Play* and *The Red Horse Animation*. Dir. Lee Breuer. *Los Angeles Times* 19 Nov. 1971: 20.

—. "Philip Glass's 'Photographer.'" Review of *The Photographer*. Dir. JoAnne Akalaitis. *New York Times* 7 Oct. 1983: N. pag.

Rogoff, Gordon. "Happy Daze." Review of *Through the Leaves*. Dir. JoAnne Akalaitis. *Village Voice* 9 Oct. 1990: 105–106.

—. "The Ravages of Modishness." *Theatre is Not Safe*. Evanston, Ill.: Northwestern University Press, 1987. 179–81.

Rosenblatt, Roger. "How to End the Abortion War." *New York Times* 19 Jan 1992, sect. 6: 41+.

Rothstein, Mervyn. "Joseph Papp Reorganizes the Shakespeare Festival to Add 'Creative Blood.'" *New York Times* 21 May 1990, natl. ed.: B3.

Rose, Barbara. "Europe Discovers America's Avant-Garde: New Physical Theater." *Vogue* July 1972: 76+.

—————. "Museum as Theater." *New York Magazine* 15 May 1972: 76.

Ruffini, Franco. "Horizontal and Vertical Montage in the Theatre." *New Theatre Quarterly* 2.5 (1986): 29–37.

Rugen, Barbara. Review of *The Balcony*. Dir. JoAnne Akalaitis. *Theatre Journal* 38.4 (1986): 473–75.

Sacks, Oliver. *Awakenings*. 1973. New York: Harper-Perennial, 1990.

Sandow, Gregory. "Whose 'Photographer?'" Review of *The Photographer*. Dir. JoAnne Akalaitis. *New York Times* 25 Oct. 1983: N. pag.

Savran, David. "Lee Breuer." *In Their Own Words: Contemporary American Playwrights*. New York: TCG, 1988. 3–17.

Sayre, Henry M. *The Object of Performance: The American Avant-Garde Since 1970*. Chicago: Universtiy of Chicago Press, 1989.

Schechner, Richard. "The End of Humanism." *The End of Humanism: Writings on Performance*. New York: PAJ, 1982. 93–106.

—. "Race Free, Gender Free, Body-Type Free, Age Free Casting." *TDR* 33.1 (Spring 1989): 4–12.

—. "Theory and Practice of the Indeterminate Theatre." Interview by Nick Kaye. *New Theatre Quarterly* 5 (1989): 348–60.

Schechter, Joel, "Notes from Under My Desk: On the End of the World and Other Spectacles." *Theater* 13.3 (1982): 38–40.

—. "Translations, Adaptations, Variations: A Conversation with Eric Bentley." *Theater* 18.1 (1986–87): 4–8.

Shank, Theodore. "Collective Creation." *The Drama Review* (June 1972): N. pag.

—. "Self as Content." *American Alternative Theater*. New York: Grove, 1982. 157–5

Shevtsova, Maria. "The Consumption of Empy Signs: Jean Genet's *The Balcony*." *Modern Drama* 30.1 (1987): 35–45.

Shewey, Don. "Art Heals." *Village Voice*. 1 June 1993: 86.

—. "Playing Around." Review of *Through the Leaves*. Dir. JoAnne Akalaitis. *New York Beat* 4 April 1984: N. pag.

—. "The Many Voices of Mabou Mines." *American Theatre* June 1984: 9.

—. "A Revue for the Nuclear Era Moves From Stage to Film." *New York Times* 9 Nov. 1986, natl. ed., sec. 2: 15.

—. "Readings in Media-Theatre." *American Theatre* Oct. 1987: 22+.

—. "Through the Turds." Review of *The Screens*. Dir. JoAnne Akalaitis. *Village Voice* 12 Dec. 1989: 120+.

—. "Rocking the House That Papp Built," *Village Voice* 25 Sept. 1990: 34–41.

—. "Playing Around: Old and New Mabou." *Village Voice* 1 Jan. 1991: 84.

—. "Playing Around: Tales from the Crypt." *Village Voice* 29 Jan. 1991: 82.

Sillitoe, Linda and Allen Roberts. *Salamander: The Story of the Mormon Forgery Murders*. New York: Signature, 1990.

Simon, John. Review of *Dead End Kids*. Dir. JoAnne Akalaitis. *New York Magazine* 8 Dec. 1980: N. pag.

Smith, Ron. "Actors, Designers Face Off: Can They Be Partners?" *American Theatre* April 1992: 49.

—. "Mabou Mines's *Hajj*: A Performance Poem by Lee Breuer." *Theatre Crafts* 17.8 (1983): 30+.

—. "Architect of Fantasy: George Tsypin's Bold Sets Defy Everything We Think We Know About Design." *American Theatre* Dec. 1990: 22+.

Snorkel. Review of *Play* and *The Red Horse Animation*. Dir. Lee Breuer. *Augur* [Eugene, Ore.] Feb. 1972: 19.

Solomon, Alisa. "Parallel Fantasies." *Village Voice* 2 Oct. 1984: N. pag.

—. "Public Execution: The Firing of JoAnne Akalaitis." *Village Voice* 30 March 1993: 95+.

Sommer, Sally R. "JoAnne Akalaitis of Mabou Mines." *The Drama Review* 20.3 (1976): 4–16.

Sommers, Michael. "Designers on Design: George Tsypin." *Theatre Crafts* Feb. 1991: 34+.

Speers, W. "Voices of '60s Raising Critical Issues of '80s." Review of *Dead End Kids*. Dir. JoAnne Akalaitis. *Philadelphia Inquirer* 20 Feb. 1983: N. pag.

"Stage View." *New York Times* 1 Feb. 1991, natl. ed.: B2.

States, Bert O. "The Anatomy of Dramatic Character." *Theatre Journal* 37 (1985): 87–101.

—. *Great Reckonings in Little Rooms: On the Phenomenology of Theatre*. Berkely: University of California Press, 1985.

—. "Playing in Lyric Time: Beckett's Voice Plays." *Theatre Journal* 40.4 (1988): 453–67.

Stelling, Lucille Johnsen. "Genet at the Guthrie: In 1966, *The Screens* Provoked Riots." Review of *The Screens*. Dir. JoAnne Akalaitis. *Theater Week* 27 Nov.–3 Dec. 1989: 39–40.

Sterritt, David. "The History of Nuclear Power—On the Stage?" Review of *Dead End Kids*. Dir. JoAnne Akalaitis. *Christian Science Monitor* 3 Dec. 1980: N. pag.

Stodder, Joseph. Review of *It's a Man's World*. Dir. Greg Mehrten. *Theatre Journal* 38.2 (1986): 218–21.

Stone, Elizabeth. "Through the Lens Brightly with Jennifer Tipton." *New York Times* 14 April 1991: 5+.

Swanson, Margaret Millen. Review of *Leon and Lena (and lenz)*. Dir. JoAnne Akalaitis. *Theatre Journal* 40.4 (1988): 554–55.

Taviani, Ferdinando. "In Memory of Ryszard Cieslak." *New Theatre Quarterly* 8 (1992): 249–61.

Teich, Jessica. "*Green Card*: An Introduction." *Theater* 18.2 (1987): 38.

Tom, Lauren. "A Public Disturbance?" Letter. *New York Magazine* 25 Nov. 1991: 9.

Tosh, Peter. "Stepping Razor." *Equal Rights.* Audiotape. Columbia, PCT 34670, 1977.

Turner, Frederick. "Storm Season: For American Directors, *The Tempest* is a Barometer of our Eclectic Age." *American Theatre* April 1988: 10-16.

Viertel, Jack. "'Dead End Kids' Charged with Nuclear Madness." Review of *Dead End Kids.* Dir. JoAnne Akalaitis. *Los Angeles Herald Examiner* 14 Feb. 1984: N. pag.

W. L., "Mabou Mines: 'A Living Cartoon.'" Review of *Play* and *The Red Horse Animation.* Dir. Lee Breuer. *San Francisco Progress* 1 Dec. 1971: 3.

Weber, Bruce. "New Theater Boss Plans Change." *New York Times* 22 March 1993, nat'l. ed.: B2.

—. "Shakespeare Festival Dismisses Papp's Heir." *New York Times* 13 March 1992: 1+.

Weiss, Hedy. "In 'Pity,' JoAnne Akalaitis Examines the Last Taboo." *Chicago Sun-Times* 4 March 90: 4.

Wetzsteon, Ross. "Improvising in Mid-Air: Kathakali and the Liberation of Discipline." *Village Voice* 31 Dec. 1991: 96+.

—. "Mabou Mines." *New York Magazine* 23 Feb. 1981: 30.

—. "Wild Man of the American Theater, Part One: Lee Breuer Turns His Life and Off-Broadway Upside Down." *Village Voice* 19 May 1987: 19-26.

—. "Wild Man of the American Theater, Part Two: Lee Breuer in the Middle of Life's Passage." *Village Voice* 26 May 1987: 33-36.

Williams, Albert. "Cool Horror." Review of *'Tis Pity She's a Whore.* Dir. JoAnne Akalaitis. *Chicago Reader* 23 March 1990, sect. 1: 38-39.

Williams, Gary Jay. "Queen Lear: Reason Not the Need." Review of *Lear.* Dir. Lee Breuer. *Theater* 22.1 (1990-91): 75–78.

Winer, Linda. "Art & Fun." *Chicago Tribune* 20 April 1975: N. pag.

Wirt, John. "Mormon Intrigue Takes Center Stage at Atlantic Center for the Arts." *Daytona Beach Sunday News-Journal.* 24 June 1990: 1H+.

Witchel, Alex. "Papp Names Akalaitis to Step in as Shakespeare Festival Head," *New York Times* 21 Aug. 1991: C11+.

Worthen, W.B. "Playing *Play.*" *Theatre Journal* 37.4 (1985): 405–414.

Zeisler, Peter. "Creative Danger." Editorial. *American Theatre* June 1984: 2.

—. "In Boards We Trust." Editorial. *American Theatre* May/June 1993: 5.

Acknowledgments

I would like to thank the many theater artists and institutions who gave generously of their time and creative energy on behalf of this book. I am especially grateful to Mabou Mines; to David Petrarca, Robert Falls and the Goodman Theatre company of *'Tis Pity She's a Whore;* and to Eric Overmyer, Kristi Zea, and the Atlantic Center for the Arts workshop of *The Mormon Project.* I am indebted to Mark Bly, Anne Dudek, Joan Elizabeth, David Leong, and Doey Lüthi for taking the time to talk with me about their work with JoAnne Akalaitis; and to Ron Russell of Theatre for a New Audience for his permission to include in this book his interview with *The Iphigenia Cycle* actors. My thanks to John Conklin for allowing me to attend his "Conceptual Foundations of Design" course at New York University, and to Andrew Lieberman for the many conversations that have helped shape my thinking about the relationship between acting and design.

I also thank Roberto Aguirre-Sacasa at the Shakespeare Theatre, Cindy Bandle at the Goodman, Dennis Behl at the Guthrie, and Katalin Mitchell at A.R.T. for providing me with rehearsal and production photographs.

I am grateful to Marisa Smith and Eric Kraus at Smith and Kraus for their interest in this project, and to Elizabeth Monteleone and Julia Hill Gignoux for their editorial assistance.

A very special thanks to Frank Galati, my teacher, director, and friend, whose presence over the years has made such a difference. I also wish to thank Craig Kinzer, Carol Simpson Stern, and Ian Watson for their insightful suggestions during the composition and revision of this manuscript.

I would like to express my deepest thanks and appreciation to Kennon McKee, Lee Roloff, María Morett, and Alvaro Hegewisch, Wendy Saivetz Schulman, Paul Saivetz, Marvin and Marilyn Saivetz, and Luis Romero for their patience, encouragement, and support.

Most importantly, I thank JoAnne Akalaitis, for allowing me the opportunity to accompany her on two fascinating theatrical journeys. Her love for the theater and those who make it have inspired this book and enriched my life.

The Author

Deborah Saivetz has directed Elizabeth Egloff's *Phaedra* for the Powerhouse Theater (Poughkeepsie, N.Y.); Caridad Svich's *Torch* for New Dramatists and New Georges (New York, N.Y.); an original adaptation of Donald Barthelme's novel *The King* for the Next Stage Ensemble of the New Jersey Shakespeare Festival; Egloff's *The Nose* for the Drama League of New York's Directors Project; an adaptation of John Cheever's *O City of Broken Dreams* for New York's Alchemy Courthouse Theater; and Wallace Shawn's *Marie and Bruce* for the Parallax Theater Company (Chicago). She is a member of the Mexico City–based company Me xihc co Teatro, and recently collaborated on the English translation of Mexican playwright María Morett's *Mujeres en el encierro* (*Women in Confinement*). She assisted lighting designer Jennifer Tipton on her production of Shakespeare's *The Tempest* at the Guthrie Theater in Minneapolis, and she has worked with JoAnne Akalaitis as her assistant on John Ford's *'Tis Pity She's a Whore* at Chicago's Goodman Theatre, and as a performer on *The Mormon Project* at the Atlantic Center for the Arts in New Smyrna Beach, Florida. She has created original theater pieces with Chicago's Industrial Theater and Oxygen Jukebox and has appeared on the daytime television dramas *The Guiding Light* and *As the World Turns*. She holds a doctorate in Performance Studies from Northwestern University and is currently Assistant Professor of Theater in the Department of Visual and Performing Arts at the Newark campus of Rutgers University.